S0-BAS-486

Also by Tim Cahill

Buried Dreams
Jaguars Ripped My Flesh
A Wolverine Is Eating My Leg
Road Fever
Pecked to Death by Ducks

Pass the Butterworms

Pass the Butterworms

REMOTE JOURNEYS ODDLY RENDERED

Tim Cahill

VILLARD   NEW YORK

Copyright © 1997 by Tim Cahill

All rights reserved under International and Pan-American
Copyright Conventions. Published in the United States by Villard Books,
a division of Random House, Inc., New York, and simultaneously in Canada
by Random House of Canada Limited, Toronto.

Portions of this work were originally published in *Men's Journal*,
Modern Maturity, and *Outside*.

VILLARD BOOKS is a registered trademark of Random House, Inc.

Library of Congress Cataloging-in-Publication Data
Cahill, Tim.
Pass the butterworms: remote journeys oddly rendered / Tim Cahill.
p. cm.
ISBN 0-679-45625-2 (acid-free paper)
1. Adventure stories, American. I. Title.
PS3553.A365R4 1997
813'.54—dc20 96-33142

Random House website address: http://www.randomhouse.com/

Printed in the United States of America on acid-free paper
2 4 6 8 9 7 5 3

To those Arizona miscreants,
my very nearly saintly brothers, Rick and David Cahill

Acknowledgments

Most of these stories appeared in *Outside* magazine, generally in a somewhat abridged and/or edited form. Many thanks to Mark Bryant, Larry Burke, and everyone at *Outside* for providing a forum and making me look good. The magazine just gets better.

"Buford's Revenge" appeared in *Modern Maturity* and "Misty Crossings" appeared in *Men's Journal,* where John Rasmus and Jann Wenner provided counsel and encouragement.

And once again, as always: Thanks to my literary agent, Barbara Lowenstein, and to my patient and enduring editor, David Rosenthal.

Contents

Thundermug: An Introduction of Sorts   xiii

Mongolia: Adventures in You-Cut Hairstyling   3

"Help, My Pilot Just Had a Heart Attack and I Can't
    Fly a Plane"   28

Buford's Revenge   38

Glacier Bay   41

A Darkness on the River   47

Uncharitable Thoughts at the End of My Rope   79

The Purple Sage, at 180 Miles an Hour   85

North Pole: The Easy Way   95

In Honduras   118

    He Who Laughs   118

    This Man Cannot Speak   124

    The Islands of Pigs   129

    Pirates   133

The Lone Ranger   140

The Ozymandias Express   145

Misty Crossings   149

Malaria   164

On the River of Cold Fires   175

In Chief Yali's Shoes   182

Bonaire   185

Geysers   191

Family Values in the Raw   195

Working the Crowd   199

The Queen Charlotte Islands: Life and Death (hee-hee)
    Tales from the Place of Wonder   202

The Tsunami Rangers   218

Therapeutic Perambulation   228

The Monks of Apnea   233

Search and Rescue   251

Among the Karowai: A Stone Age Idyll   258

Thundermug: An Introduction of Sorts

Out where I live, in Montana, we'd call it a mild cussing.

I could do that for this nice lady writer who lives back east somewhere and makes a living as a contrarian. She recently wrote an article in a New York literary magazine that said, in essence, that the current crop of travel writers sucked real bad and just bored her spitless. She managed to slag me in the same paragraph as Redmond O'Hanlon, Jan Morris, and Paul Theroux, which I regard as a compliment. That's distinguished company.

The woman, as I say, is a contrarian: Her last book—I'm forced to admit that I thought it was rather good—was titled *Talk Dirty to Me* and generally took the view that pornography was sorta spiffy and enriched her fantasy and sex life. This, of course, is a position at odds with the conventional wisdom. Everyone knows that women, without exception, hate and despise smut of all varieties. Simply not true, she said. Not in her case.

Apparently on the prowl for other instances in which the conventional wisdom is mistaken or wrongheaded, she fastened on travel writers, who, she felt, had become darlings of the literary scene and were unjustifiably celebrated by reviewers in influential journals both here and abroad. She seemed to feel the conventional wisdom is that, over the past twenty years, a kind of golden age of literate travelogues has developed.

Poppycock, she said, or words to that effect. The woman complained of feeling that she herself might not be welcome on a journey undertaken by any of these writers, which, I think, is not an unreasonable assumption.

I was also taken to task for the manner in which I titled my three previous collections of travel-related writing, all of which remain in print and continue to sell. The first, *Jaguars Ripped My Flesh*, was a joke, meant to rile colleagues with whom I'd worked closely.

Over twenty years ago, in 1975, I was among a group of editors assigned to develop a new magazine about nonmotorized outdoor sports. It was to be a literary effort, and I suggested that we might include articles about remote travel in difficult situations. The other editors objected vociferously. Such articles were then found in magazines with titles like *Man's Adventure* and were directed, apparently, at semiliterate, semi-sad bachelors interested primarily in the "nymphos" who, in this genre, seemed to populate the jungles and mountains at the various ends of the earth. The events reported in these stories were generally of dubious veracity and the authors were not darlings of the literary scene. If in 1996 we are living in a golden era of literary travel writing, 1975 was pretty much the stone age.

The articles in *Man's Adventure,* my colleagues said, were "subliterate" and always had imbecilic titles like "Jaguars Ripped My Flesh." I argued that it was possible to write well about travel and the outdoors, that writing about wilderness of all varieties was a staple of American literature, and that, goddamnit, I'd just bought a good backpack and a stout pair of hiking boots.

The magazine we developed was called *Outside*. It very quickly became the literate forum we envisioned back in 1975. (And, for what it's worth, *Outside* is not, and never was, a man's magazine. Its readership, and my own, is about 45 percent female.) For over twenty years, I've written about remote travel for *Outside,* which in 1996 won a second National Magazine Award for General Excellence.

When publishers first approached me about collecting some of my work in book form, I knew the title right away: *Jaguars Ripped My Flesh*. It was an inside joke, meant to be a poke in the eye with a sharp stick for all my friends who said the kind of work I preferred to do couldn't be done or, if it could, would never be accepted.

The next collection, a stinging left jab at those same colleagues, was titled *A Wolverine Is Eating My Leg*. I cribbed it directly from a story in an old magazine actually titled *Man's Adventure*. My third anthology, *Pecked to Death by Ducks,* took the joke about as far as it wants to go.

The contrarian writer found my titles "precious." This, mind you, from the author of *Talk Dirty to Me*. Still, the woman does have a point. Readers don't know what to expect from these oddly titled books. I've found them filed on bookstore shelves under "humor," or "fiction" or "literature," and sometimes even "travel." Worse, an animal-protection society in upstate New York once demanded that my publisher send them a copy of *Jaguars*. The letter was rather forcefully stated, and I believe they imagined the book was about some guy who battled tigers with a penknife. That sort of thing. I'm happy to say that the group, after a close perusal of the text, saw fit to review the book in a glowing manner in their newsletter. Ignore the title, they said; this guy's mostly on our side.

Well, I thought, maybe this time I should try for a perfectly descriptive title, something you might see hanging from a wooden shingle in Kansas City circa 1890, when people needed to know exactly what it was that happened behind the storefront. Such shingles might be emblazoned CHARLES WELLINGHAM CURTIS, ESQ., ATTORNEY AT LAW, or PETE WATSON, GOOD BLACKSMITHIN' DONE CHEAP. Mine reads: TIM CAHILL, REMOTE JOURNEYS ODDLY RENDERED. It's what I do. Exactly.

But did this reformulation of the titling process please my discriminating editor, the ever tasteful David Rosenthal? It did not. Missives flew out of his office in New York: "Smart-ass titles," he averred, tastefully, "help make you palatable to America."

Palatable? I thought about the word for a bit. And it occurred to me that there was something of an epicurean subtext to the book at hand: Aside from my recommendations for the Malaria Diet, the book contains descriptions of a sautéed sago beetle lunch in Irian Jaya and a drinking session featuring premasticated manioc beer in the Amazon basin. Delicacies. The book's full of them. Hey, pass the butterworms.

And the question came down from the New York editorial office: Shouldn't the animal in the title rip your flesh, or eat your leg or something? Don't the creatures in your titles tend to cause you distress?

Precisely, I replied. Ever eaten a big mass of butterworms?

So there you have it: another precious title.

But, hey, if the contrarian writer from New York still wants someone to talk dirty to her, I could do that. It'd be sort of a mild Montana cussing and would probably feature the precious noun *thundermug*. (This is the local euphemism for a container found under the bed in certain cabins that lack running water. You could use it, I suppose, to pass the butterworms.)

August 27, 1996
Hideout Cabin
Montana

Pass the Butterworms

Mongolia: Adventures in You-Cut Hairstyling

There were a dozen of us, riding the immense central Asian grassland on sturdy Mongolian horses. When I glanced back for a view of the glacier and the sacred mountain we had just visited, I saw two tiny specks inching down the steep windswept hillside, moving in our direction. I turned on my horse and glassed the hill with a little four-power Russian monocle. The pursuing riders were coming toward us at a stiff trot. They were at least two miles back and about a thousand feet above us. Each man held something in his right hand. I could plainly see the glint of metal.

"They carrying?" one of the Americans asked.

"Yeah," I said. "Both of them."

Bayaraa Sanjaasuren, our translator, conveyed the information to the Mongolian wranglers. This was serious: We had yogurt riders on our tail. Again.

"Tchoo," half a dozen men shouted at once.

Tchoo is the Mongolian equivalent of "giddyap." Mongolian

horses respond smartly to *tchoo*, no matter who says it. Guy next to you says *"tchoo,"* you're off at a gallop. We were riding a dozen men abreast because Mongolians do not ride in single file. A defeated army, they say, rides single file. And now, with the dreaded yogurt riders in pursuit, our little party sounded like the whole first grade trying to imitate a locomotive.

"Tchoo, tchoo . . .

"Tchoo, tchoo, tchoo . . ."

Significantly, there is no Mongolian word that corresponds to "whoa."

We'd been riding eight to twelve hours a day, every day, for a week, and I was fairly comfortable in the old Russian cavalry saddle I'd been given. It was a pair of metal hoops on a wooden frame, covered over in peeling leather stuffed with horsehair. The stirrups were metal hoops connected to the frame with rawhide straps. The Mongolians in our party rode ornate hand-carved wooden saddles, the best of them festooned with beaten silver medallions.

"Tchoo," I said, and stood up a bit in the saddle so my horse could stretch into his long gallop.

The ground we were approaching, however, was humped up in the marshy tussocks characteristic of soil that is permanently frozen a few feet below the surface. We were only at about 48 degrees north—about the latitude of Seattle—but cold fronts originating in Siberia, to our north, seem to flow down the great Yenisey River, northern Asia's Amazon, and funnel into Mongolia. Nowhere else in the hemisphere does permafrost extend so far south.

Trees cannot grow in permafrost, and here, in the shadow of the mountain called Otgontenger, with bare hillsides rising to ten thousand feet on all sides, we were sitting ducks. We could run, but we couldn't hide. There were no fences, no roads, no trees, no telephone poles, no buildings, no cattle or livestock of any kind. It was just us: a dozen or so men, one woman, along with several pack horses and a string of remounts, all of us dwarfed under the immense vault of the sky.

If our party had consisted solely of Mongolians, it might have had a chance. But there were seven Americans in our group and—with one exception—we couldn't outpace a pair of determined Mongolian horsemen with only a two-mile lead.

As we hit the hummocky marshland, our horses settled into a short hammering trot, which is the gait favored by Mongol riders who want to make time. Mongolian herdsmen churn butter by strapping a jug of milk to the saddle and trotting for ten minutes. This is the truth. I had a bottle of aspirin in my saddle kit, and it had long ago been reduced to powder.

Every night, as I tried to massage whatever it was that was sore and measured out my dose of powdered aspirin, I thought about this: Mongols have a reputation of being the best horsemen on earth, while their horses have what must be the world's most punishing gait. It was, I concluded, the nature of the land itself that produced this jackhammer trot.

Often the ground was marshy but studded with grassy hummocks, so a horse either ran tussock to tussock or it stayed in the equally uneven footing of the marsh. Additionally, there were marmot holes everywhere. In places where springs flowed out of rock walls, the relatively warm water melted the permafrost below, and on a warm summer day, a horse could sink into mud up to its withers.

The horses knew the land, and they made their way over it in a jouncing weaving sort of way. The short, punishing gait—I wasn't the only American who called it the Mongolian Death Trot—fit the terrain perfectly. A horse that extended—that stretched out his trot or gallop—was a horse that was going to break a leg, which is to say it was a dead horse. Mongolia is a harsh land, and only the fittest survive.

Our Mongolian companions, raised in the saddle, simply stood up in their stirrups on legs made of spring steel and pneumatic shock absorbers. The trot was too jouncy for me to raise and lower myself in the saddle, as Western riders do. I could stand, like the Mongolians, but for only a few minutes at a time. Sitting, I had the sensation of internal organs shaking loose. When I looked back after an hour, the yogurt riders had halved the distance between our parties.

Mongolia, sometimes called Outer Mongolia, is an independent country. Inner Mongolia, which borders Mongolia on the east, is part of China, and it was the Chinese who coined what has become a hated terminology: Inner Mongolia is closer to Beijing; Outer Mongolia is further away.

In fact, the country isn't outer to anywhere. Mongolia is set square in the center of Asia, and lies between Russian Siberia to the north and China to the south. It is protected by impressive natural boundaries: The Altai Mountains rise to fourteen thousand feet in the west; to the north are the dense forests of the Siberian taiga; to the south and east is the Gobi Desert, the coldest, most northerly desert on earth, a place where trekkers still find dinosaur bones scattered across the wind-shattered gravellike sands. These natural boundaries protect the grazing lands of the steppes, in the interior of the country. The average altitude is just about a mile above sea level, making Mongolia one of the highest countries in the world.

Landlocked, mountainous, and far from the moderating influence of any ocean, Mongolia offers some truly operatic weather: 90-degree summer days, 60-degree-below-zero winter nights, and twenty-four-hour temperature swings of 80 degrees and more. A European friar, John of Plano Carpini, who visited Mongolia in 1245, called the weather "astonishingly irregular." He experienced "fierce thunder and lightning" that "caused the death of many men, and at the same time there [were] heavy falls of snow." Carpini lived through an absurdly fierce hailstorm, which was followed by such warm weather that the resultant flash flood killed 160 people. He thought the country "more wretched than I could possibly say."

There was a time when geographers, expressing a kind of universal medieval dread, called Mongolia "the dead heart of Asia." The people who survived there were supposedly barbarians, nomadic herdsmen with no culture and no interest in agriculture. Every few centuries, throughout the whole of recorded history, these "uncivilized" Mongolians came bursting out of their high, cold plateau on horseback to conquer any peoples who stood in their way. Once, in the thirteenth century, they conquered the known world.

Mongolians, like many people who live in cold climates, tend to be physically bigger than their southern neighbors, and I imagined them pouring down on, say, the smaller Chinese: merciless barbarians, armies of huge men on fast horses wearing boiled-leather armor, their faces smeared with sheep fat against the cold and wind and sun.

So thundering across the steppes on a Mongolian horse in company with Mongolian horsemen carried a certain savage hormonal rush, like tearing up the highway on a Harley with a pack of Hell's Angels.

But the horses, when I first saw them, didn't inspire confidence. They were small and ratty, with big gawky heads. No animal was of any one single color. They were all about half wild and there was a rodeo every morning when we tried to saddle them up. Flapping rain jackets spooked them. Shadows cast by the campfire set them bucking. A sneeze could start a stampede.

On the other hand, they were fast, and by far the toughest horses I'd ever ridden. They could survive in conditions that would kill any other horse on earth. The animals graze on their own—they are never fed—and yet live through 60-below-zero winter nights, cutting through snow and ice with their hooves for something to eat. Unshod, our horses routinely put in thirty-mile days, accumulating as much as eight thousand feet of altitude change. And they did it day after tireless day.

The herdsmen inspected their horses for sores or bruises. They doctored them when it was necessary and rested them when they were tired. They knew each horse intimately—probably saw it born; probably broke it—but they were never sentimental. Mongolians name their horses about as often as Americans name their cars.

And the horses serve the same function as cars. They are transportation devices, meant to be kept in superb running condition. Out on the roadless grassland, a horse is the essential link to the outside world: to the market, to the nearest town or school or hospital.

Mongolians in the countryside literally learn to ride about the time they learn to walk. Not one of them has ever attended Miss Prissy's Academy of Equine Etiquette. They gallop right up behind you and give your horse a smart swat on the backside if they want to race. And, in my experience, they always want to race.

For what it's worth, I thought the seven of us from America made a fairly impressive group. Arlene Burns, a well-known river guide, had been Meryl Streep's rowing coach in the film *The River Wild*. I believe Meryl does Arlene in that film: I recognized the confidence, the feminine athletic swagger, even the hairstyle.

Christoph Schork was a pilot and ski instructor in Idaho. He rode his own horse in marathon hundred-mile mountain races and was the only one of us who might have had a chance against the yogurt riders.

Photographer Dave Edwards was working on a photo book about men who hunted with eagles in the Altai Mountains. He guided horse trips out of northern Mongolia to pay his expenses. Jackson Frishman, eighteen, was the son of a woman Dave had guided with when he worked the Grand Canyon. Jackson had a lot of white-water experience and wanted to be a river guide himself. Michael Abbot, a computer networking expert, was an avid fly fisherman who'd spent a good deal of time camping along salmon and steelhead streams in Alaska.

Kent Maiden, of Boojum Expeditions, was our guide. We were all getting a break on the price of the trip because it was an exploratory. Kent had never been to this area of Mongolia before and couldn't vouch for the quality of the horses we'd ride. Or the wranglers who'd ride with us. There were no guarantees. Whatever happened, happened.

What happened was yogurt riders.

For my part, I'd been trying, and failing, to get to Mongolia for over fifteen years. And now, in my saddle kit, I had eight Ziploc bags, full of human hair—hair cut from the heads of Mongolian herdsmen and herdswomen.

It was what I had traveled to Mongolia to get. I am a member of the advisory board of the Center for the Study of the First Americans, located at Oregon State University, where it is believed, fervently, that the earth is a giant hair ball.

Although no one knows the absolute average number, humans naturally shed an enormous amount of hair every day. Cosmeticians figure that number at about 170 daily strands. If so, the average human being sheds a little over 3.5 million hairs over a sixty-year life span. The figure is significant to the cutting edge of archaeology.

Not far from my home in south-central Montana, for instance, there are several "early man" sites. One was populated by humans as early as fourteen thousand years ago. There's a lot of naturally shed human hair buried at that and other sites. Previously, archaeologists, searching for the first Americans, discarded human hair in their digs. They tended to study bone fragments and stone artifacts.

There were problems with this approach. The first was cultural: Some Native American groups saw the exhumation of bone fragments as a kind of grave robbing. Second, stone artifacts, such as Clovis points, could be dated by standard techniques, but isolating the technology in time sheds very little light on the identity of the people who embraced the culture. If Clovis points were effective, wouldn't various groups of people adopt them, humans being human. Is someone who drives a Honda Japanese or American, African, or Latin?

The study of naturally shed human hair at prehistoric campsites does not desecrate graves and provides important, confirmable information as to the identity of the people who populated those sites. Race can be accurately determined by microscopic and DNA analysis of human hair. That is the work being done by Dr. Rob Bonnichson at the Center for the Study of the First Americans. Field and lab work are focused on the single question: Who were the first Americans?

The theory, of course, is that during the last Ice Age, when great volumes of water were concentrated at the poles and in various glaciers, the sea level was perhaps four hundred feet lower than it is today. The Bering Strait, today a fifty-three-mile water-way separating Asia and the Americas, was left high and dry. It was probably a vast grassland, alive with woolly mammoths, which humans, acting in concert, could kill and eat. They likely used spears tipped with Clovis or other points.

The folks who crossed the Bering Land Bridge were probably Asians. My mission, for the Center for the Study of the First Americans, was to collect samples of Mongolian hair, bring 'em back through customs, and send them to Oregon State University, where they could be compared with ten-thousand-year-old strands dug up outside Melville, Montana. It is possible that the ancestors of the people who today call themselves Mongolian— the ancestors of the men I was riding with, of the men pursuing us with pails of yogurt—were "the first Americans."

The air route to Mongolia required a three-day layover in Bei-jing. There, I hired a taxi and drove two hours through the countryside to visit a section of the Great Wall, the largest building construction project in the history of the world. It's fifteen hundred miles long, about thirty feet high, with towers rising to forty feet, and it has everything to do with Mongols, and the fear of Mongols. In the fourth century B.C., the Chinese began suffering the attacks of fierce nomadic herdsmen living to the north and west. Almost immediately, they began building parts of what we now call the Great Wall.

The ramparts I saw ran along the razored ridge tops of mountains rising several thousand feet above the rich agricultural lands to the east. There were guard towers every hundred yards or so, slitted windows for archers, and the land to the west—terrain attackers would have to traverse—was little more than a steep talus slope. No way could archers on horseback breach that wall.

Those ancient marauding horsemen—the Hsiung-nu—are thought, by some accounts, to be ancestors of the people who were to call themselves Mongols. The Hsiung-nu, sometimes called Huns, would be the same folks who brought Europe the Attila the Hun Show in the fifth century A.D.

Still, in the mid-twelfth century, the people living in what is now Mongolia were a fairly diverse group of warring tribes, living rather like the American Plains Indians. Superb horsemen, they believed all things possessed a spirit: mountains, rivers, rocks, hillsides. They particularly worshipped the sky, which they called Tengri. Mongolia's continental climate produces 260 clear days a year: the sunniest spot anywhere on earth at that latitude. The sky, a brilliant blue dome, arches over the rolling grasslands of the steppes. It is a felt presence: Asian Big Sky country, with a vengeance.

The ancient peoples of Mongolia lived in round felt tents, and the archaeological record suggests it was a way of life that stretched back to at least 10,000 B.C. The clans warred among themselves, engaged in shamanistic rituals, stole horses and women, put great stock in personal courage, and were terrifyingly accurate archers.

It was Genghis Khan, born in 1167, who unified all of these feuding tribes—the hunter-gatherers of the northern forests; the people who skied across the frozen lakes on polished animal bones; the camel breeders of the Gobi Desert; the herdsmen of the grasslands. In 1206, after years of tribal warfare, Genghis Khan, triumphant, declared himself "the ruler of all those who live in felt tents."

Illiterate and probably alcoholic, Genghis Khan was, according to many historians, the greatest military genius who ever lived.

The people who lived in felt tents probably numbered two million. This was the Mongol Horde. The great Khan, directing an army of only 130,000 Mongols, conquered the known world, and established the largest empire that ever was and probably ever will be. Genghis and his sons and grandsons ruled from southern Siberia to Syria, from the Pacific on the shores of what is now China all the way to the Adriatic Sea.

His horsemen sometimes rode eighty miles a day over deserts or mountains others thought to be impassable. In Europe, they were known as Hell's Horsemen. To the east, the Great Wall was little more than a speed bump on the way to Beijing, where Kublai Khan, the grandson of Genghis, built his Xanadu. He said, "A wall is only as good as those who defend it."

• • •

Probably because of the harsh, irregular climate, Mongolia, the fifth largest country in Asia, is also the least populated: 2.3 million people inhabit an area larger than England, France, Germany, and Italy combined. About a third of all Mongolians live in the capital city of Ulan Bator.

This was a little hard for me to figure out, because Ulan Bator did not sing sweetly to the soul. What I saw was a town of rectangular gray cement buildings—Soviet-style apartment blocks—with peeling, pockmarked facades, all of which appeared to be bleeding to death, the result, I saw on closer inspection, of rusting fire escapes. Packs of starving dogs slunk about in the alleys, cringing and snarling.

Our group had been picked up at the airport by the director of the Mongolian Democratic Party Travel Company, the estimable Batchyluun ("call me Baggie") Sanjsuren, thirty-seven, a big, hearty man with big, round muscles. He looked remarkably like a Crow Indian artist I know in Montana.

Our translator, Bayaraa Sanjaasuren, was a few years younger: a slender, elegant, and highly educated fellow. One of the first things these men taught us how to say was—I render this phonetically—"Mee Mer-ee-koon," which means, "I'm an American." Caucasian people, Baggie explained, were often taken for Russians and sometimes had the snot kicked out of them on the street by roving gangs of angry, unemployed young Mongolians. Americans, on the other hand, were highly welcome in Mongolia for a variety of reasons.

To wit: After the fall of the Khans, Mongolia fell under Chinese domination. By 1911, Inner Mongolia was already Chinese. In Outer Mongolia, just after the Russian revolution in 1917, defeated anti-Communist forces, led by the "Mad Baron" Ungern-Sternberg, took Ulan Bator, then called Urga. The Mad Baron specialized in citywide arson and mass executions. Mongolian freedom fighters, notably D. Sukhbaatar, Mongolia's national hero, sided with Russian Communists, defeated the remnant Chinese warlords in Urga, and eventually captured the Mad Baron, who was promptly executed. The capital was renamed Ulan Bator

(Red Hero), and in 1921, Mongolia declared itself a Communist state, the second country in the world to do so.

Very quickly, Mongolia became a Soviet client, marching in lockstep with Russia and possessed of its own secret service, its own purges, and its own little Stalin, a mass murderer named Choybalsan. Religion was outlawed. For centuries, Mongolians had been Buddhists, of the Tibetan variety. Under Choybalsan, soldiers burst into the lamaseries, marched the older monks out back, shot them dead, and buried the corpses in mass graves. Nomadic herdsmen found themselves members of collectives. They were encouraged to move to towns, where they could become industrial workers, striving for progress. Mongolian writing was outlawed, and Russian, "the international language," was taught in schools.

Discussions of Mongol heritage were discouraged. The very mention of Genghis Khan was an embarrassment to Moscow in that the great Khan and his descendants had ruled large parts of Russia for over three hundred years. For the last seventy years, Genghis had been a name to be whispered in Mongolia. In 1962, for instance, a party official named Tomor-ochir made the mistake of attending an ill-advised ceremony designed to rehabilitate the image of Genghis Khan. The man was accused of "wrong thinking," dismissed from his post, expelled from the party and, eighteen years later, mysteriously hacked to death in his own apartment.

People had to be circumspect: They hid their Buddhist beliefs, and they found it expedient not to mention Genghis Khan. Ever. Politically correct thinking was the order of the day. Here, from a 1987 book entitled *Modern Mongolian Poetry*, is the celebrated poet Tsevegmidyn Gaitav (1929–1979), with a stirring effort entitled "Our Party":

> *Radiant,*
> *Boundless,*
> *Thinking so clearly and*
> *with perspective*

> *Steering wisely*
> *The state*
> *and the people*

> *Illuminating our road*
> *By the teaching of Lenin—*
> *Sagacious, meaningful,*

> *Daring, straightforward,*
> *You are leading our people,*
> *Forward, along the socialist road*
> *Our Party!*

And so on, until the people got pretty damn sick and tired of all that sagacious illumination. The first demonstrations started in the spring of 1990. Many people carried signs reading MORINDOO, which means "mount up" and was the battle cry of Genghis and his warriors. The Mongolian Communist party, perceiving that it was riding a razor edge on the arc of history, voted to dissolve itself.

Soviet soldiers pulled out of the country. Russia cut its subsidies to Mongolia. By 1992, the country was in a poor way, unable to feed itself or employ its workers.

Baggie, driving down the muddy streets on the outskirts of Ulan Bator, said the country was grateful for an influx of foreign aid from the U.S., among others. "We know," Baggie said, "that the money comes from taxes American people pay. Mongolians want to thank the American people."

We passed Sukhbattor Square, where the demonstrations had begun. Baggie and Bayaraa were among the organizers, and both had been active early on in the Mongolian National Democratic party, which advocated democratic reforms, a free market economy and, inexplicably, I thought at the time, a national diet that included more vegetables.

Looking out at the street scene, it was clear that the times had changed. Robed Buddhist monks strolled across the square; a vast expanse of stone stood where there had once been a statue of Stalin. I could hear, faintly, the tinny sound of someone playing "Lucy in the Sky with Diamonds" on a boom box. The Beatles were very popular in Ulan Bator. Huge hawks buzzed the statue of D. Sukhbattor, and men with ancient cameras took black-and-white souvenir photos of herdsmen in town for what might be a once-in-a-lifetime visit.

At dinner in a new hotel, one of several springing up around town, Baggie explained how he'd fallen into the travel business. In 1993, as a member of the Mongolian National Democratic party, he'd visited the U.S. on an international goodwill trip. One of the stops was in Bozeman, Montana, where he met Kent Maiden and Linda Svendsen, who, through Boojum Expeditions, had been running horseback trips in Chinese Inner Mongolia for over a decade. The couple had even been legally married there, in a Mongolian ceremony. International goodwill led to business arrangements.

Prior to 1992, only one institution could issue the written invitations necessary to obtain a Mongolian visa. Juulchin, the government tourist agency, was essentially in the business of soaking the capitalists. When I inquired about a visa in 1980, the price of a three-week trip was $25,000. Expensive, yes, but you got to hunt and kill Marco Polo sheep, among other exotic and possibly endangered animals. I passed on the deal.

By 1993, with the demise of the Communist party, Baggie was free to team up with Kent and issue his own written invitations to visitors. Prices are a small fraction of what Juulchin used to charge.

Before and after and during dinner, we drank toasts to the ordinary American taxpayer, to free speech, to a free market economy, to the Mongolian National Democratic party, to the American Republican party, which was advising the MNDP on grassroots organizing, and to the new Mongolia altogether, a country finally free to consume more vegetables. The vodka was Mongolian, a popular new brand called Genghis Khan.

• • •

The next day, we flew from Ulan Bator to a town called Uliastai on a Mongolian Airlines jet. At the airport there, one of seven in the country with a paved runway, a young Mongolian fellow walked toward me, dropped a shoulder into my chest, knocked me back a step or two, and kept right on going. Five paces later, he turned smartly and started back. It was going to be a series of slow-motion assaults.

"He thinks you're Russian," Bayaraa explained.

"Hey," I said sharply, "Mee Mer-ee-koon."

"Ahh!" The young man stopped and smiled. *"Saim bainuu?"* he asked politely. How are you?

"Saing," I said. Fine. *"Saim bainuu?"*

And then there was a lot of Mongolian-style handshaking, in which you grab each other's elbows, both of them, and nod and smile a lot. The guy ended up helping us load our luggage into a dilapidated slick-tired bus. He was glad to help. We weren't Russians. We were Mer-ee-koons.

Presently, the bus was bashing its way into the mountains along a narrow, rutted dirt road. We made our way through herds of sheep; and goats; and yaks, which looked to me like fringed Herefords. There are twenty-five million head of livestock grazing in Mongolia, about ten times the human population, and according to my Mongolian-language tapes, the third thing a polite person says to another—after "How are you?" and "How's your family?"—is *Tania mal saim bainuu?* How's your livestock?

In the pasturelands rising up on the other side of the road, men on horseback worked the yaks very much the way Montana ranchers deal with cattle. But instead of ropes, the Mongolian herdsmen used rawhide loops set on the end of long poles. The poles, Bayaraa told me, serve a double purpose. Stick one upright in the ground, and no one will approach. In this treeless grassland, it was one way for a man and woman to ensure themselves a little privacy. It was also a symbol of virility.

Above, hawks and falcons and huge griffons drifted in great circles, silhouetted against Tengri, the sacred sky, which was a brilliant shrieking blue filled with billowing white clouds. A herd of horses galloped across a nearby ridge, their long manes flying in the wind.

Baggie said he approved of my hairstyling mission and had always thought that Mongolian people, his ancient ancestors, may have been the first Americans. It is a theory strongly promoted by the Museum of Natural History in Ulan Bator.

Fifty miles east of Uliastai, the cruel joke of a road ended in what was an attempt at a hot springs resort, a series of whacked-together wooden buildings originally built for Communist party bigwigs. The place looked embarrassed, like a man in a tux at a beer party. All the other habitations in the countryside, without exception, were round felt tents, basically unchanged since the time Genghis declared himself "ruler of all those who live in felt tents." They looked like white puffball mushrooms and were called gers. Don't say *yurt*. Russians say *yurt*.

At the end of the road, wranglers, hired for the trip, watched as we set up our American tents. The men thought our gers were flimsy, but they liked the portability. It took, they said, several hours to take down a Mongolian ger. The wranglers seemed shy, and they smiled constantly, nervously.

In the saddle, though, these same men laughed and sang unselfconsciously, utterly at home on horseback. In Montana, we'd call them can-do cowboys.

Our head wrangler, Lhagra, a lean unflappable man in his fifties, took it upon himself to coach me in matters Mongolian. The wraparound jackets all the men wore were called dels. The sleeves could be rolled down to warm the hands in cold weather, and the sash that held the garment together was a handy place to stash a knife. The oversize boots with turned-up toes were called gutuls. For the past seventy years, children had been taught in school that gutuls were a symbol of Mongolian subservience to religion. You can drop to your knees so much easier in boots with turned-up toes. Actually, Lhagra explained, the boots are designed to slip easily into the stirrup, and to show respect for the earth: Turned-up toes don't tear into the ground.

I learned a Mongolian saddle song about a young camel in the Gobi Desert, just starting off on his first caravan. It is late in the day, and the shadows fall long across the sands. The camel is leaving his mother for the first time. Here the song breaks into a lot of mournful ululation, which is fairly easy to do given the jouncing gait of the horse. The singer then expresses a similar love for his own mother. Mongolian songs never concern death, divorce, or unrequited love. Life is hard enough.

We were circumnavigating Otgontenger (Young Sky) Mountain, which was, at 12,982 feet, the highest point in Mongolia's central Hangay range. The peak itself was hidden behind other, smaller, mountains and we got our first clear glimpse of it when we topped out on a pass at 10,300 feet. A millennium of tradition required that we stop and pay our respects to the mountain at an elaborate ovoo, a construction of sticks and poles, piled tepeelike on an altar of stones. Tattered blue prayer flags tied to the poles snapped in the wind. There were cigarettes and banknotes and pieces of hard cheese piled on the stones. We walked three times around the ovoo, tied hairs from our horses' manes to the poles, and left our offerings.

As we led our horses down the steep slope on the other side of the pass, a cloud passed over the sun, the temperature dropped thirty degrees, and the wind drove a sudden snowfall directly into our faces. It was August, but it felt like winter. Then, maybe half an hour later, the sky cleared and the sun seemed to boom down on us. It wasn't hot, but there was a harsh, unfiltered quality to the light. I could feel my face burning.

We mounted up and rode down into an enormous river valley. There were wind-sculpted boulders on the ridges of the hills that framed the valley, and these ornate rock formations looked like Oriental dragons. It was impossible to estimate distance or to figure the size of the river below, because there were no trees or gers or livestock to measure against the immensity of the land. Lhagra said he saw riders moving along the riverbank. I couldn't even see them with my pocket telescope.

The riders, two men in their early twenties, joined us for a short time, which in Mongolian terms meant two days. We named them for their looks: the Movie Star, and Bad Hair Day, who had about a dozen swirling cowlicks on his head. The strange style made him look perpetually startled.

The men were out marmot hunting, and would sell the skins for a good price at a market in Uliastai. The Movie Star carried a Russian .22 rifle and a bipod strapped to his back. He wore a white sheet over his del, and a kind of white doo-rag hat topped with ludicrous rodent ears. Marmots, I was given to understand, stay close to their burrows and disappear into them at the slightest hint of danger. They were, however, curious, and might stand still for a moment when faced with the eerie specter of a man dressed like the marmot angel of death.

Hunting these bucktoothed rodents was a serious business. An animal that was too easy to shoot—one that was slow or stupid—could kill you and your family. The marmot disease was a bad way to go: ten days of delirium, swollen glands, fever, and screaming pain. In the West, the same misery is called bubonic, or black, plague. In the fourteenth century it killed a third of the population of Europe: twenty-five million people.

The theory is that ship-borne rats brought the plague to Europe. But Tim Severin, in his book *In Search of Genghis Khan*, notes that the first European reports of the plague came in 1347, when it broke out among the troops of the Kipchak Khan, who was besieging the Black Sea port of Kaffa. The Khan, in what must be the first instance of biological warfare in history, catapulted infected corpses over the city walls. There were Italian trading vessels in the port, and they returned to Genoa. Carrying plague.

In a book of Mongolian folktales, I found this cautionary narrative:

A hungry wolf comes upon a horse mired in the mud. The wolf prepares for a feast, but the horse asks him if he shouldn't pull his meal out of the mud first. So the wolf performs this chore and prepares, once again, to eat. The horse resorts to sanitary arguments. Shouldn't the wolf clean his food before he eats it? The wolf acknowledges that this might be a good idea, and licks the mud off the horse. Finally the wolf is ready to eat, but the horse says, "Hey, there's some writing on the hoof of my hind leg. Before you eat me, read that please." The curious wolf walks around the horse, who lifts up his hind leg and bashes in the wolf's skull with a single kick.

The wolf, alone and dying in the mud, howls to himself (and I quote directly from the book here): "I was a blockhead . . . Am I owner that I should have pulled the horse from the mud? Am I the mother who should have licked and cleaned the horse's body? When did I learn to read and write? I'm stupid and now I am dying."

It seemed to me that much of the etiquette I was learning had to do with never having to tell yourself "I'm stupid and now I'm dying." The Mongolian handshake, for instance, the grabbing of elbows, assured each party that neither was carrying a concealed weapon. In a ger, a man took his knife out of his sash and let it hang on a long cord, so it was not within arm's reach. Snuff bottles were accepted in the right hand, while the left hand was placed on the right elbow.

And then there was the matter of the dogs. There were always several around any ger, snarling and snapping at the horses' hooves. These dogs, called Brown Eyes, for the golden eyebrows most of them have, were big German shepherd–shaped animals, with enormous heads, deep chests, and tails that curved up over their backs. When approaching a ger, it is polite to yell "Tie up your dogs!"

A government pamphlet said that this courtesy gives people time to prepare for a visit. Tim Severin thought it had to do with plague: If the people in a ger are infected, they will not answer. That silence, Severin thought, is a signal to ride the hell on out of there. In point of fact, the dogs all wore collars, with a short length of rope attached, and the owners always came out and tied them up. These were not the cringing dogs of Ulan Bator. They were well fed, powerful, and protective: dogs that guarded livestock and sometimes fought off wolves. A couple of them could easily kill a man. It was stupid *not* to yell "Tie up your dogs."

Our friend Bad Hair Day, it turned out, had been mauled by a dog when he was younger. I felt a little bad about the name we'd assigned him when he let me examine his scalp, which was a mass of angry scar tissue.

Mongolia is one of the most sparsely populated countries on earth, and we sometimes rode days between gers. The ones we did see were usually clustered in groups of four to eight. There was always a single wooden pole out front, a hitching post brought in from somewhere else where trees grew. A saddled horse was tethered to every pole I saw: the Mongolian equivalent of leaving the car running. Often, handmade ox carts with wooden wheels were parked beside the ger, and sometimes they were piled high with the dry dung of sheep or horses or yaks, which is burned as fuel.

Bayaraa and Baggie, mindful of what they'd learned from representatives of the U.S. Republican party, stopped at each of the gers and talked about the Mongolian National Democratic party. They used the term *grassroots organizing,* which seemed particularly appropriate.

The gers had no windows and a single low door, always facing south. About eighteen feet in diameter, the tents were supported by a latticework wood frame that folded up like an accordion. Woven rugs, always red, covered the floor, and each ger was arranged in precisely the same manner. The man keeps his saddle and tack to the right of the door. To the left are cooking utensils and children's things. The entire family sleeps in the bed against the left wall, children at their parents' feet. The bed on the right is for guests. Against the wall opposite the door are two low chests of drawers, painted orange. On the chests are framed black-and-white photos: the children at school; the man in his army uniform; the family posing stiffly in Sukhbattor Square.

A tin stove stands in the center of the ger, under a flap at the top of the tent that can be opened or closed. A rope drops down from the upper framework of the ger. It can be fastened to a small boulder beside the hearth, to keep the ger from blowing away in the wind.

People we met said they moved their gers two or three times a year. Families tend to winter a couple thousand feet above their summer pastures. Cold air settles in the valleys and it's always warmer higher up.

We tried to observe the household rules—don't lean against the wall; don't point your feet at the hearth—but Lhagra had reason to critique one aspect of American manners. We were always saying *"bayarala,"* thank you, and it was unnecessary. Almost insulting. Every Mongolian has been forced to take refuge in someone else's ger at one time or another. The tradition, then, is one of unthinking generosity. Guests are fed and feted as a matter of course, and there were numerous small niceties in the rituals. The tea, for instance, had to be made in the guests' sight. It contained mare's milk and salt. An acquired taste. The yogurt, on the other hand, was sweet and delicious, the best I've ever tasted. It was thin enough to drink from a bowl.

Sometimes we drank a liquor of distilled mare's milk, and ate salty rock-hard cheese formed into medallions about the size of silver dollars. I was never able to leave a ger without accumulating gifts amounting to several pocketfuls of the stuff. In return, we gave our hosts what gifts we could: extra flashlights, batteries for the short-wave radio, T-shirts, bandannas, a few spoons of powdered aspirin. We were down to essentials, almost completely out of gifts, but by God we had enough cheese. I could hear the pieces clacking together in my jacket and saddle kit when I rode. It was noisy cheese.

Every single day, without fail, we consumed two massive meals of boiled mutton.

I can say this: The mutton was always fresh. We'd ride into a ring of gers, buy a sheep, and watch the Mongolians slaughter it. The animal is flipped onto its back, and held down. A slit is made in the belly. The butcher inserts his hand, punctures the diaphragm, and finds the vena cava leading out of the heart. Hooks the finger around the vein and yanks. This was said to be the

Buddhist way, the most humane way to kill, and indeed, the sheep was generally dead within thirty seconds.

When Genghis Khan unified the Mongol nation, he established a system of laws, some of which involved penalties for rustling. If a man steals another's livestock, Genghis ruled, he must return the animals, or similar animals, one for one. If he could not, or would not, his "heart" would be "squeezed" until he died.

So the method had the force of tradition behind it.

Mongolians eat every part of the sheep. They crack the bones for the marrow. They boil the head, and make blood sausage from the intestines. The fat, our wranglers said, is the best part. A sin to waste it. Once, when the American contingent cooked dinner, we cut away the fat. The Mongolian herdsmen gathered up the white-and-yellow mess, put it in a pot with water, boiled it, and drank the results down like a thick tea.

Kent had had the foresight to buy several sacks of potatoes imported from Russia, but most of the Mongolian wranglers said they tasted "like dirt." There was an enormous prejudice against vegetables of any kind. The whole idea of farming was disgusting to a herdsman. Being tied to a single plot of land was no life for a man. In any case, the growing season where these men lived, at about eight thousand feet, was about two months long. And much of the ground was permanently frozen a few feet below the surface anyway.

A government pamphlet tried to put the best light on this situation. "Mongolia," it said, "is totally self-sufficient in vegetable production."

Some people, it seemed, thrived on the diet. Herdsmen and their wives lead hard, active lives and we met plenty of folks in their eighties. Still, life expectancy in Mongolia is below the world average: 64.6 years for men; 66.5 for women. Which is why the newly formed Mongolian National Democratic party platform has a plank that essentially reads "Eat your vegetables."

There were ovoos everywhere, at every pass or narrow canyon a rider might care to traverse, and I was leaving huge handfuls of hard cheese medallions as offerings. It was a losing proposition.

By my calculation, we were still carrying over fifty pounds of noisy cheese, and we sounded like castanets on horseback.

Michael Abbot, our fly-fishing aficionado, was getting grumpy about angling opportunities. There were grayling in the waters above eight thousand feet, and lennick—a four-to-ten-pound ugly brown trout-looking fish—lower down. Wherever we stopped, however, there was usually some religious prohibition about fishing that stretch of the river: A famous lama had once walked the banks, and we don't fish there out of respect. Or, the river provides water for cooking and washing and drinking so we don't fish as a way of showing our gratitude.

In point of fact, we never saw anyone from the gers fishing, anywhere. Mongolians don't enjoy fishing as a sport, and they don't eat fish. They eat boiled mutton and yogurt and noisy cheese. Michael Abbot thought the sacred fishing regulations were a fairly low rent form of religious sacrifice, like giving up Limburger for Lent.

He had good luck fishing on the banks of remote rivers, in unsanctified places. But even then, miles from the nearest habitation, there were sometimes restrictive rules. On the back side of Otgontenger, for instance, at about eight thousand feet, we camped at a lake called Doot Nur. It was set in a grassy basin and surrounded by hills rising to ten thousand feet, which hid the mountain ranges beyond. Above nine thousand feet, the hills had accumulated a dusting of snow. Michael Abbot stood watching the evening hatch and muttering about Limburger. Doot Nur, the Lake of the Voices, was off-limits to fishing. In the spring, people gathered around the lake and listened to the ice break up. Sounds echoed in the basin, and sometimes you could hear voices, often the voices of your ancestors.

So . . . you could drink from the waters of Doot Nur, okay, but you couldn't bathe there and you certainly couldn't fish.

The lake was large, maybe five square miles. Christoph pointed out several dozen tiny specks moving slowly on the opposite bank and handed me his binoculars. The specks were camels: huge, shaggy double-humped animals. They moved up through the green grasses and looked exceedingly strange trudging across the snow above.

The camels, Lhagra told me, were domestic beasts, not wild, and were used as pack animals when a family moved its ger. Deduct a few dozen karma points from my cosmic account: I rode around the lake, cut out the lead camel, and spent fifteen minutes frustrating his instinct to get back to the herd. I thought, Well, here I am in Mongolia cutting camels in the snow. Arlene said it looked like a cigarette ad.

And then we were riding up another endless valley that dropped directly down out of Otgontenger. At about nine thousand feet there was a huge ovoo, the most elaborate yet, and I saw it as an appropriate place to offer up several big handfuls of noisy cheese.

We rode and walked the horses up a steep, rocky slope to eleven thousand feet, where there was a small lake at the base of the glacier on Otgontenger Mountain. We hobbled the horses on a level grassy spot. Mongolians ride carrying a long rawhide rope, attached to the bridle. A Mongolian herdsman may fall off his horse, but he never drops the rawhide rope. A man on foot in the grassland is a dead man. The rope is also used to tie a horse's two front legs together, and the hobbled animals graze placidly in a series of festive bunny hops.

It was about five hundred yards over boulder-strewn ground from the grass to the lake. There were mini-ovoos every ten feet: a small cairn, a couple of twigs, each of them worth one, maybe two pieces of noisy cheese. Lhagra advised us to drink from the lake, for our health. The water came from the glacier, which was everlasting. Drink from the lake and live forever.

Ominous clouds moved over the peak above us. A wind rolled down the glacier. It swirled and whistled over the lake. I could hear the sound of distant muttering voices, which came, I saw finally, from a series of small waterfalls on the far side of the lake. The sun was setting and the place seemed just a bit spooky to me. One man's spooky, I suppose, is another man's sacred.

We rode three more hours, through the dark, to our campsite.

Naturally, it snowed. In the morning, the sky was crisp and blue and the sun glittered on the glacier above. The light was very nearly blinding. The wranglers said we must have done okay by the mountain, shown proper respect. Otgontenger had washed its face for us.

That day, we began retracing our route, riding endlessly and wailing in the saddle about lonely camels. The plan now was to top another pass, dump some noisy cheese at the ovoo there, and ride down through the Ider River valley to the town of Toson Cengel, where we'd catch a flight back to Ulan Bator. Just below the headwaters of the Ider, there was a ring of about eight gers, where we stopped to talk with the people about hairstyling matters. Baggie explained the scientific nature of my request. Followed here much murmured intensity among the Mongolians. They didn't want me to touch their heads. Their concerns were a complicated amalgam of Buddhist and shamanistic beliefs that I didn't fully understand.

But hey, Baggie said, no problem. Or words to that effect. I didn't want to touch their heads anyway. I wanted them to cut a few strands of their own hair, using their own knives. Baggie said that I feared DNA contamination, which he attempted to explain. The Mongolians regarded me tolerantly, as if to say, Well, there's no accounting for other folks' religion.

So the people cut strands of their own hair, with their own knives, and placed them in separate Ziploc bags for me. One of the families gave us a thirty-pound tub of noisy cheese as a gift. The tradition was to give back the tub, filled with our own gifts. We sorted through what was left of our dwindling gear. Give 'em a couple of rain jackets: We only had a few more days, and the weather might hold. Give 'em a few flashlights: We would be able to set up our camps by moonlight.

We rode off, my mission accomplished and our packs considerably lighter. Unfortunately, all up and down the Ider River valley, the word was out about the strange Mer-ee-koons who worshipped hair. People rode out to visit with us, and they never came empty-handed. Generally, they carried metal dairy pails full of yogurt. We stopped, visited, ate the yogurt, rinsed the pails, and returned them full of polar fleece jackets. If it got cold, we could wrap ourselves in sleeping bags.

And then, finally, only a few days outside of Toson Cengel, when we were completely out of anything at all that might be construed as an appropriate gift, I saw a pair of yogurt riders, two miles back and a thousand feet above. We fled, thundering over the grassland, galloping where we could, and simply enduring where we couldn't. We fled in a deafening clatter of noisy cheese. We fled the smiling beneficence of Mongolian generosity.

When the yogurt riders caught us, as they surely would, we'd give them the shirts off our backs.

"Help, My Pilot Just Had a Heart Attack and I Can't Fly a Plane"

"I think I ate some bad fish last night," your pilot says.

You don't even know the guy's name. Freddy somebody, and you've hired him to drop you off at a remote fishing camp on a lake in northern Wisconsin. You're in a little tiny four-seater plane, but you don't know what kind. You know dick about airplanes.

So you're sitting next to Freddy, on the right-hand side of the plane. There's a kind of little steering wheel in front of you and some rudders at your feet. It's all the same stuff Freddy has in front of him, and you can see your steering wheel move in and out and twist around as the pilot horses the little plane through the sky. It's a bright, clear day, and the fish you're thinking about are muskie. They say it takes fifteen hundred casts to catch a . . .

"Damn!" Freddy burps out an anemic little burp, puts his hand to his chest, grimaces, and says, "Jesus."

You turn to your fishing partner in the backseat. His name is Joe. Anyone who reads any of the hook and bullet magazines knows that everyone's fishing partner is always named Joe. "Me and Joe," the articles begin, "were flying up north to hook the monster muskie of Lake Mishikobi . . ."

"Joe, you got any Pepto for Freddy?"

"Unghhhhhh," says Freddy, whose face suddenly looks ghastly.

You are developing a very bad feeling about all this. Freddy's eyes roll up in their sockets and his head drops onto his chest. He pitches forward in his seat and kind of hangs there, restrained by his chest harness.

Freddy is dead to the world. Freddy may, in fact, be dead.

"Me and Joe crashed in a ball of flame and were incinerated somewhere a few hundred miles short of Lake Mishikobi and didn't catch any muskie at all. The end."

This sort of thing happens every once in a while. On August 21, 1988, for instance, a small plane went down near Wall township, New Jersey. According to an aircraft accident report filed with the Aircraft Owners and Pilots Association (AOPA) Safety Foundation, "The private pilot of a Piper PA-28-150 took off with one passenger and a few minutes after takeoff, he became unconscious. The passenger gave the pilot mouth-to-mouth resuscitation: however the pilot was not revived. The nonpilot passenger attempted an off-airport landing and struck trees." The passenger received serious injuries. An autopsy on the pilot showed "severe occlusion of his coronary arteries."

Or: On November 13, 1985, just after takeoff at Fayetteville, Arkansas, a fifty-three-year-old pilot "released the controls and threw his head back." The only passenger, the pilot's wife, who had no previous flying experience, "kept the aircraft airborne for almost two hours with help from an airborne pilot that [sic] was talking to her. Both engines quit from fuel starvation and she made a forced landing three miles from the Fayetteville Airport." The wife was seriously injured. "She later stated that she felt that her husband had died just after takeoff."

Or: From another report about an accident in which both pilot and passenger died: "The autopsy report indicated that the pilot had a 'patchy healed myocardial infarct' prior to the accident."

The FAA does not keep records for incidents in which there are no injuries or no property damage. Sometimes, however, a pilot becomes incapacitated for some reason, and a passenger with no previous flying experience miraculously brings the airplane in to a safe landing. On October 19, 1991, for instance, sixty-two-year-old Patrick Sharp died of a heart attack while piloting a Piper Cub over eastern Oregon. His daughter, twenty-three-year-old Patti Sharp, who had never flown before, put the plane down safely in a field outside the ghost town of Shaniko.

On November 23, 1983, Jane Turner, of Phoenix, assumed control of a Cherokee when her husband suffered a fatal heart attack. She was in the right rear seat and coached the right front seat passenger, Editha Merrill, a seventy-eight-year-old great-grandmother, in the use of the controls. Mrs. Merrill brought the plane down at Luke Air Force Base. There were no injuries.

Jane Turner, as it happened, had taken what is called a pinch-hitter course from the AOPA. The course is designed for nonpilots: people who frequently fly as passengers in small planes and who want to know how to land the damn things. If they have to.

I took the weekend course in Concord, California. There were several hours of classroom work and four hours of actual flying time in company with an iron-nerved flight instructor. I racked up twelve takeoffs and twelve landings. The takeoffs were easy. A few of the landings were not bad at all.

One day, after the classes were over, I sat with George Rhodes, my classroom instructor, and John Speuernagel, my flight instructor, and I asked what would happen if a pilot suddenly became incapacitated and none of the passengers had any flying experience. I wanted to know what would happen to me and Joe. Now that Freddy's dead.

"We're going to die," Joe says.

(This can be either a nightmare or a fantasy of competence and courage. The fantasy is preferable. In it, you're incredibly cool.)

"I don't *want* to die," Joe whines. He disgusts you. (This guy's a dithering simp. I don't even know why you'd want to go fishing with him in the first place. Let's make Joe piss his pants and pass out so we won't have to listen to him anymore.)

The plane seems to be flying level. You take the little steering wheel in your hands and push in very slightly. The plane's nose dips slightly. You pull back and the plane levels out. Well now, if you can keep her level, there's some time to think.

You are looking down into the Wisconsin forest. There is some kind of settlement in a clearing up ahead. It's a northern Wisconsin town: one gas station, a general store, twenty-nine taverns. The plane is so high you can hardly see the buildings. So there's lots of time to think.

Maybe you should use the radio. Maybe you should try calling for help. Just put the headphones on and pick up the little doodad. Push the button on the side and talk. That's the way you saw Freddy do it.

"Uh, hello? Hello? Can anyone hear me?"

Should you say "mayday" or something? Don't people always say "mayday" in the movies? Instead, you say: "I'm in trouble up here. I think my pilot just had a heart attack and I can't fly a plane. Hello? Hello?"

And a voice comes back over the radio: "Aircraft in distress calling Dulles approach. Say again."

It was at this point, as we were constructing the me-and-Joe scenario, that my flight instructor, John Speuernagel, and I had a brief disagreement.

"Dulles," I spluttered. "What's Dulles doing responding to these poor guys up in northern Wisconsin?"

"Well, I don't know northern Wisconsin," Speuernagel said reasonably. "Let's put them down in the Washington, D.C., area. Just because I know the terrain."

"Can't do Wisconsin at all?"

"Nope."

• • •

Suddenly, inexplicably, you are somewhere over the Washington, D.C., area. Joe is still passed out—the weenie—and another message is coming through on the radio.

"Aircraft in distress. This is Dulles approach. Stand by. We'll coordinate an effort here and see what we can do to help you. I'm going to ask you some questions, and I would like you to give me the answer to those questions as you are able."

The voice, which is remarkably calm, asks if the plane is going up or down or if the thing seems to be flying level, which it is. What kind of plane is it?

"I don't know." But wait. Didn't Freddy have a clipboard? With a partially completed bill on it? Didn't he put it behind his seat, in a little net compartment?

"The plane's a Cherokee 180. Registration number N5330N."

"Very good. We'll refer to you as Thirty November from now on."

And then there are a lot of questions about the radio. There seem to be half a dozen radiolike gadgets stacked up just to the right of Freddy. You describe lots of digital readouts, one on top of the other.

"Thirty November, you have a digital stack. Take a look and see if one of those radios is showing 120.45."

The top one does.

The controller cautions you not to adjust that. It is the radio. "We don't want to lose you. Okay," he says, "now look to the bottom of the radio stack. You're going to see one of two things. You may see an instrument that has a knob on the left that says ALT or SBY . . ."

"I see it."

"And you may see four numbers to the right of that knob."

"It says 1700."

"Good. Go to the numbers on that instrument and adjust them to 7700."

"I've got 7700."

"All right. On that instrument, you will see a button that says IDENT. Have you located that?"

"Got it."

"Okay. Push that button. You should see a light. Do you see a light?"

"Yes."

"Okay, Thirty November, perfect. You just lit up like a Christmas tree on our screen. We've now got radar contact. I show you at fifty-five hundred feet. Now, we're going to turn you around toward Dulles and we're going to bring you in for a landing. Can you hold level at your heading for a bit?"

"I think so."

"I'm going to do a bit of coordinating and get back to you."

It occurs to you that they're probably going crazy down there. They'd have to reroute commercial traffic. Assemble a team of ambulances. Fire trucks.

"Thirty November. Take a look at the panel in front of you. Do you see the control yoke? It looks like a steering wheel, but it has two handles. Do you see it?"

And the controller takes you through some easy maneuvers. Push for descent; pull for ascent. Piece of cake. Turn the wheel gently to the right and the plane banks easily to the right. Try it on the left side.

"Okay, Thirty November. Don't overcontrol. Just a very light pressure."

After each maneuver, the controller has you level the plane so that the whole machine is precisely parallel to the ground. You are going to want to be parallel to the ground when you try to land.

"Thirty November, you now have control of the plane and we're going to do a little housekeeping here. Can you locate some fuel gauges?"

There are two of them. The one on the right says 20; the one on the left, 10.

"Thirty November, you're probably flying on the left tank. We're going to switch to the right tank and give you a little more fuel to get into Dulles."

With the controller's help you locate a bank of switches on the subpanel and snap on the red one that reads FUEL PUMP. You then

switch tanks, which is not any fun at all because the switch—
actually a large red lever—is on the pilot's side, on the frame of
the plane, next to dead Freddy's left shin.

"Thirty November, we're going to start you down pretty soon.
The easiest way to do that is to just reduce the power a little bit.
So we're going to look at the power controls now. They are in the
center of the panel between the two control yokes, and you
should see three controls there. The black-handled one is the
throttle. The red-handled one is the mixture control. For our
landing, I want you to move the red one forward as far as it will
go."

And when you've done that, the controller asks you to locate
the altimeter, which is one of six instruments in front of dead
Fred. It's not hard to identify since it's labeled ALTIMETER.

"Thirty November, what's your altimeter reading?"

"Uh, 4, 9. 4900 feet, I guess."

"The big hand is on the four and the little one on the nine?"

"Yes."

"Thirty November, you have plenty of clearance. Can you see
the ground from there?"

You can see it just fine.

"Okay, Thirty November. You're twenty-five miles northwest
of Dulles. In another ten minutes you should be able to see the
airport very easily. Now, I want you to go to the power handle.
The big black T-handle, next to the red fuel-mixture handle. You
got it?"

You pull back on the handle, just move it an inch or two as
instructed. The engine noise decreases a little. There's a tachome-
ter over near the pilot, and you read off the numbers to the controller.

"Twenty-two rpm. Good power setting, Thirty November.
That will get you into a nice gentle descent. I show you presently
at forty-five hundred feet. Now we're going to arrest that rate of
descent. Push gently up on the black power lever."

The nose of the plane levels out and the altimeter seems steady.
There is a ridge ahead—plenty of clearance—and then you can see
a huge airport complex spread out in front of you.

"Okay, Thirty November. You're about ten miles northwest of Dulles. Let's go back to the power control and bring it back to twenty-two rpm and continue our descent. We want to go down to about three thousand feet. Big hand on the three, little hand on the zero."

And the plane, indeed, does seem to be very gradually dropping. It takes several long minutes to reach three thousand feet.

"Thirty November. Look out the right side of your airplane and you should see another airplane right beside you. That's an airplane from the Army Guard unit and we're going to go ahead and let them check in with you."

"Thirty November? This is Army Guard 403. We're going to get you down safe and sound. We'll be able to tell you what to do, and we'll be able to tell you if your nose is too high or too low. We'll bring you down at the proper speed."

There is a short pause while you think about the rest of your life.

"Hey, Thirty November," Army 403 says, "relax. We're from the United States government. We're here to help you."

"You're from the government and you're here to help?"

"Thirty November, I've been in two wars and believe in the power of laughter."

"Well, uh, thanks Army 403."

You can actually see the pilot of Army 403. He's a man in his forties, some colonel probably, and he's smiling and waving. Just now, he's back on the radio.

"Thirty November, we're going down to two thousand feet. Just pull back on the black T-bar, the throttle. Very, very gently now."

And slightly later: "Thirty November, your nose is only slightly down. Do you see the vertical speed indicator right under the altimeter? It says VSI on it. Is the needle position just a bit under the big five?"

It is.

"That's good. You're descending at about four hundred feet a minute. Which means your power setting is just about right."

And then there's a lot of chatter between the controller and

Army 403 about leveling off at two thousand; about flying past the airport and approaching from the south. You look down and notice that you are flying right by the airport.

"Thirty November, we're in good shape here. I want you to take the control yoke and very gently move it to the left. Good."

You are making a 180-degree turn. "Stay with it," says Army 403. "Very good. Okay, you've almost come around. And . . . perfect. Now, just a slight pressure to the right. That'll level your wings." And you are looking down at a runway, very far away.

The controller says, "Army Guard, you're five miles southeast of Dulles, heading one hundred. Descend and maintain twelve hundred. Looks real good. We're going to sequence you for one right. Thirty November? Good luck."

You seem to be lined up with the runway just right. The altimeter reads 1100 feet. There is no traffic at all, just a row of ambulances and fire trucks revving up next to the terminal.

"Thirty November," your personal colonel says. "We're going to go down again. Reduce power a little. We'll descend at four hundred feet a minute. You have the runway on your nose?"

"Yes."

"Looking good. Looking good."

It occurs to you that everyone has forgotten something very important. "Are my wheels down? Do I have to put the sons of bitches down?"

"Negative, Thirty November. You have fixed landing gear and everything looks very good. Uh, Thirty November, have you ever used landing flaps?"

"What are landing flaps?"

"Nothing important. What is your speed now?"

"Looks like just under ninety."

"Okay, Thirty November, we've got about two miles of runway down there for you and we don't need flaps."

As the ground approaches, Army 403 advises you to get your feet on the rudders. He says that if the nose turns right, you push gently on the left rudder. If it turns left, hit the right. He says this will compensate for ground winds, but all of this is a little academic because the runway is rising up to meet you and you are going ninety miles an hour and everything is beginning to happen way too fast. Rudders? Ground winds?

Army 403 says, "Keep descending, Thirty November. You see the lip of the runway? It's just under you now. You're only sixty feet in the air and leveled out real good. Okay. Your nose is a little right. Give me a gentle push on the left rudder. A little more. Yesssss. You've straightened out. Real good. Now, in a few seconds I'm going to tell you to chop the power: Just pull that black T-bar, the throttle, pull it all the way back. Not yet. Get ready. You're almost ready to hear those tires squeak. Little bit of right rudder now. Yes. Okay, aaaaaand chop the power."

The engine virtually stops and the plane keeps gliding along on its own inertia, gliding level, parallel to the runway, but it is dropping gradually, very gradually, and you realize that you could, in fact, walk away from this one.

"Thirty November, you're only about fifteen feet in the air. Pull gently back on the yoke to put your nose in the air. Good. Hey, did you hear those tires? Thirty November, you're on the ground, pal."

But now you're going ninety miles an hour across the tarmac in an awkward vehicle that you have no idea how to steer. Or stop.

"Just let her roll out, Thirty November. Give me a little right rudder. Good. And pull that red handle all the way back. It'll make the prop stop. Okay."

And you are sitting on the runway, not moving at all and entirely alive.

This is the way it would go in the best of all possible worlds. It would turn out that Freddy survives, and that when Geraldo Rivera calls to ask you to be on his show, you get to turn him down flat. Joe writes a best-selling book on stress management and passes out on Geraldo's show. At Lake Mishikobi, you catch a muskie on the first cast, return home to discover that you are, in fact, married to Sharon Stone and that you've won millions of dollars in a multistate lottery you forgot entering.

This is your fantasy.

Either that, or you could crash and burn.

Buford's Revenge

"Hey," my companion said, "look at that spider's nest."

I turned to where he was pointing and saw a beehive. There were no bees in evidence, only a spider—a daddy longlegs—crawling over the hive.

My companion and I were both thirteen. He was a city kid, very smooth, and knew how to smoke cigarettes in an extremely sophisticated manner, by which I mean he could do it without coughing. He beat me at pool every afternoon and we both liked the same girl, whose name was Cherry B. He often made her laugh, mostly at my expense.

At this point, however, it was just me and him, walking through the woods at a Virginia resort that catered to vacationing families: mine; his; Cherry B's.

"Watch this," the guy said. He picked up a stick. "I'm going to bust the hell out of that spider's nest."

"Don't do that," I shouted.

"What's the matter? You scared of spiders, Buford?"

He called me Buford. I was a country kid, and kids from the country were all named Gomer or Buford in this guy's experience. We were slow and stupid. I longed to invent a retaliatory nickname for him, something clever and annoying, if not actually humiliating. Something to make Cherry B laugh.

"You know what's going to happen when I bust this nest?" He smiled in a bullying manner. "About a million spiders are going to come out and crawl all over your butt, Buford."

He shouldered the stick and made as if to whack the hive.

There was time. I could have told him. I have, over the years, been entirely unable to justify this moral failure to myself. What I learned in my fourteenth year on my summer vacation is that I will not always do the right thing and that women, remorseless creatures, will not only forgive but sometimes actually reward such character flaws.

The beehive hung from a tree on a steep hillside. I figured that the guy would run downhill when it happened, and that he'd take the bees with him. So . . . I'd run uphill.

What I did next could probably be described as a full Buford: I gibbered in fear and ran uphill as fast as I could, my hands in the air, screaming about spiders.

I never saw him whack the hive. I could hear his derisive laughter, and I believe I may have even heard the sound the stick made when it hit.

Thirty seconds passed. I was still running, sprinting hard, when the screams started. They were more or less continuous and seemed to be moving downhill, diminishing in volume, like the wail of a retreating police siren.

That afternoon, I played pool with Cherry B in the common room, and told her the story of the spider's nest, which made her laugh.

The next day, he was back. Same swagger, same superior manner. But no one looks very cool with lumpy bee stings all over his face and neck.

"Run into some bees, did you?" I asked.

"Why the hell didn't you tell me, Buford?"

"Geez," I said, in a kind of slow, brain-damaged drawl, "I thought you was just funnin' me there . . . Spiderman." Cherry B laughed out loud.

That night I kissed her, and she kissed me back.

It was a summer vacation on the dark side.

Glacier Bay

You know how guys in beer ads are always pictured doing stuff you wouldn't do—or shouldn't do—when you've been drinking beer? In the Beer Ad Universe, guys continually engage in potentially dangerous activities like bungee-jumping or roofing their houses or talking to women.

Recently I discovered that last year, I was a beer ad guy.

It was a print-ad campaign, and apparently there was a poster, along with a lot of those little cardboard tents they put on tables encouraging people to buy beer. The picture on the poster and on the cardboard tent was of me. I am a small speck of a guy in a kayak, surrounded by floating icebergs and dwarfed before an enormous tidewater glacier looming two hundred feet above me.

I suspect the ad campaign was designed to suggest that this beer is as cool and refreshing as a couple million pounds of ice grinding down a mountainside.

The picture was taken in Glacier Bay National Park and Preserve, located about seventy miles north and west of Juneau, Alaska. A guidebook I read before my visit encouraged folks to book midsummer trips, but it was late September and snowing moronically when I arrived at Park Headquarters, at Bartlett Cove, near the mouth of the bay.

The next day I rented a kayak. The concessionaire said there was only one other kayak rented out: some crazy guy paddling around all alone in the snow. That was my partner, photographer Paul Dix, the future beer photo entrepreneur.

I was a day late—several flights had been canceled due to snow—but Paul had said he'd meet me about fifty miles north, up Muir Inlet, near the "snout" of McBride Glacier. Despite the delay, I suspected he'd still be there waiting, because Paul takes his commitments seriously. Also, I was bringing the food.

I lugged my kayak through ankle-deep snow down to the tour boat, which, for a small fee, would drop me at a gravel bar near McBride Glacier, a place, I learned later, Paul had renamed Hungry Point. It was a five-hour trip up the inlet, and, of course, it snowed. You really couldn't see anything. Then the wind picked up. I figured it was a katabatic wind, the kind that comes howling down off mountains of ice because of the simple physics of gravity: Cold air is heavier than warm air, so it sinks to flatland and squirts out horizontally. Sometimes at fifty or sixty miles an hour.

The tour boat dropped me off at the gravel bar. Here, predictably, the snow was being driven horizontally by the wind. Worse, it was falling as corn snow, which consists entirely of exceedingly hard little white pellets, so the situation as a whole was rather like being sandblasted with crushed ice.

The few tourists on the boat regarded me with that somber homage our society pays to the visibly deranged, which is to say they were pretty much doubled over laughing in the snow on the deck. So the boat pulled away, and I was left standing alone on a gravel bank, unable to see more than fifteen feet in any direction and feeling quite sorry for myself, when Paul Dix came paddling out of the ice storm, and greeted me with a hearty "Where in hell's the *food*?"

We sat in a tent for most of the rest of the day, and Paul filled me in on his adventures to date. There were black bears and Alaskan Brown bears all over. The Browns were like the grizzlys we were familiar with in Yellowstone Park, only bigger. Yesterday Paul had paddled into a sandy cove, looking for a place to camp. A bear had recently padded across the beach, and Paul was measuring his own foot (diminutive and pitiable) against one of the prints (colossal and appalling) when he noticed the bear had left something else on the beach. What it had left wouldn't fit in a gallon pail and was still steaming. Paul decided to paddle on.

"Good thing you weren't carrying any food," I said.

"Yeah," Paul replied pointedly, "I sure was lucky."

In fact, we *were* lucky. The next day dawned clear. The sky was cobalt-blue, there was not a breath of wind, and the sea was like glass, a mirror to the sky and the mountains on either side of the inlet, which was about a mile wide in that spot. We paddled over the reflections of snowcapped peaks, on our way to Muir Glacier, as the sun shone and the temperature rose to a little over 70 degrees, which is about as warm as it ever gets in Glacier Bay.

And then, there in front of us was the glacier, pouring off the mountain and into the sea. The enormous wall of ice, the terminus of the glacier, is called the snout, and this one looked to be about two hundred feet high and maybe a mile across.

The whole of Glacier Bay is shaped a little like a horseshoe, open end to the ocean, with the inland section surrounded by mountains that rise from sea level to ten-, eleven-, and fifteen-thousand-foot-high peaks. Snow falls in the upper elevations, never melts, is compressed by the next year's snow—and the next decade's—until it turns into heavy, dense ice, which flows downhill, as all water must. The ice makes pretty good time, too, sweeping down to the sea at the rate of four to seven feet a day.

The terminus, that great wall of ice with its foot in the sea, is subject to tides that rise and fall up to twenty feet, and these tides eat away at the base of the glacier so that great slabs of it "calf" off the main body and crash into the ocean in an explosion of spray. The sound of the glacier calving can be heard for miles, and the mountain across the inlet from Muir Glacier is called White Thunder Ridge.

Paul and I camped on a gravel slope below White Thunder Ridge, and we might have gotten some sleep were it not for the damn northern lights, which arced across an ebony starfield like phosphorescent green smoke interspersed with dozens of red lightning bolts running in ultra-slow motion. All the while, the sound of calving ice rumbled off the ridge above. It was like having the whole damn philharmonic orchestra come over to play Beethoven for you at midnight: The mindless and ungrateful go to sleep so they can rise up in the morning fully rested and spiritually impoverished.

For the next few days, Paul and I played chicken with the glacier. Kayakers are cautioned to stay at least half a mile from the snout, but distances were impossible to calculate. I'd get in there, way too close, and hear what sounded like the magnified cracking of automatic-gun fire. Then a great two-hundred-foot-high block of ice would separate itself from the glacier and fall, slowly it seemed, into the sea with a roar that echoed against the mountains for a full minute. And afterward, maybe five minutes later, a small ripple of a wave would roll past my kayak, and I figured I could maybe move in a little closer.

It was at this point that I saw glaucous-winged gulls making for the glacier and diving for stunned fish brought up by the falling ice. They were tiny in my vision, like children's drawings of birds, and I thought again that I might paddle up a little closer.

I avoided the icebergs, big as mansions, and made my way through a watery field of "bergy" bits, smaller slabs of ice, that pretty much covered the surface of the sea. There was a strange sound all around, a crackling, like static electricity, and it was getting louder as I paddled toward the foot of the glacier before me. It took a while until I understood that it was the bergy bits that were crackling, in the manner of a very cold ice cube dropped into a glass of water.

There were harbor seals basking in the sun on the larger slabs of ice, and some of them dropped into the water, disappeared for a time, then surfaced near my kayak. They had heads like wet Labrador retrievers—that same friendly curiosity—and one came close enough for me to touch with my paddle had I wanted to. He tilted his head in a quizzical manner, dove, then surfaced again on the other side of the kayak. I thought he wanted to play tag, and I paddled toward him, at which point my kayak was rocked by a sound so loud it could actually be felt.

I looked up to see a block of ice the size of a twenty-story building falling in my direction. Time slowed down, as it does in these situations, and I had the leisure to fully appreciate what an enormous horse's ass I was. Eventually, about a month later it seemed, the ice thundered into the sea far in front of my kayak. It threw up a wave that rolled toward me in a ten-foot-high crest of dirty brown water, capped off with pieces of ice ranging in size from fist to Ford. I paddled forward, to take the wave at a run so that it wouldn't crest over me. My kayak rolled easily over the top and slipped down the back side. The last rumble of the calving echoed off White Thunder Ridge, and I could hear the bergy bits snapping all around. Some insane person was beating a drum hysterically inside my chest.

Which, I think, is when Paul—who was quite a ways behind me—snapped the picture that someone thought might sell beer.

The weather held for a week, and we paddled back down the inlet toward Bartlett Cove and the mouth of the bay, a trip that is a time-lapse lesson in plant succession. Two hundred years ago, the explorer Captain George Vancouver mapped what was then Glacier Bay: a ten-mile inlet, capped off by a four-thousand-foot-high wall of ice. Over the past two hundred years, since the end of "the Little Ice Age," that immense glacier has retreated almost sixty-five miles, and the land it exposed was all barren rock and sterile gravel.

But the planet is modest and she quickly clothes herself with life.

Even under White Thunder Ridge, on land that had been ex-posed perhaps ten years ago, Paul and I found "black crust," an algal feltlike nap that retains water and stabilizes silt so that, eventually, mosses grow. They in turn support hardy pioneers, like fireweed and dryas. These plants are plentiful a few miles from the retreating glaciers. Further down the inlet, alder breaks spring out of thick beds of dryas. The alders drop nitrogen-rich leaves, building a soil that enables spruce to take hold and eventually shade out the alders. At Bartlett Cove, which was under four thousand feet of ice two hundred years ago, there is a hemlock and spruce climax forest.

Paddling down the Muir Inlet, moving forward through time, Paul and I often saw Alaskan Brown bears padding across golden sand beaches. One day, a pack of killer whales came steaming up the mile-wide inlet, about eight abreast. Orcas, sometimes called the wolves of the sea, hunt in packs, and they are not often seen far up the inlet or near the ice. The twenty-five-to-thirty-foot-long whales swim fast, almost thirty miles an hour, and they don't like constantly colliding with bergy bits, not to mention full-on icebergs. This pack must have been hungry. I figured they were on their way to visit our friends the harbor seals, currently basking unaware on the ice at the foot of Muir Glacier.

We heard wolves howling in the backcountry at night. Once, down inlet from the alder breaks, we saw a kayaker, far out ahead of us, his paddle dipping from side to side. This was the first human being we'd seen in a couple of weeks, and we called out to him. The kayaker failed to respond, probably, we decided later, because he turned out to be a bull moose. It was his antlers swaying from side to side as he swam that had looked like a kayak paddle.

Paul, had he known he was going to sell a photo to a Canadian beer company, might have taken a picture of that moose's head. Instead, he got a horse's ass. I never did see the poster, but you'd think those Canadian beer execs would send me a few cases of their fine product so I could go bungee-jumping and talk to women. At least get my roof fixed.

A Darkness on the River

The Marañón River drops out of the Peruvian Andes and flows into the Amazon, some six hundred miles to the east, near Iquitos. In the state of Amazonas, in the province of Condorconqui, just below the eastern foothills of the Andes, the Marañón is wide and fast. Between the towns of Imacita and Santa María de Nieva, just past the place where the Cenepa River flows into the Marañón from the north, there is an island about a quarter of a mile long and perhaps one hundred yards across at its widest. On the evening of January 18, 1995, two twenty-six-year-old Americans, Josh Silver and Patchen Miller, floated past the island in a large balsa-wood raft they had built several days earlier. They tied off in the eddy at the downriver tail of the island. About nine-thirty that night, Patchen Miller and Josh Silver were shot and left for dead.

Josh Silver survived and was treated for his wounds at an army base, then transferred to a hospital in the town of Santa María de

Nieva. The American consul general in Peru, Thomas Holladay, was notified by radio telephone that two Americans had been attacked. One was being treated for his wounds; another was missing and feared dead.

Holladay notified the parents of Patchen Miller, Sandra Miller of New Hampshire, and Paul Dix, a Montana photographer and human-rights activist. At the time, Dix was in Nicaragua. He'd driven down to that country from the U.S., carrying a truckload of clothing and medical supplies to be distributed to the poor.

Dix immediately flew to Peru. The arrangements he made were a blur. Had he flown from Managua to Houston first? Or Miami? He was caught in a spiral of obsessive thinking: Patchen was only twenty-six, and therefore he couldn't be dead. Patchen was an experienced traveler. He'd been to Central America with Paul. Traveled there for six months. He'd been to Nepal and Thailand. He was sensitive to the people he met, and those people loved him. He made lasting friends everywhere he went and he was good on rivers and in the wilderness and he could live off the land and he was Paul's son and he was only twenty-six years old and he couldn't be dead.

The Peruvian army, the police, and many of the good people of Santa María de Nieva searched for Patchen's body. By the time Paul Dix arrived in Lima, there was no longer any hope.

Thomas Holladay's office was in the fashionable Miraflores district of Lima. Hotels there are expensive, most rooms running to over $100 a day, and Paul checked into a youth hostel—a fifty-nine-year-old man living cheap in a ten-bed dormitory room. He had to be close to Holladay, who was receiving occasional reports over the scratchy radio telephone linkup from Santa María de Nieva.

Holladay's office was set on a Miraflores side street that was blocked off to traffic by large cement pillars, which were guarded by soldiers with automatic rifles. There was still a lingering threat of car bombs, or attacks by the remnants of the Sendaro Luminoso (Shining Path), the Maoist rebels whose campaign of terrorism stalled in 1992, when its leader, Abimael Guzman, was finally captured.

Paul Dix made his way past the pillars and shoved his passport through a window covered over in bullet-proof glass; he was given a numbered visitor's pass and escorted to Holladay's office. The consul general was a burly man with a full beard, just going to gray. He wore immaculate suits, spoke softly, combed his hair straight back from his forehead, and had the slightly pugnacious look of an Irish bar fighter.

Holladay didn't have much information yet. The assailants were said to be Indians. But they could just as easily have been armed revolutionaries or drug traffickers. Additionally, the tensions were building between Peru and Ecuador, its neighbor to the north. War was a very real possibility. If it came, it would be centered around the Cenepa River, not far from where Patchen had been shot. It was possible that the Americans had been caught in the crossfire in some unreported border conflict. Or mistaken for spies. Or shot by spies from Ecuador in an effort to discredit Peru.

Thomas Holladay is a busy man, but he began researching the incident and made time to see Paul Dix often. Together they planned to travel to Imacita, then travel downriver to the island where Patchen had been shot. The place was very remote, and there was no reliable information about how to get there. Meanwhile, newspapers in the United States had picked up the news: NEW HAMPSHIRE MAN FEARED KILLED IN PERU.

Paul Dix lives in Montana, in my hometown, and I've known him for many years. We've traveled together on numerous magazine assignments: kayaking in Glacier Bay and Baja; sailing in Hawaii; climbing and dinosaur-bone hunting in Montana. We're friends.

When I heard that Paul was in Peru—and why—I called the American embassy there and was connected to Thomas Holladay. "Is Paul okay?" I asked. "I mean emotionally."

Holladay said he thought he was. "Paul Dix is a strong man," he said. There was a pause. "He mentioned you," Holladay said finally. "You're the writer."

I told him that I was, and Holladay suggested I might want to accompany him and Paul to the place where Patchen was killed. It

was unclear whether we'd need to go in with armed guards—
Peruvian police or soldiers—but two American citizens had been
attacked, one was likely dead, and Holladay wanted to focus
some international attention on the place. The strongest possible
expression of outrage was in order. A visit from a high-ranking
American diplomat would help do that, as would stories in the
media, both in Peru and in the U.S.

That was why Holladay was going. Paul, he gave me to believe,
had his own reasons, which were private and deeply conflicted. In
that context, it wouldn't hurt at all if he had a friend along.

I said I'd get down there as soon as I could.

Not long after that conversation, Paul Dix was sitting in
Thomas Holladay's Miraflores office when Josh Silver hobbled in
on crutches. He'd been transported by speedboat back upriver—
past the island where he'd been shot—and had then traveled by
bus over the Andes. Paul knew Josh. They'd spent nearly six
months together, along with Patchen, in Nicaragua in 1989 and
'90, at the height of the contra war.

Both Paul Dix and Thomas Holladay took extensive notes as
Josh described what had happened on the Marañón River on the
night of January 18.

Josh's Story

The tropical night came down hard, bang, like that, and the light
didn't linger in the western sky as it does in more temperate
zones. The raft was tied off at the downstream edge of a long, low
island covered in dense brush. There was a large sheltering tree,
like a ceiba, at the foot of the island, and it balanced itself in the
marshy soil on huge woody buttresses. Vines dropped from the
branches, and the forest beyond was a vertical canopy, a dark
carpet of vegetation.

Josh Silver and Patchen Miller had rowed a couple of hours
that morning, but the river had risen six feet the night before, and
the raft they'd built was ungainly in the higher water. It was a ten-
by-fifteen-foot monster, mounted on six 55-gallon oil drums.
There was a roof, and rowing station with ten-foot-long oars.

The Rio Marañón is one of the rivers that can be considered the headwaters of the Amazon. Miller and Silver planned to float five hundred miles to Iquitos, Peru, then continue down the Amazon in passenger vessels. They were three days into the trip, and they were being careful.

The river between the towns of Imacita and Santa María de Nieva was Indian country, and the Indians had reason to hate and fear outsiders. The two Americans could see for themselves what was happening: There was an oil pipeline road, built in the 1970s, that cut directly through traditional Indian hunting grounds. The road brought settlers from the mountains down to the lush, more easily farmed jungle. Other outsiders were just beginning to exploit the land for timber, for gold, for oil. And the government of Peru was encouraging even more settlement. There was a long-standing border dispute with neighboring Ecuador. That country claimed *it* owned the land along the Cenepa River, which flows into the Marañón, not far from Imacita. Some Peruvian politicians had proposed a policy of "living borders," a strategy of moving so many Peruvians into the area that Ecuador's claims would never be realized.

And all these forces, the Americans knew, were slamming up against the indigenous people, despoiling their traditional lands and eroding their way of life. Miller and Silver believed in Indian rights, and respected traditional ways. They wanted to learn from the Indians, to support them in their struggles to hold on to their lands.

But they weren't stupid. In the upriver town of Muyo, where they built their raft, the settlers—people of Spanish heritage and mestizos, of mixed Indian and Spanish blood—told them that these Indians, the Aguaruna, were dangerous people. There had been several European people killed on the Marañón a few years ago. Or maybe it was ten years ago. Anyway, two—or four, or six—people had been shot to death. By Indians. It was a little fuzzy in the details, but everyone—all the settlers they met in the new towns along the oil pipeline road that paralleled the river—said to stay out of the Indian villages. Don't get off the river, and don't talk to the people. Just keep moving.

And so they had.

The river at Imacita, where they put in, was wide and deep. It changed colors as the sun moved across the sky. Sometimes the Marañón was the color of strong green tea, and sometimes it looked as thick and brown as chocolate milk. But even then, at its darkest, the water reflected the sky, so often the raft seemed to be floating over puffy white clouds. The banks were dense with vegetation—mostly forest trees, but there were some banana trees, and a few fields of sugarcane standing fifteen feet high, like green fuzzy-tufted pussy willow. Where the banks were steep, small waterfalls tumbled down mossy rocks, and when the sun's light hit these falls at a slant, they glittered like polished silver against the various shades of green.

Occasionally they passed well-constructed split-cane huts, with thatched roofs. The Indians didn't live together in groups. There seemed to be some areas that were more densely populated, but the houses were always separated, one from the other, by half a mile or more. Most of them weren't even visible from the river, but you could kind of calculate the distance by the evidence of cookfires, by the plumes of smoke rising above the trees.

Everything looked well kept, exceptionally clean, and you could see that these people had it together. There were no electrical wires, no roads, and no garbage heaps anywhere. Sometimes they saw young Indian children, in clean shorts and T-shirts, fishing along the bank with bits of string. The shirts had NBA logos on them, Ninja Turtles, Batman—missionary clothing-drive stuff. In the calm stretches between rapids, Indian people of all ages moved across the river in dugout canoes. They used single-bladed oval paddles. There was also some commercial traffic: speedboats full of passengers and cargo going downriver, others coming up, but none of the white or mestizo passengers ever stopped at any of the Indian villages.

Miller and Silver weren't in the Amazon basin. Not yet. The altitude was about nine hundred feet. There were mountains beyond the banks rising to three thousand and four thousand feet, and the peaks were covered over in perfectly white clouds that contrasted sharply with the impossibly blue sky. It was hot at midday but relatively cool at night. Every afternoon, it seemed, there was a brief rain, one of those tropical torrential deals that lasted an hour or two, and then there were rainbows. Always rainbows, every day.

The river was three hundred feet wide in places, and it wound through the land in wide sweeping curves. The curves could be a little hairy. You had to set up for them about half a mile ahead: Read the river, avoid the "V" of hard current that would pull the raft into the worst of the rapids, and be sure that you still had enough river to clear the rocks on the outside corner of the curve. The river kept trying to slam the raft into those rocks.

And then, at the end of the waves, just where the river began to straighten out, there might be a whirlpool. If the river was narrow and the curve tight, the whirlpool could be as much as forty feet wide. Some of them were actually concave, and you could see where the center of the vortex lay several feet below the surface of the river proper. Fallen trees, twenty feet long, swirled around in the whirlpools like matchsticks in the toilet bowl. Then, *thrrrp,* a tree would be sucked into the vortex and you'd never see it again. It just never came up.

Local people called these treacherous sections of the river pongos. A bad section was said to be *feo,* ugly. Some were *feo, feo,* and in these doubly-ugly pongos, many people had drowned. Their bodies were seldom found.

The morning of the Americans' third day on the river, the Marañón was six feet higher than it had been the day before. Miller and Silver floated for about two hours, then hit a pongo that was much uglier than any they'd seen before. The raft got caught on the outside lip of a big whirlpool, and Patchen, at the rowing station, spent almost fifteen minutes fighting the vortex. Finally, they spun out of danger and the river swept them past a long island, where there were fields of sugarcane interspersed with patches of forest. Ahead, there was another pongo, not quite as big as the last one, a "pongito," really, but they decided to eddy out in the lee of the island. Tie off for the day. Wash clothes. Fix the roof of the raft. Get organized and wait for the river to subside a little. Study the maps and try to figure out where they were.

Because Ecuador claims this land along the Marañón—and because several border disputes have erupted into full-scale combat over the past fifty years—good, detailed maps have military significance and are hard to obtain. The tensions were evident in all the military checkpoints along the river. The Americans had to stop, show their passports, and watch some soldier who looked about thirteen years old write their names into a big ledger book. The checkpoints were tight, nervous places, and it seemed as if the soldiers expected another war with Ecuador to break out at any minute. The soldiers weren't in the business of giving potential spies information about the river, and as a result, the Americans weren't precisely sure of their position.

Wherever the hell they were, Josh Silver thought it was an "amazing" place. Very few gringos had ever seen this stretch of river. Some adventurous souls have rafted the Marañón, but almost all of them put in dozens of miles downriver, past the ugliest of the uglies, the Pongo de Manseriche, a twisting canyon of crashing water and orchid-laden walls half a mile high.

Silver and Miller, however, had studied the port at Imacita where they put in. They reasoned that if commercial traffic—thirty- and forty-foot-long dugout boats, with low-power outboard motors, carrying heavy loads of passengers and cargo—was coming *upriver,* through the pongos, they ought to be able to float it downriver. Patchen was especially good on the water; he'd been building rafts and floating the rivers of New England since he was a kid. Later, he ran several rock-'em, sock-'em stretches of white water in the western USA, including the Colorado through the Grand Canyon.

But now the water was high, and it was time to tie off and wait. The island seemed a good place. Earlier, they'd pulled up to a covelike section of bank and asked some of the Aguaruna people there if they could tie off for the night. The folks seemed friendly and curious, but they said no. Just like that. "No."

There was, as far as the Americans could tell, no one living or working on the island, and tying off there didn't seem like trespassing. They wanted to be sensitive to the Indians' concerns. Josh felt he and Patchen "shared a compassion" for the rural poor in Third World countries. In college, Josh had studied political science, international economy, foreign policy. It seemed to him that, all over the world, various powers had a political and economic stake in the poverty of the people.

And that was Patchen Miller's take on the world of power and money as well. He had spent a year in the Friends World College, which as a graduation requirement obliges students to live in two cultures other than their own. The college provides students with "narrative evaluations rather than grades." In his Global Political Economy class, the instructor wrote that "Patchen's term paper on the costs of deforestation in the tropics was well researched and clearly written. Excellent work."

Josh believed that he and Patchen shared a "world paradigm." The six months they'd spent together in Nicaragua during the contra war had shown them how the policies of various governments impacted on the poor. It was always the rural poor who suffered.

They wanted to do something about it. Alleviate poverty. Expose injustice. That sort of thing. But neither of them was naive. They knew you couldn't do it all at once, and maybe there was very little you could do at all. A guy had to start with the little shit. Which is why Josh and Patchen had spent the first part of their trip to South America working at an orphanage in Ecuador. They were there for ten days or so, over the Christmas holidays.

The orphanage was called the Garden of Eden, in the town of Salcedo, and was an evangelical Christian kind of place—not exactly Josh or Patchen's cup of tea—but the kids were great. Mostly, they were street kids abandoned in the bigger cities, presumably by prostitutes and drug abusers.

Patchen built a chicken coop out of bricks and mortar. Josh put together a medicine cabinet. They welded a broken door, regraded the driveway, and spent a lot of time playing games with the kids. The place wasn't exactly a model of hygienic food preparation, and Patchen got pretty sick for a while, which, he figured, was pretty much par for the course when you ate out of the kitchen at the Garden of Eden.

At night, they played music. Josh was okay on the mouth harp, but Patchen was, in Josh's view, "a brilliant, unbelievable percussionist." It was like he'd grown up in Jamaica instead of an A-frame in the New Hampshire woods. He'd played professionally for a while, in bar bands that toured around New England, but Patchen didn't drink or smoke, he loved being outdoors, and the rock-and-roll life wasn't for him. Still, the man could play pots and pans with a pair of spoons. In one of his college courses, the Quest for Human Meaning, Patchen submitted an audiotape of his music as part of his final project. He thought rhythm had a lot to do with human meaning. The kids who gathered around him at the orphanage seemed to think so, too.

Patchen and Josh left the Garden of Eden, hitchhiked south, crossed the border into Peru, bought provisions at the town of Bagua—rope and soap and six weeks' worth of food—then built their raft in a settlement called Muyo. They used tools and a workshop lent to them by a friendly local carpenter. It took them two days. Then they had to arrange for a big truck to take the raft down a muddy dirt road to the Marañón port city of Imacita.

The raft had been mostly Patchen's idea. He thought a fairly stable platform would be the best way to get photographs of the people and wildlife along the river. There was a chance that he could sell some of his photos, maybe even make it as a professional photographer, like his father. That kind of life would allow him to travel the world, experience what he saw as a vanishing wilderness, and, yes, maybe even expose injustice. Help people.

Or . . . it was just possible that he could make a living as a writer doing the same sort of thing. Patchen kept a journal. People who read his work always said he ought to think about writing as a career. "Excellent essays, demonstrating considerable analytical skills," one of his Friends World College professors wrote.

Another professor thought that "Patchen . . . demonstrated a solid understanding of complex text and lecture material in the course Topics in American History. One of those topics was "The Expropriation of Native Americans." As part of his course work, Patchen Miller had spent two months living with an American

Indian family in New Mexico. He had been interested in shaman-ism, and ended up herding sheep for a born-again Christian Na-vajo.

And now here they were in Indian country, and it was probably not a good idea to stop and talk with anyone about shamanism or anything else. Hell of a way to learn about Indian culture.

Still, they weren't sure exactly where they were, and needed some local expertise. Had the river crested, or was it going to rise some more? How far were they from the Pongo de Manseriche? About dusk on that third day, a young Indian guy in a dugout paddled by, and Josh hailed him. They spoke, in Spanish, at a distance; about the river. Slowly the guy pulled closer, until he was sitting right up next to the raft.

Eventually, this shy young Indian fellow got up on the raft, and they were all shooting the shit, in Spanish. He was a kind of nondescript-looking guy, maybe twenty years old; it was hard to tell. He wore his hair cut short in front, long in back, and had a strange kind of nose that came flat out of his forehead, made a perpendicular turn to the world, and formed a kind of box, right there in the middle of his face. It looked, to Josh, "like the guy had a Dick Tracy nose."

The Americans gave their visitor a few small presents: some matches, batteries. The three drank some coffee and by then it was dark, about eight in the evening. Another dugout came by. The two Indian men in it must have known the kid on the raft, and they spoke for a while in their own language: a lot of long and short vowels separated by sharp consonants. *Aw waka nepeenakata.* Those weren't the real words, but it sounded like that. There was none of the soft sibilance of Spanish.

The two men in the dugout were drunk, "fully inebriated," in Josh's view, but they were friendly enough in the you're-my-best-pal-wanna-fight manner of drunks the world over. Mostly they just spoke with the kid in that Indian language.

The men left. There was a big rainstorm then. When it was over, the kid wouldn't leave. He wanted to see everything on the raft: the clothes and tents and boots and backpacks and headlamps and cameras and binoculars and all the provisions they'd bought for a trip that might be six weeks long. It seemed like the kid looked everywhere, just searched every storage place on the raft.

They traded songs for a while, and this kid with the Dick Tracy nose sang some beautiful, haunting melodies in his own language. The melodies, the strange rhythms, reminded Josh of the South African singers on Paul Simon's *Graceland* album. Ladysmith Black Mombasa, from the black townships. Remarkable similarities.

It was now about nine-thirty, and the two men in the dugout came back. They weren't nearly as friendly this time and only spoke to the kid for a few minutes before they left.

About ten minutes later, both Josh and Patchen heard some rustling in the bush, beyond the big tree at the end of the island.

"What's that?" Josh asked the kid, in Spanish.

"It's my father," the young man said. "He's an evangelical minister. He wants to meet you." The kid yelled into the bush, something quick and sharp, in his own language.

Patchen got up and walked to the back of the raft with his headlamp. He'd light the way for this kid's father.

Josh Silver heard the shot: the booming blast of a shotgun. He saw the muzzle flash in the foliage. He didn't see Patchen get hit, just saw his body pinwheeling off the raft. Josh reached for him in the dark water—there were bubbles there—but he came away with nothing. And then he was fighting with the kid, screaming at him, and there was another shotgun blast in the night and something tore into Josh's left thigh.

The kid wasn't surprised, wasn't shouting; nothing. He'd set them up: Josh knew that at a level of instinct, where there were no words. He knew that the shotgun was a single-shot model and that the killer in the bush was reloading even as Josh dove into the waters of the Marañón.

They were there, behind him, on the raft, shouting into the jungle night, that Indian language—crack, crack, crack—and there were probably flashlights scanning the water. He didn't look back. The kid's dugout was still tied up to the raft. They could come after him at any time.

Josh swam sidestroke, holding his leg with one hand, applying direct pressure to stop the bleeding. He made for the near bank, the north side, away from the major current, which ran along the south side of the island and into the pongito about three hundred yards, downstream. The north bank was one hundred yards away, and the water was fairly calm.

Josh Silver hid in the foliage there. He found a vine and tied it above his wounds. He'd taken a dozen or more pellets—birdshot, it looked like—and one of them had passed directly through his thigh. An entry wound and an exit wound.

Josh couldn't believe the kid with the nose case had set them up. He'd looked at everything. When he yelled to the man in the bush—the one with the shotgun—he was probably telling him that there were no weapons on board. "They're not armed. Kill them!" Something like that.

The man in the bush hadn't stumbled, and the gun hadn't gone off accidentally. He had stood there in the darkness, taken aim at Patchen—illuminated by his own headlamp—and shot him at point-blank range. They meant to kill, and now they'd have to kill Josh.

The Indians must have thought: Two gringos on the river; they disappear. Who's to say that they weren't sucked down into some ugly pongo? And if that's your plan, Josh thought, you can't leave a living witness. So they were looking for him, and they were going to kill him, and Josh could hear their voices calling across the water.

Time passed. Then Josh saw a man moving along his bank of the river, shining a flashlight back and forth, as if he were looking for someone. The beam of light passed very close to where Josh was hiding.

He couldn't stay there, and he needed to find help. The last military checkpoint he and Patchen had passed was, Josh thought, about four miles upriver. It was two nights after the full moon, and black clouds were scudding across the sky. Josh was wearing river shorts. That's all: no shoes, no shirt. His skin, in the moon-light, looked impossibly white. He smeared mud on himself and started upriver.

He ran for a time, jarring the hell out of his wounded leg, then slowed down to a walk. Sometime later, Josh saw a dark figure moving along a path beside the Marañón. The man was carrying a rifle or shotgun of some kind. Josh didn't think the guy had anything to do with the people who were looking for him. They were too far back, and Josh had heard that these Indians generally carry guns at night and that they are night hunters.

Still, he didn't know, and he hid from the man.

He was, he knew, never going to make it to the military check-point. He'd have to stay deep in the foliage, off any trails, away from men with guns; and traveling that way—barefoot, with a wounded leg—was impossible.

But . . . if he let the river carry him, he could swim down-stream, staying close to the banks and out of the pongos. There was sure to be another checkpoint where he could get help. Seemed like they had checkpoints about every five or ten miles. Just stay in the water all the way past the island. He had to keep his head low and make as little movement as possible.

The water was cold, and Josh could only stay in it for half an hour or so at a time. He'd pull out on a bank, warm up with some push-ups and some sit-ups, then swim again until he began shak-ing.

Nine hours after he dove off the raft, at about dawn the next morning, Josh took a big chance. There was a man working on his boat, an Indian doing something with the tiny outboard, and Josh spoke with him. The guy put the wounded American in the dugout, fired up the engine, and together they sped across the river to the military checkpoint at a place called Urukusa.

He'd been shot by one Indian and rescued by another.

At the army base, they put him in some kind of medical place and patched up his leg. There were sixteen pellets in his thigh. Josh was feverish, and his leg was badly swollen, infected from the river water.

Later in the day, Peruvian police from the town of Santa María de Nieva arrived. Josh was transported downriver to that town. Someone called Lima on the radio telephone, and the news was relayed to Consul General Thomas Holladay: An American citizen had been shot and was being treated for his wounds. Another was missing and feared dead. The assailants, apparently, had been Indians. Aguaruna.

The Aguaruna

Late in January, while Paul Dix was in Lima, pitched battles broke on Peru's northern border. It wasn't the first time.

In 1941, Peru fought an undeclared war with Ecuador over a persistent boundary dispute. In 1995, the dispute erupted into a mini-war, like the one in 1951–1952 and the one in 1981. The fighting was centered on the upriver sections of the Cenepa, which flows into the Marañón not far from the island where Patchen Miller was shot. Though official figures were lower, it looked as if several hundred soldiers on both sides had been killed.

Paul Dix and Thomas Holladay were forced to postpone plans to visit the Marañón ambush site. Paul, working out of the youth hostel in Miraflores, began researching the Aguaruna people. He made several visits to the Indian-run Center for Amazon Anthropological studies in Lima. I spoke by phone with people who'd visited the area: anthropologists, botanists, missionaries, and Indian-rights advocates.

The Aguaruna were part of the Jivaro linguistic-cultural group and had never been conquered by the Incas or by the Spanish; nor had they been militarily vanquished by the nation of Peru. They were a proud people, unconquered, and perhaps unconquerable.

Until about fifty years ago, the Jivaro had been headhunters. The only eyewitness account of a Jivaro head-hunting raid I was able to find was written by F. W. UpdeGraff, an American who tramped around the area in 1894. It is fair to say that the book he wrote, *Head Hunters of the Amazon,* lacks a certain degree of cultural sensitivity.

UpdeGraff was living in an Aguaruna village. There was a battle with a rival Jivaro group, the Huambiza. The victorious Aguaruna lopped off the heads of the dead and dying. UpdeGraff felt he couldn't interfere, in that "we were but five in a horde of fiends, crazed by lust and blood."

UpdeGraff waited almost twenty-five years to write his book, which is to say that he lived through the First World War, in which millions died, killed in a more sanitary fashion, and not by blood-crazed fiends at all but by patriots: white people, for the most part, who, clothed in glory, dispatched the enemy for God and country. Fiendish blood lust hardly entered into it.

According to UpdeGraff's account, skulls were removed from the Huambiza heads; the skins were sewed and soaked and heated, and generally shrunk down to about a third of their size. The heads, he learned, were brandished only during the victory festivities, after which they were discarded. UpdeGraff knew that such trophies were of value to American collectors and pointed out, in pornographic detail, the authentic markings of a genuine Aguaruna shrunken head.

It is not clear to me exactly where UpdeGraff was, but he was probably very close to the Marañón. Today, a large portion of the Aguaruna people live along the banks of that river, in the area between Imacita and Santa María de Nieva. There were, at last census, about thirty-eight thousand Aguaruna, and they had combined with their traditional Jivaro enemies, the Haumbiza, about six thousand strong, to form a political organization called the Aguaruna Huambiza Consejo.

The Aguaruna and Huambiza tend to live in family clans of thirty to forty people. They are hunters and small-scale farmers, who sometimes sell produce at markets. Their language, unlike Spanish, uses a lot of sharp consonants: *yugkipak* for forest pig; *ikamyawaa* for jaguar.

The men hunt and weave. The women tend children, grow manioc, and make pottery. The men sing songs for success in hunting; women's songs encourage the manioc to grow. Some Jivaro songs use a five-note scale. The rhythms are complex and irregular, a bit like the music that comes out of the black townships of South Africa.

Masato, or manioc beer, is an Aguaruna dietary mainstay. Women boil the tubers, pound them, chew the pulp, then spit the mash into a large pot to ferment. Masato, called *nijamanch* in Aguaruna, is nutritious and intoxicating.

Each traditional village has its shaman. When people fall ill, the Aguaruna use herbal cures along with what might be called household magic, but are in no way opposed to modern medicine. In cases where these methods fail, a shaman is called in to remove "spirit darts," likely implanted by a sorcerer, who is an ordinary man motivated by spite or envy. The shaman performs various ceremonies, under the influence of a powerful herbal hallucinogen called *ayahuasca*.

Michael F. Brown, an anthropologist who spent two years living with the Aguaruna, cites a 1976 case in which a village elder died suddenly of unknown causes. The village shaman was pressured to identify the sorcerer responsible. "From the images of his *ayahuasca* vision," Brown wrote, "he drew the name of a young man from a distant village. . . . The man was put to death in a matter of days. Because Yangkush [the shaman] was widely known to have fingered the sorcerer, he became the likely victim of a reprisal raid by members of the murdered man's family." Brown rarely saw Yangkush leave his house without a loaded shotgun.

These conventions—cycles of vengeance, family feuds—persist despite the work of various missionaries who have been working and living among the Jivaro for generations.

One of my contacts had the phone number for the Aguaruna Huambiza Consejo in Lima and I gave it to Thomas Holladay. The consejo speaks with a voice that is heard internationally. It was formed in the late 1970s, and quickly found itself at odds with Werner Herzog, a German film director obsessed with the idea of making a historical film in the area. The producers of the film refused to enter into negotiations with the consejo and its head, Evaristo Nugkuag. They argued that hundreds of Indian workers were being paid twice the going wage and that the Aguaruna opposed the film solely because Huambiza people had most of the jobs. Evaristo Nugkuag replied that the movie, *Fitz-*

carraldo, showed the historic oppression of Indians without ever addressing itself to that issue. The film set, which was located at the confluence of the Marañón and Cenepa rivers, was destroying the forest and disrupting people's lives. Or so the consejo argued. On December 1, 1979, a party of Aguaruna men burned the set to the ground. The film crew fled to Iquitos.

When I spoke with one of the principals involved in the film, he said he didn't want to get into it again. Not with Evaristo Nugkuag. The *Fitzcarraldo* burning had brought the man international fame. He was politically astute and knew how to focus the world's attention. You couldn't fight the consejo.

Thomas Holladay called and spoke with Evaristo. He said that as soon as the war cooled down, he wanted to visit the site where a young American had been killed. He would be bringing along a couple of journalists and the murdered man's father. Holladay called me and said Evaristo had been very helpful.

"You identified Paul as Patchen's father?" I asked.

"I thought it was best to tell the truth."

"Ah geez, Thomas." I had to hook up with the one American diplomat on earth who thought it best to tell the truth. What Thomas and I both knew about Aguaruna culture was this: A murdered man's father seeks revenge. The people would assume Paul was there to find and kill the people who had shot Patchen. Which put us in danger of a preemptive strike. On the other hand, anyone who knew anything about the area said that the consejo could guarantee our safety.

"Evaristo says we're welcome to come," Holladay said. "He'll help us in any way he can."

Paul Dix flew back to the U.S. for Patchen's memorial service, a celebration of his life, held in the woods of Vermont. There were six hundred people in attendance. What struck Paul about the ceremony was the sheer diversity of Patchen's friends. There were rough-hewn backwoods loggers, young musicians, hippies, yuppies, Dartmouth professors, rich people, poor people, and hundreds of children. Patchen and his mother ran a summer program teaching children about the woods, a kind of mini-ecology camp. The children loved Patchen, and came back year after year.

Patchen's mother, Sandra Miller, put together a brochure that included excerpts from "Growing Up in the Woods," an autobiography Patchen wrote in the fifth grade. "Our bird feeder has the most action around, with chickadees that eat from our hands, flying squirrels that eat from my hands, chipmunks that eat from my hands. . . . They all like to come through the window into our house. The voles and mice wash their faces after eating peanut butter."

The last bit of the autobiography was titled "Chapter IX: The Future." It read: "I would like to be active outdoors, explore, go places, have experiences, live with and study people from other backgrounds. Anthropology sounds good."

In Peru, the war dragged on. Paul and I, working together in Montana, combined our notes on the Aguaruna. The missionaries, we agreed, had enjoyed a large measure of success. Today, each village is likely to identify itself as either Protestant or Catholic, but the new religions are sometimes understood in a manner singular to the Aguaruna. The most hallucinatory book in the Bible, Revelations, is the most significant to the Jivaro.

This fact has led to strange interpretations of outside culture. Canned goods, for instance, which can be purchased in stores that serve the army checkpoints along the Marañón, are carefully examined by the Aguaruna and Huambiza. It is thought that bar codes have dangerous significance and must be carefully counted. If they add up to the number 666—the mark of the Beast in Revelations, the sign of the devil—the food is demonic and not to be eaten.

The Aguaruna and Huambiza people, especially those in remote river villages, have ample reason to fear outsiders and their customs. The new oil pipeline road has brought in many mestizo farmers, who use an indiscriminate form of slash-and-burn agriculture. The Indians, by contrast, slash but don't burn, and have much smaller fields. The Aguaruna believe, quite rightly, that their ancestral lands are being destroyed, despoiled.

It is true that Peru has taken steps to guarantee the Indians these lands, but the model for land titling was taken from high mountain villages, where people live together in towns, not separated from one another by half a mile or more. On the Marañón, land is titled to Aguaruna "villages" that hardly exist, and settlers are moving into the spaces between. In addition, the Aguaruna Huambiza population has doubled since 1976, but these people are now being forced to live on less land.

People are angry, and the Aguaruna sometimes resort to a form of self-defense that trades on their fierce reputation. When a settler builds a house on what is considered Indian land, Aguaruna men have been known to dress in their traditional costumes and surround the place at night. They scream and brandish weapons. No one is ever injured, but the settlers generally find it prudent to move, usually the next day.

Still, despite such efforts, the influence of the outside world has reached deep into the guts of Aguaruna society. The army needs Aguaruna soldiers, familiar with the jungle trails near the border. Getting them to enlist isn't much of a problem. Young Aguaruna men of seventeen, who might be in Imacita or Santa María de Nieva for a festival, are simply rounded up by soldiers. The "enlistment" is a two- or three-year proposition.

And when these young men come back to their villages, they are filled with strange ideas; they are sometimes contemptuous of their own culture, angry, and often dissatisfied. Villagers speak of "bad influences."

People in the most remote villages most fear outsiders. That fear is embodied in a ghoulish night creature called the pishtaco. Not every white man is a pishtaco, but it is only white men who kill in the night and then plunder the corpses for their life force, which is focused in the "grease," or body fat. This grease is used to lubricate the white man's machines, and explains the efficacy of such technology.

Michael F. Brown sees the "*pishtaco* fears . . . as a powerful metaphor for the experience of . . . people whose lives have been twisted and foreshortened by what they see as mysterious power emanating from the gringo world." Every missionary, botanist, doctor, or anthropologist I talked to knew the pishtaco myth. It wasn't a quaint bit of folklore. The Aguaruna believed in pishtacos who stalk the night.

The dread of pishtacos is invariably mentioned as a possible motive whenever any white person is killed in Indian country. On October 8, 1989, on the Marañón, three French citizens and a Peruvian were shot and killed by Indians, near the place where the Cenepa flows into the Marañón. They were floating on a raft and shooting videotape. According to Charles Pittaluga, the French consul in Lima, the killers were never found and a motive was never established. Some settlers who lived in the area blamed the harsh rhetoric of the consejo for creating a climate in which unwitting trespassers could be murdered. There is also a persistent rumor that the killers believed the video camera was a pishtaco device that could extract a man's grease from a distance.

In collecting information on the Aguaruna, I too was looking for a motive—a reason why Patchen Miller died—and that fact may have colored the tenor of my questions. Edmond Hammond, a twenty-six-year-old Indian-rights activist, asked me, please, not to "mythologize the Aguaruna. They're different," he said, "but not inhuman or unhuman. They have a right to live as they choose. They're people." The Aguaruna Hammond knew were proud, honest, clever, generous, and fond of jokes.

Michael F. Brown said that in two years living among the Aguaruna, "I never had as much as a pin stolen. Theft was nonexistent." He thought the Aguaruna "were incredibly admirable. When you depend on people for your survival—unless you're a complete blockhead—you develop a very real admiration for them. They've never been conquered, they're proud, they're resourceful: they're not beaten down Indians. The Aguaruna are like the Lakota Sioux of the Amazon: very forceful and straightforward. Other Indian groups might find them too forceful, but Aguaruna culture didn't collapse when it came into contact with the outside world, as many others did."

What Edmond Hammond said was that if the Aguaruna were "demonized," it would play directly into the hands of certain Peruvians, who want to open up the land for more colonization. They want to do this because of the tensions with Ecuador, and they want to do it for financial gain. Colonists will bring in mercury-based gold mining, and will poison the rivers. The forest will be slashed and burned for cattle farming. The present small-scale timbering will give way to large international schemes. "If the Aguaruna are slammed as a people because of the actions of one or two men who should go to jail," Hammond said, "it will be an ecological and civil rights disaster."

Which, I thought, would not at all be a fitting tribute to Patchen Miller, considering the way he lived and the things he believed.

Vision Quest

By late April the war had wound down, and on April 30, Paul Dix and I, along with Thomas Holladay and a Peruvian photographer, Victor Chacon, of *Caretas* magazine, boarded a commercial flight in Lima on the first leg of our trip to the Marañón ambush site. The Russian twin prop banged and crashed its way over the Andes, and as we dropped into the vast green expanse of the Amazon, Paul said, "People talk about closure, that I'm coming here for closure." He shook his head slowly. "There's no closure. You don't just cry for a few days and then it's over." He paused for a moment, then said, "Every once in a while a wave of grief just washes over me and I know it's never going to stop happening." Birds ate from Patchen's hand. That was a thought that could trigger him. "It'll get better," Paul said, "but it's never going to be over."

Paul is a photographer and tends to see his emotions visually, as a picture. When he thought of Patchen, he saw a globe, with a dark spot—an invincibly evil area—centered in the jungles of Peru. He disliked the image, thought it was twisted with hatred, and he couldn't get it out of his head.

There was little chance we'd ever find out who killed Patchen. Paul just needed to understand, to talk with the Aguaruna. Shake the dark image, if that was possible.

Of course, if there was a group of robbers along the Marañón who killed for profit, they should be punished. But Paul hoped the Aguaruna would do that themselves, in their own way. That's what Patchen's mother, Sandra, wanted. Just leave it. Sandra had raised Patchen. She was suffering terribly, and as Paul saw it, she had all the rights in this matter. But there was that dark spot on the globe, and Paul needed to sink into its depth. Something beyond grief, or even justice, was pushing him. He couldn't explain it.

We landed at Bagua, on a military gravel airstrip. It wasn't a scheduled stop, but Thomas Holladay had pulled a few strings, and the four of us stepped out of the plane into a blinding light. There were a couple of hundred uniformed soldiers sitting under a tin-roofed palapa, waiting for their flight home from the war.

A group of Peruvian National Police, who had been notified of our arrival, met us on the runway and asked how they could help. Take us to Imacita, we said.

Presently we were thumping and sliding down the gravel oil-pipeline road in a white police Nissan pickup truck. The rain was falling in sheets when we pulled into Imacita about dusk. It was a small town, with muddy gravel streets set around a tiny public square constructed entirely of cement: cement walkways; cement benches; a cement sculpture of what appeared to be a soccer ball on a pedestal. Men and women—mestizos, whites, and Indians—sloshed through the streets in high-top rubber boots. The shops were all open to the street, and consumer goods were piled in racks: soap and canned food and aspirin and rope and pails and towels and toys, all covered over with blue tarp awnings. It was a town of shiny blue tarps in the rain.

A distinguished-looking man stepped out of one of the cafés and hailed us. He wore gold-framed aviator glasses, a light green dress shirt, beige slacks, and dark leather shoes. I had seen pictures of Evaristo Nugkuag taken around the time of the *Fitzcarraldo* incident. Then he wore colorful handmade ponchos, and his hair was cut in the traditional Aguaruna fashion, short in front, long in back. Now, he had a typical Peruvian businessman's haircut; he was in Imacita on consejo business.

Evaristo welcomed us. He and Thomas exchanged diplomatic pleasantries in Spanish. The rain let up, and we stood in the muddy street under a light drizzle. Two little boys ran by, screaming with laughter, chased by an angry young girl in a pink frilly dress that looked as if it had been in a mud-ball fight. Evaristo shook Paul's hand and held it in his own as he expressed his sympathy. He said that the killers were probably "outsiders."

Very gently, Paul said he didn't think that was so. The incident happened in the middle of Aguaruna country, the killers were Indians, and they spoke Aguaruna. Evaristo dropped Paul's hand, pivoted about in a circle, as if agitated, and said, "Oh, this is bad. This is very bad for the Aguaruna people." He said that the murder could only be the work of "individuals." There were many "bad influences" now.

Paul said he understood a little about the problems the Aguaruna faced. Evaristo nodded. That was good, he said, and he wanted Paul to know that what happened was not "political" and wasn't meant to be a message of any sort. "We work," Evaristo said, "with many Americans. We work with people of all nationalities."

That night Paul and I spoke for a while, in private. "When Thomas introduced me to Evaristo," he recalled, "he said that I wasn't looking for the killers or coming for vengeance, and that's right. But then . . . he said I came to forgive."

"And you didn't?" I asked.

"I'm not Mother Teresa," Paul said.

We sat in silence for a moment. "What do you think Evaristo meant," I asked finally, "when he said 'this will never happen again'?"

We speculated for a bit. Evaristo was a politician. He had traveled widely in Europe, raising money for the consejo, and had visited the U.S., where he was received in the White House. The man owed his power and position to the fact that he was able to mobilize international opinion on the part of his people. I truly believed Evaristo when he said that the January 18 incident was "bad for the Aguaruna." The killing diminished his effectiveness in the international marketplace of ideas. It was entirely possible that Evaristo knew who pulled the trigger that night, and that steps had already been taken, punishments meted out. Not that he would ever tell us.

Paul and I agreed that the presence of Thomas Holladay on this trip was crucial, and demonstrated that Patchen's death was being taken seriously at the highest levels of the U.S. government.

"I suppose Thomas has a file on me," Paul said. Dix has been highly critical of U.S. involvement in Central America, very vocal about it, and he tends to see the government as a monolith— diplomats in league with the CIA in support of death squads. That sort of thing.

"This is a tough trip," I said. "It's dangerous. Thomas didn't have to come."

"I know," Paul said. "The man's been nothing but a source of support." He thought for a moment, then allowed that maybe, in spite of his position, Thomas Holladay was one of the good guys.

"Probably just fell through the cracks," I said.

That night at dinner, Paul took a stand: He did not want to visit the Aguaruna with an armed police guard. No police at all. We asked Thomas what he thought. A thin, venomous-looking spider, about half the length of a big man's hand, was crawling across the front of Holladay's shirt, and he brushed it to the floor with the unconscious reflex of a man who's used to hard living in hot climates. In fact, Thomas Holladay had spent two years in the Peace Corps in Yap and served one year in Vietnam. "No police," he said, and shrugged. "I don't have a problem with that."

Victor Chacon, for his part, liked the idea. Victor was an Amazon Indian by birth, but he was really a member of the tribe of Tim Page and Sean Flynn, which is to say he was a combat photographer. Once, on assignment, the Sendero Luminoso kidnapped him: a man put a gun to his head, then pulled the trigger on an empty chamber. It was a warning. Victor thought, The dumbshits didn't even confiscate my film.

By ten the next morning, we were at the island where Patchen and Josh had been shot. Evaristo had said that people all up and down the river knew we were coming and that we were free to visit any of the villages. He didn't believe the police would allow us to do that in their absence, and helped us put together a complex connivance in which we would book passage to Santa María de Nieva in a commercial passenger craft, then call an unscheduled stop at a place where a member of the consejo, Yuan Unupsaan, would be waiting for us in a small speedboat.

The water was lower, but the island was just as Josh Silver had described it: the eddy, the ceiba tree, the wall of foliage. Thomas Holladay and I crashed through the underbrush, looking for a trail. I was sweating and sunburned, and when I rubbed my hand across the back of my neck, there were dozens of nasty little stinging ants balled up in my palm. Yuan Unupsaan, with the perverse pride of people who live in challenging environments, began describing the infinite varieties of ants in the Amazon: the little red ones that crawl up your pants legs and sting like fury, and the big black ones that leave welts the size of a man's fist, and the . . .

"There might be a trail here," Holladay called.

It wasn't much, but we followed it twenty or thirty feet to a hole in the ground, where it ended.

"*Iruich,*" Yuan said in Aguaruna. Armadillo.

"It doesn't take Sherlock Holmes, does it," Thomas Holladay said.

There was no trail through the foliage. The assailant hadn't just been strolling through the forest. It had to have been the two drunken men in the dugout. And since they had arrived in a hand-paddled dugout, they couldn't have come very far. The river had been almost twenty feet higher in January. No one could paddle upstream against that current, and the big pongo above us, the one Patchen and Josh had battled for almost fifteen minutes, was very ugly. So the killers came from the village across the river to the south, Huaracayo, or the smaller one to the north, Ajachim.

Paul had already figured it out. He was sitting on the sand beach above which Patchen's raft had been floating four months earlier, when the water was that much higher. The sky was perfectly blue, there were a few white puffy clouds, and the river was clear and fast and clean. Sunlight dazzled off its surface. Paul was miles away, fighting against one of the waves that rolled over him from time to time.

I sat some distance away, with Thomas and Victor and Yuan,

who was telling us about the rabid vampire bats up the Rio Santiago.

"Can you take us over to Huaracayo?" Thomas Holladay asked.

In that place, there was a sort of village green, with a soccer field, a medical clinic, and a schoolhouse. The buildings had thatched roofs, or tin roofs, and were built of split cane, tied together with vines. There were gaps between each bit of cane so that the buildings were cooled by breezes. This was an administrative center, and the people lived in similar houses some distance away. The only man present told us that everyone else was out working in the fields. We gave him a gift of several dozen spiral notebooks for the children, and he told us we could meet with the people of Huaracayo the next day.

And so we made our way downriver, checking in at two army posts, and arrived at Santa María de Nieva early that afternoon. It was a larger version of Imacita, and entirely unlike the immaculate village of Huaracayo, there was a faint odor of rotting produce and human waste. We were met there, with great fanfare, by the local police. The commanding officer was a bundle of energy and looked a bit like the late actor Sal Mineo. He said he'd just been assigned the post, that there wasn't a lot of mysterious crime in Santa María de Nieva—whenever anything happened, it was generally pretty clear who did it—and that he was very keen to find Patchen's killers.

It has been Paul's experience that cops in rural Third World posts are often corrupt, and use their positions to bully the poor and powerless. So it was with something less than complete enthusiasm that he sat with the officer for three hours, going over an inventory that Josh had made of all the gear on the raft: a Leatherman tool, an MSR cookstove, an orange Therm-a-Rest air mattress, two blue Lowe backpacks, a green Patagonia canvas shirt, a pair of Ray-Ban sunglasses, a pair of Eddie Bauer suede hiking boots. Paul drew out the logos of the various brands, and the officer copied everything down in a growing state of excitement. Oh yes, this was a big break, he said. Sooner or later someone would show up wearing something on the list. He'd hear of someone showing off a cookstove or knife. The killers had probably taken the covers off the oil drums on the raft and sunk it in some pongo. But . . . they may not have considered the fact that Josh could produce such a complete and identifiable inventory.

It was clear to me that this officer of the Peruvian Investigative Police, assigned to a jungle backwater, desperately wanted to solve a crime with international implications. It was a career maker. There was just this one thing holding him back. A detail. The police in Santa María de Nieva—it pained him to say it—did not have a boat. He'd never actually been to the ambush site, which was several hours upriver. And if we were going there tomorrow—if we'd already hired a boat—was there any chance he could come along? As an observer. He wouldn't be in the way at all.

Paul didn't like it. We discussed the matter over a dinner of stewed chicken and rice. I asked Paul why he had spent three hours with the cop if he didn't want the killers caught and punished.

"There's part of me that wants that," Paul said. And it was decided that the officer could come along, provided he came out of uniform, unarmed, and left the meeting while we talked with the people.

We slept in a hotel that had eight-foot-high cubicles for rooms. The roof was tin, supported on heavy wooden beams twenty feet overhead. About one-thirty that night, there was a godawful racket, the thumping, thundering sound of that tin roof dancing a fandango on top of the beams. The earthquake, I learned later, measured 6.2 on the Richter scale. It was over a few minutes after it began. Paul and I shined our lights on the beams to see if there was any structural damage. I saw something—a bit of brown fur—moving across the wood. A rat? Maybe a spider monkey.

I went back to bed thinking, for some reason, of a spider monkey I'd seen at one of the army checkpoints. It was a pet, pampered and overfed. I'd made some witless joke about *"negocios de monos,"* monkey business, and a soldier said, "That's what we call the Ecuadorians. *Monos."* Monkeys. I thought, Easier to kill a monkey than a human being.

And that thought stayed with me all the way back up the river the next day. At Huaracayo, we were met by the mayor, called the Apu, whose name was Victor Yagkuag. The people were gathered in the schoolhouse. There were about fifty of them, sitting three abreast on benches built for schoolchildren. The women sat to the left, and several of them were breast-feeding babies they carried in slings. The men wore clean T-shirts with shorts or dark slacks. Most of them didn't wear shoes.

Yuan Unupsaan, of the consejo, seated Paul and me in the front of the room, on tiny children's tea-party chairs. He introduced Thomas Holladay, who in turn introduced the police officer, Victor, Paul, and me. He said that Paul had not come to seek vengeance. He had come to understand the context of his son's death. He had come for emotional reasons. He had come for spiritual reasons.

The Aguaruna, perhaps, thought it unlikely that Paul wasn't seeking vengeance, but they seemed to nod with a kind of forlorn wisdom when Thomas talked about death and spirituality. It was the formulation Paul had been looking for as well. Spiritual reasons. You could grasp some tragedy with your mind, but until your soul understood, you would forever be in pain.

Thomas Holladay excused himself from the meeting. He said that he, as an official of the United States, and the police officer, as an official of the Peruvian government, would go back down to the boat so that people could speak freely.

And when they were gone, Paul and I got caught in a quick blast of Aguaruna political discourse. "Here," the Apu said, and he showed us a neatly handwritten document festooned with signatures. The police had come to the village directly after the murder, and everyone said then that they didn't know who did it. See, it's all written down.

This demonstration was conducted at high volume, with many emphatic gestures. No one had heard the shotgun blasts that night. The river was too high, too loud for the sound to carry. And what motive would someone from the village have?

Paul stood and waved his arms. He wanted to speak. Victor was in the back of the room, shooting pictures.

A woman stood and said, "We too ask our God why this happened."

"We didn't know your son," a man shouted. "Why would we kill him for vengeance?"

"Wait, wait, wait," Paul said, in his fluent Spanish. *"Esperan."*

Yuan translated Paul's words into Aguaruna, though it was clear to me that all but the oldest men and a few of the women understood Spanish.

The people settled down, and Paul thanked the consejo for helping make this trip possible. He thanked the people of Huaracayo for taking time off from their work to speak to him, and he told them that they lived in one of the most beautiful forests he had ever seen, alongside one of the most beautiful rivers on earth. He emphasized, again, that he hadn't come for vengeance. He was not looking for *los culpables,* the guilty ones. He had come only to understand, and to resolve the situation for himself spiritually. He had suffered much pain since his son was killed, he said, but he wanted the people to think about Patchen's mother and the pain she felt. For the mother, he said, it was very bad. Very bad.

The people now sat in complete silence. Paul spoke slowly and sincerely, using simple words and short declarative sentences for an audience that spoke Spanish as a second language. The care he took gave his sentences the force of poetry.

He said that he was beginning to understand the customs of the Aguaruna people and that he had great respect for them. He understood their fear of people coming in from the outside—people who wanted to take their land, their hunting grounds. He knew they loved their children and feared bad influences.

Perhaps there were Aguaruna people who had fallen under the spell of these bad influences, he said. Perhaps there were people who killed not for vengeance but for profit. This was very bad for the Aguaruna people. To rob and kill—this had never been the Aguaruna way. It was a sin against the soul of the people.

Paul paused. There was a stirring on the women's side of the room. The Santa María de Nieva policeman was standing outside, listening. We could see him through the split cane. Paul walked outside, and the people heard him tell the officer to "go back to the boat. Do it now, please."

There was a certain rumbling of satisfaction when Paul came back into the room. He sat back down next to me on his tiny chair.

"I am not a citizen of Peru," Paul told the people, "and there is nothing I can do about my son's death. Perhaps the police will do something. I would prefer—and the mother would prefer—that you do something about it in your own way, according to your own customs. Perhaps that has already been done."

I could not read the people's faces.

"You did not know my son," Paul said. "His name was Patchen. Patchen Miller." And he told them that Patchen had loved rivers and mountains, that he had loved the forest and all the animals in it. He told them how Patchen had lived and what he had believed. "If you should find out who the guilty ones are," Paul said, "I want you to tell them that they killed a brother."

There was utter silence in the room, and now I could read the people's faces very clearly.

"Patchen Miller was your brother," Paul said.

What I saw in some of those Aguaruna faces was a sudden shock of sorrow, and I believe that, for a moment, they grieved for their brother.

I thought about that as we ate the chicken and yucca and plantains the people of Hauracayo brought us for lunch. The advice Patchen and Josh were given—don't talk to people on the river—was wrongheaded, and maybe fatal.

It's a simple thing to sit around a campfire, drinking, and discuss what to do about a couple of men you don't know; men who you haven't spoken to, and who won't speak to you. The killers may have thought, These two men could be pishtacos, and they are on our land, and they are like the others who come and steal from us, and they have things we want, and we can steal from them, and this is only fair. We don't know these men. They are not our kin, and they are not our brothers. They are like *monos,* monkeys, not even human, and we can kill them.

After lunch, the Apu broke out some manioc beer, that tuberous mess the women spit into buckets to ferment. It was quite white, lumpy like buttermilk, sweet and cool.

Thomas Holladay passed the wooden bowl to me. "Did you see the two young guys in the T-shirts?" he asked in English.

"One red, one green?"

"Yeah. Hair short in front, long in back."

"Both of them with the Dick Tracy nose."

"I told Victor to shoot some close-ups of those guys," Thomas said. "Portrait shots. I thought Josh might like to see them."

A woman filled the bowl after I drank, and I took it over to Paul, who was talking with the Apu.

"This stuff is really good," I said.

"Especially if you don't know how it's made," Paul said, in English.

He was feeling better—good enough to joke around, anyway— and when we said good-bye to the people of Huaracayo, Paul thanked them for speaking with him. He said they'd helped him deal with his pain and that he felt *tranquillo,* peaceful, calm.

Later that day, we flew out of the Marañón River basin in a small single-engine plane chartered from a missionary group. We rose above a series of rain squalls, then passed over the island across from the Aguaruna village of Huaracayo. The sky was clearing to the west, but it was still raining in the east. There were half a dozen rainbows arced out over the place where our brother, Patchen Miller, died.

Uncharitable Thoughts at the End of My Rope

I am hanging from a rope affixed to a diaper, which I am wearing in the place where diapers are most often worn. The diaper is, in fact, a ten-foot-long runner made of nylon webbing and is wrapped about my legs and crotch in a manner most familiar to mothers and climbers. The ends of the runner are hooked into a pair of carabiners, which in turn hook into a small piece of metal containing two holes called a figure eight.

With my diapers and carabiners in place, I can run a doubled over climbing rope through the figure eight, step backward off the lip of a cliff, and slide safely down the rope. This is the fastest nonfatal way to get down off a mountain. Since most cliff faces are higher than the average climbing rope is long, numerous slides are required to reach flatland. Ropes are expensive, however, and in order to retrieve them after each slide, they are usually wrapped around an anchor—a tree, a horn of rock, a sling affixed to a chock—and dropped double down the face of rock below. The

ends of the rope should dangle over a stand-up ledge at the very
least. There the climber can pull on one end and bring the rope
down after him. The process is called rappel, from a French word
meaning "recall."

I am out recalling over the side of a cliff this spring day because
the summer is shaping up heavy on rope work. I have been invited
to help some people place a pair of peregrine falcons on a rocky
ledge rising high over the Pacific Ocean. I have promised to join a
caving expedition where we will be expected to slide down a rope
in absolute darkness some four hundred feet. "You can rappel,
can't you?" I was asked in both cases.

"Does a chicken have lips?" I lied. "Is a bear Catholic?"

The last time I slid down a rope was six years ago. As I remember, it seemed a painless procedure after the first-time terror of
trying to scale a 5.7 climb called the Grack in Yosemite. Slide
down a rope? No problem. Rappel off a cliff holding a delicate
peregrine falcon in a sweatsock? Piece of cake. Drop off into the
darkness of the earth's abysmal depths? I could handle it.

As time ground slowly onward, it occurred to me that—what
the hell, a little practice with the rope wouldn't actually hurt. God
helps those who help themselves. Be prepared. Better to be humiliated in front of friends than go plunging into the darkness with
bats like falcons swooping all around.

My friend, photographer Paul Dix, has been climbing for almost thirty years and owns all the requisite ropes and hardware.
As it happened, Paul didn't mind taking an afternoon off for some
rope work. I would be perfect, he said, for "some rappelling
photos." Paul says things like that with a straight face. He would
use the shots to build up his stock file. Dix said he would be
happy to supervise my practice sessions if he could shoot photos.

Which is how I came to be hanging over the lip of a cliff in
Yankee Jim Canyon, just above the rapids of the Yellowstone
River. Other men have hung from the neck until dead; I was
hanging from my diapers and dying of boredom. This is the curse
of going anywhere with an outdoor photographer.

"Just hold right there," Paul said, diddling with his Nikon.

"Okay, now drop down about two feet. Good. Now turn your face out of the shadow. Lift your right foot about four inches. Perfect. Hold it there. Look natural."

This was my first drop in six years, and a natural look would have been one of intense apprehension, but after hanging in various positions one ordinarily sees only in East Indian sex manuals, a certain ennui takes hold of the soul.

"Can I go now?" I called. The diapers were beginning to chafe.

"Uh, wait just a minute please. I'm changing film."

Using Paul's gear and relying, as I was, on his expertise, I was in no position to argue. I was in no position at all. I was hanging by my diapers, thinking uncharitable thoughts about photographers.

"Oh my God," Paul called. "You think you can hold there another few minutes? Five more minutes." Dix was in a lather of anticipation. "There's a couple of kayakers upriver." The photographer was scrambling up the side of the cliff, dragging thirty pounds of camera gear in a frenzied quest to find the perfect angle. "If I can just get you and the kayakers in the same shot . . ."

Paul was muttering to himself, hard at work. Someday he'll be sitting at home, in his office, and his agent or some magazine art director will call and ask, "You wouldn't have a photo of a scared-looking guy rappelling down a cliff with a couple of kayakers paddling by below, would you?"

And Paul Dix will say, "Of course," in a way that suggests all good photographers have that shot.

There was a nice little rapids upstream, and the kayakers had no idea that I was hanging in the wind, waiting for them to pass so that Paul could be nonchalant with art directors about his rappelling photographs. The kayakers were probably nice guys. I bet I'd like them if I met them in a bar somewhere. What I didn't like about them this particular day is the way they kept . . . diddling around. Drop into a big hole and paddle furiously in order not to move. Anybody who would work that hard to go nowhere, I thought, twisting slowly in the wind, was an imbecile of heroic proportions.

"Can you drop below the overhang so you hang free?" Paul asked. So I hung there, working hard to go nowhere and feeling vapid as a kayaker in a rapid. The diaper was cutting into my thighs and there was a sense of paralysis in my legs from the hips down. I mean, it had begun to hurt, hanging there for half an hour at a crack, and I began to think of Paul as a Kodachrome sadist.

Okay, I admit that photographers, as a rule, are probably wonderful people, as likable as the idiot kayakers probably were, but while at work, the average outdoor photographer could piss off the pope. Once, in South America, I stood under a heavy waterfall wearing rain gear made of a "new-generation" fabric while photographer Nick Nichols took shots for a catalogue designed to show that this stuff was impervious to water. It was a cold day on the high plateau known as El Mundo Perdido, the Lost World, and the fourth time I walked through the falls, I called up to Nick that I was soaking wet and cold.

"This stuff doesn't work," I screamed. "Not even a little bit."

"Gimme one more walk-through," he shouted back. "I haven't got the shot."

"But the stuff doesn't work." A bit of logic and fine good sense howled into the empty space between a working photographer's ears. "It leaks like a sieve."

"I don't know that," Nick shouted. "Gimme one more walk-through."

"This stuff is the fabric of betrayal . . ."

"Looks great," Nick yelled. "Real good. One more walk-through."

Nick has actually asked people to give it one more walk through a bed of coals. That was in Surinam, where he was working on a story about the people who live deep in that country's tangled jungle. Their ancestors, brought over as slaves, had immediately escaped into the bush, where they lived as they had in West Africa. Anthropologists study the bush people of Surinam in an effort to understand eighteenth-century West African culture. Nick spent three weeks in one jungle village—long enough to count the people he met there as friends.

The villagers finally agreed to perform their fire dance for the camera. "I still don't know how they do it," Nick told me, "whether they go into a trance or whether their feet are just so callused they can stomp the fire out. Anyway, the head fire dancer goes first, then his assistant comes on, then a trainee comes out and stomps out the rest of the fire."

It was a difficult lighting situation—shooting into a fire, at night—and Nick was worried about the shot. He asked his friends to give one more walk-through the next night. "I think," Nick said, "they thought I was disappointed at the size of the blaze, because this time they built a bonfire. The head dancer didn't stay in very long, and neither did his assistant. The magic wasn't there that night. Something. When the trainee came in to put the thing out, it was still blazing away and I could tell he was definitely getting burned."

And so they learned in Surinam what it means to have a photographer as a friend.

Far and away the worst of the breed are underwater photographers. I've got enough scuba experience to know that in any given group, the person with the camera is likely to be the best and most knowledgeable diver. Just don't get buddied up with him. The scuba photographer drops down the anchor line, swims ten yards, and finds something to engage his or her interest. As likely as not, the fascinating stuff involves a couple of tiny organisms the size of your thumbnail swimming around a coral knob no larger than a coffee cup. The rest of your group is off hanging on to the backs of manta rays or watching green turtles mate, but the inflexible rules of diving won't let you leave your buddy, the motionless photographer. No use even swimming over to see what it is the camera is focused on. You'll stir up the sand or frighten the organisms and spoil the shot.

After the dive, the photographer will be in a state of near sexual excitement. "A feeding phenomenon no one has," he'll mutter in ecstasy. "No one's ever seen it before."

"Especially not me," you point out.

"Hey," the photographer says, "I've got it on film," as if photography is somehow superior to experience. "I'll send you a copy." The shot, when you get it, will be beautiful, suitable for framing, a photo you could label "the conservation of underwater experience."

I was thinking about the treachery of photographers—some shots of me actually make it look as if I might be a few pounds overweight, a rank distortion I firmly believe can be corrected in the darkroom—when Paul said it was okay. I could go ahead with my practice rappels. When I was just about at the end of my rope, he called, "Hey, Tim, could you hurry back up here? There's a big raft coming down the river."

I clipped out of the rappel rig.

"They're coming pretty fast," Paul called. "Could you run, please?"

The Purple Sage, at 180 Miles an Hour

Four or five years ago, I was interviewed by a Swedish photographer who leveled what I considered to be a bizarre accusation. "You are cowboy," he told me.

Hey, smile when you say that, pardner.

The man was visiting the small Montana town where I live. He was working on a photo essay about the American West and seemed to believe that anyone who'd want to live in some tumbleweed tank town, of necessity, had to be a cowboy.

I endeavored to set my Swedish friend straight on those individuals who labor in the field of bovine animal husbandry. Cowboys, I said, are men and women who work with cattle on horseback. Such persons tend to share a certain philosophy; a courtesy; a prickly pride; and a tendency to, oh, sometimes exaggerate events, often to humorous effect. Many of my neighbors are, in fact, ranchers or working cowboys, and yes, you can tell them by their outfit. Wannabe buckaroos always get it wrong:

wrong hat, wrong length pants, wrong boots, wrong life, big pathos.

So no, I told the Swedish photographer, I am not cowboy.

Oh sure, I ride horses now and again, but the awful truth is I keep falling off the sons of bitches. It happened again just last spring. For reasons that have never been satisfactorily explained, I failed to stop when the horse did. Just kept going right over the horse's neck and landed, boom, on my back in a cloud of dust.

It occurred to me then that I was rather like those English seamen of a century ago who, shipwrecked in the Arctic, failed to adopt Inuit survival techniques and consequently froze to death. Just so. If I ever wanted to ride a horse with any degree of dignity, I was going to have to learn from a cowboy.

Which is how, some months later, I made my way to the All 'Round Ranch, in Utah, where Al Brown runs a kind of horseman's clinic on the sage-littered slopes of the Blue Mountains. You don't need any experience; you don't need to know the first thing about horses. Al swears he can have you galloping around barrels in an arena within a week. He'll have you herding cows. Rounding up strays in brushy draws. Running down obstreperous calves at a gallop, through knee-high sage.

So there I was in Utah, three months after my spring horse-wreck, galloping along on Josh, a horse that had once run at Ruidoso Downs, home of the richest horse race in the world. Josh was a quarter-horse gelding, eleven years old, and just coming into his prime as a saddle horse. He was easily the finest and fastest horse I had ever ridden—*Dios mio* was he fast.

It was pouring down rain in the Blue Mountain plateau, near the border of Utah and Colorado. There was a rainbow behind us to the east, some blue sky to the south, and a black thundercloud directly ahead. Bolts of lightning danced on a distant ridge that marked the horizon. The trail was a narrow rut, running with water, and the horse's hooves threw up clods of mud. Al Brown, galloping easily beside me, shouted some words of welcome instruction. "Settle down a little deeper into the saddle," he called. I did that, and it smoothed out the ride some.

Josh was steadily gaining speed, however, and I was steadily losing confidence. Unfortunately, I know this drill well: The horse just keeps running, faster, then faster still—it's really a barely controlled runaway—until a kind of dumb terror informs me that it's time to stop or die. The stopping process involves pulling back on the reins and shouting "whoa" several dozen times as the horse shifts down through several bone-jarring gears to a final stop.

It's like driving some kind of hot sports car—a Ferrari, for instance—but the car is rigged in such a way that once you punch the accelerator, you have to run it all the way up to 180, or hit the brakes in a panic stop. There's no cruise control, no way to drive the beast at a safe and sane 85 miles an hour.

As Josh gained speed, Al said, "Hey, give him a little tap." By which he meant: Pull back once, quickly, gently, on the reins. Josh immediately settled back into his previous pace. If the horse had been a Ferrari, we'd be doing, oh, 55 or 60 and—hey, what's this?—I could keep him right there, with an only occasional tap on the reins.

"All right," Al shouted. "Now touch his ribs." That's what you do on a horse like Josh. No need to kick. You just touch his ribs with your boot heels. When I did, my head snapped back and we were doing a figurative 85, instantly.

"You get unbalanced," Al shouted, "grab your saddle horn." Al didn't buy into the dictum that a "real cowboy" never grabs his saddle horn. He'd worked with cattle, "a-horseback" all his life, and was, he said, always grabbing the saddle horn.

He pointed off to the right, to a place where the trail probably branched to the north. We were going to turn "just beyond that big stand of sage." Which was probably hiding the trail.

And I thought about what Al had said about turns, about how a horse running in the wild turns in a sinuous curve, winding its body into the motion. In contrast, a horse carrying a rider will turn stiffly, all in a block. The back end of the animal tends to come around too far, like a car losing traction on an icy curve. "A-horseback," as Al would have it, you correct the tendency to come around by touching the animal far back on the ribs on the outside of the turn.

Which is what I did, and pretty well, too. Josh wound around the stand of sage, which stood five feet high, wrapping the turn so tight that stiff branches scraped against the outside of my thigh, and I was glad, for a moment, that I was wearing leather chaps. I say for a moment because rather quickly after that, I wasn't glad about anything at all. We weren't on any trail but were galloping at 85 over a gently rising plain littered with sage so thick that if I fell off, no part of my body would actually hit the ground.

You can't ride horses through thick sage. This ought to be self-evident to anyone. It's not possible. The horse is going to get its legs tangled up; he's going to go down, hard, and take you with him. This was dangerous. It was irresponsible. I was maybe a little scared.

Al Brown was out about fifty yards ahead, shouting cowboy shit like "Yee-hah" and "Ya-hoo," and he wasn't on any trail either. Rain was sluicing off his oilskin slicker, and his horse was moving smoothly, splashing through standing water and kicking up dry dust underneath. Thunder rumbled in the distance, and there was no way, at this speed, that I could direct Josh through the sage. He was making tiny adjustments that I could feel in my inner thighs, moving miraculously through the heavy brush, and I kept my right hand close to the saddle horn, just in case. It occurred to me, in a panicky way, that I ought to discuss responsibility with Al, and I touched Josh once, gently, on the ribs so that, instantaneously, we were doing 120 and closing in on Al Brown. I realized with a start that Josh had at least two more gears in him and that he could do 180, easy. Even through the sage.

Josh wanted to run, to leave Al's horse in the rain and dust, but I tapped back on the reins so that Al and I were riding side by side at about 100 miles an hour, through the deadly sage. I wanted to tell him that what we were doing was impossible. It didn't occur to me at the time that such a statement is ridiculous.

"Al," I shouted. "Hey, Al!"

He turned to look at me: Al Brown with the front brim of his cowboy hat blown flat against the crown, Gabby Hayes style; Al Brown with his goofy mop of a mustache mostly covering a maniacal grin; Al Brown with the rain in his face, the rain running in sheets down his slicker; Al Brown at 100 miles an hour, sitting his horse like he was part of the animal. We were topping a gentle ridge, and out ahead, in the distance, a sea of silver-green sage fell down toward the Green River in a series of long, gentle swells.

"Al," I shouted into the wind, *"there's no damn trail!"*

The man regarded me for a moment. He was squinting against the wind and rain, but there was a strange luminescence in his eyes, something that seemed to transcend joy altogether and to rise up into realms of spiritual ecstasy.

I thought perhaps he had misunderstood me.

"No trail here," I screamed.

"Yeah," he shouted back. "Ain't it grand?"

The point here is that I completely missed the point.

There were seven of us riding with Al Brown that week, including three women from Switzerland. One was a good rider, the other two were experts, and they had all read about the All 'Round Ranch in a German magazine specializing in, yes, Western riding. The style, they said, was all the rage in Europe. In Switzerland, the women rode English saddles. In the English tradition, folks ride with their legs folded up under them like jockeys; they hold their reins up under their chins, in the manner of a squirrel with a nut.

It's a tough, demanding way to ride, very stylized, but the women wanted to learn Western riding—the buckaroo style—because it allowed you to sit in the saddle all day. It seemed to them "more natural." In Switzerland, they told me, there are plenty of places to ride, but it's all trail riding. What the western United States offered was vast tracts of prairie and desert and mountain meadow. It was ranch land or public land, and you could ride anywhere. You were not confined by trails. This was a freedom not available anywhere in Europe.

So the women had come to "ride the range": to do the very

thing that had frightened me that day. Which is to say they wanted to get off the trail. To go loping at 150 miles an hour through the sage.

We were sitting around a campfire, discussing the matter, and Polly Golins, Al's partner in the business, pointed out that wild horses live, and run, through sage-littered landscape every day. Horses didn't get tangle-footed in sage any more than B'rer Rabbit gets tangled up in the Briar Patch. Sage was a horse's natural medium.

Oh, sure, you had to look out ahead. While the rider made major decisions in terms of direction, the horse micromanaged the ride. Which meant, in essence, that if there was a big stand of sage looming up in front, you had to be prepared for the horse to zig right, zag left, or simply jump the brush. You had to pay attention.

If I was embarrassed by my expressed fear of off-trail riding, Polly and Al pretty much made me feel at ease. They did this by purposely making complete fools of themselves in the bad joke department.

"Say, Polly, I heard you had to shoot your dog."

"Yep."

"Was he mad?"

"I reckon he weren't too pleased."

The next morning, our third with Polly and Al, we were all up at about seven, building the fire and making ourselves breakfast. At the All 'Round, clients are not called dudes. Dudes, Al explained, get waited on. By contrast, we enjoyed the privilege of setting up our own canvas tepees, digging rain trenches around same, and making breakfast. Help was always available, but in general, we caught our own horses in the corral, cleaned their hooves, and checked the animals for saddle sores or suspicious swellings in the legs. We saddled them ourselves, and there was none of this single-file trail riding, the horses all bunched up nose to butt.

The first two days, we had walked our horses, mostly in deference to John, a young insurance executive from New Jersey who had never ridden before. The afternoon of the second day, Al had taken me out for a run through the sage. My stirrups seemed to be too short. I had figured this out when Al said, "Your stirrups are way too short."

In buckaroo-style riding, the stirrups are run long, leaving just an inch or two between you and the saddle. I had always ridden with the balls of my feet in the stirrups, carrying a lot of the weight of my body in the knees. My knees have always ached after riding.

With the longer stirrups, the knees barely bend and they never ache afterward. If you have a good pair of boots—a pair made with heavy leather, a steel shank in the sole, and heels at least an inch high—you can use hoop stirrups, which are simple metal rings. Slip the smooth-soled boot into the ring, right up to the heel. When you stand to smooth out the ride, you are standing on the bottom of your foot, on the steel shank.

With good boots, hoops, and stirrups at the proper length, you feel welded into the saddle. Secure. There's no talk about posting or cantering at the All 'Round. Al and Polly start you off in a slow lope, riding beside you, offering advice—"settle back a little deeper into the saddle"—and things seem to progress naturally.

This day, we'd be riding mostly at a stiff trot, a gait that has always been problematic for me. Al explained that it was, in fact, the gait favored by men and women who work cattle on horseback. Walking is too slow to get anything done; a gallop will tire any horse; but the animals can trot all day long. You smooth out the jarring ride by watching a shoulder of your mount. It's a little like dancing. The horse sets the beat, and you adjust from side to side, walking along in your stirrups to a rhythm that is more easily felt than described.

We were trotting out over the range when half a dozen sage hens rose before us and fluttered off to the east. Al and I were chatting about hats. I asked him why he seemed to disdain stampede strings, strips of rawhide that are tied under the chin to keep the hat from blowing off at full gallop.

Al Brown thought for a moment, than launched into a full half hour on the philosophy of cowboy hats. The shape of the crown and brim, the curl, would all be expressive in some way of a rider's personality. And although Al didn't precisely say it, there was an element of initiation—of real pain—involved in any hat. It is purchased small, and should, brand-new, feel like a band tightened around the skull. A week of constant headaches will stretch the thing out a bit, especially if there are rainstorms involved. Sleet and hail.

The hat becomes a part of the rider. It keeps the rain and snow out of his face, shades him from the sun, and keeps him warm in the cold. If the rider has to do some brush-popping, that is to say, ride through high, thick brush rising up over his head—service berries or choke cherries—he ducks down, holding the hat on his head with one hand. The wide brim protects his face from snapping branches.

The hat, as Al saw it, was a mystical thing. Kings wear crowns, Indians wear feathered headdresses, proper Englishmen wear bowlers. There was a weight of symbolism invested in any hat, a character and a philosophy. Cowboys understand this and associate their headgear with good fortune. No buckaroo ever lays his hat brim down: Hey, the luck just runs out of it that way.

When there's difficult work to be done, a cowboy wants to pull the hat down low, tight. If it still blows off his head, he has to understand that nothing is accidental. The missing hat is a matter of some significance, a signal winging in at him from the cosmos. Maybe it blew off because he was cocky or unprepared. Maybe he didn't need to be in that particular place at that particular time. When a cowboy's hat blows off, he is obliged to think about it. To philosophize.

With a stampede string, however, Al said finally, and in answer to my original question, your hat never blows off. Therefore there is never any need to review your life, such as it is. Al seemed to believe that persons who wore stampede strings failed to live sufficiently contemplative lives.

A cowboy's outfit is all cotton and wool and leather. Nothing much has changed in 150 years, primarily because the system works. This is a lesson those shipwrecked English seamen never learned from the Inuit. There's a reason and a purpose for everything. Cowboys wear boots, for instance, because boots slide off the foot. This won't seem important until you fall off a galloping horse with one lace-up shoe caught in a stirrup.

Frankly, the functionality of the gear surprised me. I wore the Wrangler jeans Al recommended because the inseam is stitched on the outside and doesn't cause saddle sores. My hat and ankle-length riding slicker kept me bone-dry in heavy rains. The way my boots fit the stirrups had a lot to do with my new confidence on Josh. The leather chaps I wore, provided by the ranch, took a lot of punishment from snapping sage. I liked the way they felt against the saddle—leather on leather—and imagined they contributed to the extraordinary fact that in over fifty hours of riding, I failed to fall off my horse even once.

Some of the riding was even a little demanding. The seven of us learned to herd cattle, to ride drag and swing, to read brands. John, the novice in our group, learned to ride at a gallop, and on our last day, we competed in an arena, racing around barrels and passing mailbags to teammates at a full gallop. The arena work seemed almost easy after a week of range riding, and I found myself doing things "a-horseback" that I thought only rodeo cowboys could do.

This is not to say that I am, or will ever be, a cowboy. I still have areas of invincible incompetence on a horse. Tight galloping 180-degree turns have me bamboozled. Josh never liked the way I did them. He would nearly stop, get all tangle-footed, and sometimes rear up a bit.

Al Brown's advice was to look at it from Josh's point of view.

"What do you tell him when you get to the turn?" Al asked.

"I tap on the reins to slow him up a bit."

"Are you perfectly balanced?"

"No, not really."

"What do you do to get your balance?"

And I saw it very clearly: On a tight turn, when I begin to feel unbalanced, I tend to clamp my legs tight around the animal. This causes my boot heels to touch his ribs, which is, of course, the signal to go. Meanwhile, I'm pulling back on the reins. No wonder Josh gets tangle-footed. No wonder he rears up.

I had to look at it from his point of view.

What I knew for sure about Josh and his point of view was this: The horse just purely loved to run. In our time together, we opened it up all the way and did 180 miles an hour out there on the range. We did it lots of times, with the rain or the sleet or the snow blowing in our faces. There were rainbows or storm clouds, or both, spread out all across the sky, and the wind blew the brim of my hat back flat against the crown, and I was welded into the saddle, shouting "Ya-hoo" or "Yee-hah" or just "Go, Josh." What I felt in those moments was something so far beyond exhilaration that it was, well . . . it was almost cowboy.

North Pole: The Easy Way

Ice.

The air was filled with a light snow that didn't precisely fall but seemed to drift aimlessly under a pearly, opalescent sky. Everything else under that crystal dome was flat, an endless prairie of sea ice, white with the newly fallen snow, and I could see the curve of the earth in the far distance of my vision in any direction I cared to look. That direction was south.

I was, for the moment, facing due south. Behind me, the direction was due south. It was due south to my right, due south to my left, and if I wanted to quarter off on my left side, I'd be facing south by south-south.

It was August 8, and the temperature stood at about 36 degrees Fahrenheit, as warm as it was ever going to be here at the geographic North Pole. So sure, several of us agreed, why not take a brief refreshing dip in the Arctic Ocean. The massive icebreaker that brought us here had formed a nice swimming hole in its wake.

I stood on the edge of the ice in my swimming suit and stared down about four feet into the open water of the Arctic Ocean, which was an uncomfortable-looking iridescent black.

It was 11:00 A.M. by my watch, but in my hometown in Montana it was much earlier. Or was it later? All the lines of longitude crossed at this point, and longitude is how human beings reckon time. So for just these few seconds I was standing on every line of longitude at once. Or none at all. Depending on how I wanted to look at it, I had no time whatsoever; either that or I had all the time in the world.

The thing is, it was cold standing around in a bathing suit at the North Pole. So I dove, because at this point, it seemed that there was no more time. The water, saturated with salts, was supercooled, which is to say it existed in its liquid state well below the freezing point of fresh water. We'd measured the temperature at 30.2 degrees.

At four or five feet below the surface of the sea, there seemed to be no light at all, and the body that I was inhabiting did not register temperature. There was no pain involved at all, which, I suppose, is one of the first manifestations of shock. Cold did not, for instance, punch the breath from my lungs. None of that.

Time, on the other hand, took an immediate 180. The world bucked furiously, then lurched into extreme slow motion and began slowly fading to black. It occurred to me that my life, such as it was, had suddenly become a malfunction at the Plaza Cinemaplex. Swimming toward the surface seemed an unreasonable chore.

When the Soviet Union collapsed of its own weight, a number of Western tour companies, among them Quark Expeditions, approached Russia with a proposition. I imagine the pitch went something like this:

Look, you guys have all these icebreakers, right? Best icebreakers in the world. You need them eight months of the year to convey freighters along the frozen north coast of Russia and Siberia, from Murmansk near the Scandinavian Peninsula all the way to the Bering Strait. But, look. That route, the Northeast Passage, it's pretty much ice-free during July and August, right? So the question is, What are you guys doing with your big icebreakers during the summer? Uh-huh. Well, what if we could come up with a summer use for those ships that could earn you guys several million in hard currency. Yeah, we're talking American dollars.

Which is how, one day late in July, I came to be standing on the tarmac at Murmansk, Russia, discussing the price of our trip to the North Pole with an elderly gentleman from Brooklyn, New York. We had just stepped off a charter flight from Helsinki, and the airport wasn't set up for tourists. There was, in fact, no terminal at all, just a single soldier in a metal shed checking passports for seventy-eight people who were standing on the naked tarmac, watching Russian workers sitting on huge tractor tires smoking cigarettes while Aeroflot refueled our charter plane. There were two wooden outhouses and some of the passengers lined up to relieve themselves.

"Figure a thousand dollars a day," the gentleman from New York said. "Twenty days. Subtract out for sleeping." He was a short, vigorous man—a sailor all his life, he said—and he expressed himself in a comical manner. He was Popeye personified. "It costs sixty dollars a waking hour."

We watched one of the passengers, an elegant-looking woman of about sixty-five, step into the left-side outhouse. There was something wrong in that one, something, judging by the faces of those who had fled previously, that was fairly disgusting. No one had ever stayed there for long.

"Time her," Popeye said.

Presently the door burst open, and the woman, who looked like she was about to be sick, ran behind a ramshackle olive-drab armored personnel carrier.

"How long?" Popeye asked.

"A minute, almost exactly," I said.

"Cost me a dollar," Popeye observed.

Buses ferried us over the countryside, which was alive with wildflowers and dwarf birch, with blueberries and wild strawberries and mushrooms. There were small lakes everywhere, over every ridge, and people were out picnicking or canoeing or collecting berries in wicker baskets on this warm weekend afternoon. The land rose and fell like ocean swells. It had, clearly, been molded by glaciers, and was dotted with drumlins and moraines and erratic boulders.

Murmansk was a town of some two hundred thousand people and until 1991 was a supersecret military outpost, a repository for the most awesome nuclear arsenal on the shores of the Arctic Ocean. The town consisted, for the most part, of blocky rectangular apartment buildings all thrown together and set against one another at bullying and discordant angles. Most of the buildings seemed in urgent need of repair: lots of peeling paint and crumbling cement. The personality inherent in the buildings was that of the Communist party and was expressed vertically. Khrushchev had built four-story apartment blocks; Brezhnev had built them to nine stories.

And then we were at the port, all of us stepping onto the icebreaker *Yamal*, which looked a bit like a snazzy Brezhnev apartment building set a bit forward on a huge whaleboat hull. The ship was newly painted, neat as Grandma's kitchen, and the passengers were offered a bit of bread and a pinch of salt on boarding. A uniformed Russian official said something about bread and salt and Russian tradition. It was hard to hear him because a young man nearby was playing a stand-up Yamaha electronic organ. He was playing "Those Were the Days," with the rhythm section set to polka.

Soon enough we were sitting in the ship's lecture room, which seated over a hundred and looked like one of the better classrooms at an American junior college. Greg Mortimer, the Australian tour director, laid out a few facts. The ship was powered by two nuclear reactors pumping 75,000 horsepower to three massive four-bladed screws.

The *Yamal* was the most powerful icebreaker on earth. It weighed twenty-two thousand tons and could crack through fifteen feet of ice at six miles an hour. The passengers were to be housed in the officers' cabins. The officers themselves had doubled up in rooms with the crew. There were over a thousand rooms aboard the *Yamal*.

We would visit a number of Arctic islands on our way to and from the Pole. It would be, Mortimer said, a historic voyage: "Only some twenty-five hundred people have stood on the ice at the North Pole." This was nice to know, though I didn't suppose it would earn me any permanent notice in the annals of polar exploration. Greg Mortimer, however, is one of the few human beings to have climbed Mount Everest without oxygen, and I figured he had a better shot at the history books than any of us.

Dinner—Dover sole, veal Oscar, that sort of thing—was served in a large, well-appointed dining room: white tablecloths, white cloth napkins, white wine. Red wine. Cognac. The kitchen staff was German and Austrian; the waiters, for the most part, Russian.

My cabin was spacious enough: good toilet, good shower, a down comforter on the starched white sheets of the bed. We were steaming north, out of Murmansk, through ice-free seas. I fell asleep at ten-thirty, missed the sunset at eleven-thirty and then the sunrise two hours later at one-thirty. Too bad. It would be my last sunrise and sunset for at least two weeks. From now on the feeble Arctic sun would simply wobble around in the sky like some guy's badly set glass eye.

It started with what is called plastic, a thin transparent sheen of ice laid over the surface of the sea in widely spaced patches. Later there was frazzle, slightly thicker ice that had formed in long, rectangular crystals. And then, after dinner on the second day, we saw a bit of pancake ice, crystal lily pads of varying sizes. Further north, winds and currents would collect the sea ice into floes, solid blocks of ice the size of football fields, of whole city blocks, of entire cities.

At about two in the morning of the next day I woke to a grinding, thumping sound. The sky was clear. The sea was flat calm, and it mirrored the pale blue of the Arctic sky. Floating in this shimmering sea were widely separated wind-driven aggregations of ice: misshapen lumps and hummocks that stretched out from horizon to horizon as far as the eye could see. Some were the size of coffee tables; others were about the size and shape of an eighteen-wheel truck.

The sun was low in the sky, balanced on the edge of the sea, and its light cast a golden trail across ice and sea.

I took a walk on deck, listened to the crash and thud of ice against our hull, went down to the small library, and read about polar bears in *The Arctic,* a book by Joseph Wallace. "One of the most completely wild and independent animals on earth," it said of the ice bear. Big males could weigh up to seventeen hundred pounds. They have been spotted within a few hundred miles of the North Pole itself; they have been seen swimming in frigid seawater twenty miles from the nearest land. They are, except when breeding, lone travelers.

The polar bear feeds mostly on ringed seals, animals that can weigh well over a hundred pounds. In the Arctic winter, when the sea freezes over, the seal maintains a series of breathing holes and gnaws away at the always-forming ice with its teeth. The seal must surface every ten minutes or so to breathe. The polar bear knows this, and he waits by a hole in the ice, standing motionless, sometimes for fifty hours straight in the bitter Arctic night. An ice bear can crush a seal's skull with a single blow.

In the summer, when the floes begin to break up, the seal likes to sleep on the ice, but always near the escape of open water. Evolution has blessed those seals that sleep fitfully; most wake every minute or so to check the ice for bears.

Wallace said there were two flaws in this system: one, each individual seal sleeps about the same period of time, almost to the second; two, the sleeping animal twitches before it awakens. And the great white bear knows these facts as well. He advances on the sleeping seal, notices the telltale twitch, and stands immobile— just another hummock of ice among many. The only thing that might give the bear away is his large black nose. Some biologists insist that as the bear draws close, he covers his nose with a large, shaggy white paw.

This is a matter of some controversy among experts, but it seemed a charming detail, whether proven fact or fond fiction. A bit grim from the seal's point of view, however. Imagine death rumbling out of that gray Arctic haze like a giggling geisha.

I wondered, then, why I saw something of my own inner life in the polar bear. Indeed, there was something of everyone's life, some universal identity. It was about three in the morning, a rather hopeless time, when you think about the loved one who died, the broken relationship that was supposed to be forever. We've all been there: wounded; weak. We retreat into isolation, perhaps self-pity. If we survive—and we will—the broken parts heal over. We are, perhaps, stronger than we were. Whatever hurt us, whatever nearly broke us—it's still gone. We're lone travelers across a barren icescape, but in time, we begin to move through it with assurance—powerful, completely wild, and independent. Like the ice bear.

With this thought in mind, I went below decks to a half-court basketball court and shot baskets for a time while the *Yamal* cracked through the ice. I rode a stationary bicycle for half an hour. It was still three hours until breakfast, and I was completely alone.

The trip was costly, in terms of both time and money, and the passengers had plenty of both—which is to say they were generally retired and wealthy. Other than that, they were a fairly disparate group. In addition to Popeye, there was the Dreaded Couple Who Did Not Share My Political Opinions; the Man Whose Luggage Was Lost; the Woman Who Climbed Mount Kilimanjaro at Seventy ("Our flight was canceled and we had two weeks free," she explained). The Swiss contingent included a man who'd climbed the Matterhorn fifteen times. The Japanese group, as if to shatter lingering stereotypes, was dominated by a female hotel owner who drank scotch straight and loved to dance. She was the Tina Turner of the Orient.

The rascular density—defined as the number of bona fide sons of bitches per hundred—was remarkably low: a mere 1.282 percent. The man in question bullied his wife mercilessly. Walking by their cabin, I sometimes heard him discussing the affairs of the day with her. "Shut up," he shouted. "You don't know anything. Shut up." The man often found himself eating alone in the dining room, while his wife was invited to sit with large, happy parties. He would look up from his lonely dinner and stare in puzzlement at the folks chatting with his wife, who didn't know anything. What was wrong with those people? He was the Man Who Didn't Get It.

Shipboard entertainment consisted entirely of lectures on the history, geology, glaciology, and biology of the Arctic. Nikolai Druzdov, a Russian biologist affiliated with the University of Moscow, was perhaps the most likable man on board. He had a gangling, goofy dignity and a gift for the unforgettable image.

He spoke of the snow geese that nest in the Arctic, on Wrangle Island, in the summer. The birds winter in the U.S. and Canada and are protected internationally, but that protection, Druzdov said, didn't apply to the tax extracted on the snow geese by polar foxes.

On Wrangle Island, Druzdov explained, the birds nest on the ground, which leaves their eggs vulnerable to the foxes. A large female, rising off her nest with wings spread, is generally enough to drive off any fox. But the bird cannot, for any reason, leave her nest. The fox is always lurking about, ready to snatch unguarded eggs.

"Sometimes," Druzdov said, "it snows in spring and summer, and then you see the geese sitting on their nests with just their heads above the snow." The next day, the temperature may rise well above freezing. The bird has been sitting for days on ground that is permanently frozen a few inches below the surface. Her body heat has formed a kind of cup in the permafrost. Snowmelt cannot drain away and is contained in that icy cup, so now the goose is sitting in water halfway up to her neck. And if the temperature should drop below freezing again, the goose is frozen up to her neck in ice. The polar fox strolls from nest to nest, casually nipping the heads off the helpless geese. Then he sits and waits for the feast of the next thaw.

The question-and-answer period at the end of each lecture was invariably dominated by the same individual. He asked questions that had nothing to do with the subject at hand; either that, or the answers he sought were so glaringly obvious that the only appropriate response would be to walk up and slap the guy, hard.

"These geese nest on Wrangle Island, right?" asked the Man Who Didn't Get It.

"Correct."

"And they winter in Canada?"

"Yes."

"So what I want to know is: How do they get across the Bering Strait?"

The pack ice was getting thicker. By ten-thirty that night it lay across the sea in great irregularly shaped sheets. Some of the floes were just large enough for a man to stand upon; others could accommodate a drag race. The larger sheets had hummocky, rolling surfaces and small oblong ponds of meltwater had formed in most of them. The ponds took on the color of the underlying ice, so that they were light blue or cobalt-blue or blue-green against the white snow-covered surfaces of the floes themselves. In places, these ponds formed their own blue or green rivers, which sometimes fell over the lip of the ice into the sea.

The water that bordered the floes was all that I could see of the Arctic Ocean. It was a strange iridescent black in the weak light of the cloud-obscured sun.

In places, the wind had stacked slabs of ice one atop the other to form slanting spires and castles and battlements. These spires seemed to rise out of the broken white plain of sea ice as we approached. The floes were so closely packed that it was possible to imagine traveling by foot across the ice, jumping from slab to slab. The very thought was terrifying; and yet the eye sought out a route.

At about 11:00 P.M., an announcement was made over the ship's intercom that there was a polar bear on the ice half a mile ahead of us. I went up to the bridge with most of the other passengers and stared out the large windows. The *Yamal* had slowed to only a few knots, but the bear, which was now only a quarter of a mile ahead of us, very sensibly fled. It was a shaggy yellow-white beast, and it shambled in its pigeon-toed fashion from floe to floe, swimming in the black water when necessary, then heaving itself back up onto the ice. We were, as yet, so far away that occasionally I lost sight of it.

From the bridge, the blue meltponds and rivers on the floes stood out much more clearly against the prevailing snow cover and the bordering black water. The bear was shuffling through a world of blue and white and black. He cut left, over a large floe, and the ship's starboard bow thrusters cut in. We plowed through the ice, over the very tracks of the bear, throwing up spray and keeping the animal directly ahead of us, so close now that I no longer needed binoculars.

An otherwise quite lovely woman loudly narrated the adventures of the bear to the bridge at large. "Look, he's swimming," she announced, as if to a convention of the vision impaired. "Now he's getting back up onto the ice . . ." She was the Lady Who Stated the Obvious, and to her credit, she asked a question that I had shamefully left unvoiced: "Do you think we're *bothering* him?"

I tried to see it from the bear's point of view. What would I feel like if I were standing out in the middle of a vast treeless snowy plain and an apartment building appeared out of nowhere and started chasing me around?

Were we too close?

I thought maybe we were.

I'd never seen a polar bear in the wild before and now here I was chasing one all to hell and gone across the ice in the world's most powerful icebreaker. It was a question of the animal's dignity.

"Look," the Lady Who Stated the Obvious exclaimed. "He's defecating."

Sea ice drifts with the currents and the winds. It moves in dense packs of floes, sometimes cruising along at two or three miles an hour. In 1596, a Dutch ship captained by Willem Barents sailed around northern Europe and was trapped in pack ice on the northern tip of the island of Novaya Zemlya, at a place called Ice Bay. Barents was searching for the Northeast Passage from Europe to the Orient and its riches. Barents's ship was eventually crushed by the drifting ice and he, along with sixteen other men, spent the winter of 1596–97 at Ice Bay. That summer, the crew set out for the mainland in small open boats salvaged from the wreck. Barents died en route.

This is the history of the Northeast Passage: always the ship trapped in the ice. The ship crushed. The howling winter. Death.

The *Yamal*'s passengers were helicoptered from the afterdeck to Novaya Zemlya. It was three in the morning. The light was pale, silver-gray, and the sun was rolling around in the sky somewhere near the horizon, a dim silver disk behind bleak gray clouds. In this spectral light, the bay seemed a ghostly place. There were no trees, anywhere. Permafrost, a few inches below the rock, would not permit a tree to sink a tap root. There were a few patches of orange and green lichen, and a gray pond or two where meltwater lay in a depression, imprisoned by the underlying ice.

The beach was brown, almost black, covered over in gravel. It rose in a series of terraces that had formed when the last glacier retreated and the land, relieved of its burden of ice, rose up in a process called glacial rebound. Of course, as the glacier melted, sea level rose as well, and thus a series of terraces was formed.

The ground was strewn with small, flat rocks chipped and flaked from larger rocks during periods of freeze and thaw. The land was literally shattered.

There was a weathered wooden cross standing huge against the gray sky commemorating Barents. The remains of the cabin his crew built was a sprawl of crumbled ship's timbers that hadn't rotted in over four hundred years. The wood had splintered in the cycles of frost and thaw. There were rusted barrel hoops and six-inch-long nails four hundred years old.

I was examining a reindeer horn when Nikolai Druzdov strolled up and told me that the Novaya Zemlya had its own distinct subspecies of reindeer feeding on the island's moss and lichens.

"Already," he said, "we are in Arctic desert." There were a few yellow poppies growing in wet rills, flowers the size of pennies clustered together in small, brave groups that hunkered down out of the wind and huddled together for warmth.

An Arctic tern hovered overhead and screeched at us. The bird had a snow-white body, red legs, and a black head, which made it look rather like a 1920s champagne dandy in terms of plumage. Nikolai thought the tern was defending its nest, which was probably somewhere nearby, among the rocks on the treeless plain.

It was about 25 degrees. A bitter wind was whipping over the frost-shattered land, and now big wet flakes of snow began to fall, driven across the rock-strewn beach at a severe angle.

At this time of year, Nikolai said, the terns already had chicks, and since winter comes early in the high Arctic, they were already preparing for their epic migration. Arctic terns nest in places like Novaya Zemyla in the summer, then, at the onset of winter, fly south, over the northern temperate zone, over the tropics, over the southern temperate zone, and spend the southern summer on icebergs, frozen islands, and the Antarctic icecap. The twenty-thousand-mile yearly round trip is the longest migration of any bird on earth. Science does not yet fully understand why the birds don't stop over in, say, Bermuda; and quite frankly neither do I.

Nikolai asked me where I was from. "Montana," I said. "It's near Canada, in the Rocky Mountains."

"Yes," Nikolai said, "I was in Bozeman this winter." He had been filming a documentary on Yellowstone Park for Russian television. "It's very much like Siberia," he said. "Bison digging in the snow to eat. Like musk-ox in the Taimyr Peninsula. Cold. I was cold there."

Cold as Siberia? A man takes a measure of strange pride in such a comment.

And then it was time to helicopter back to the ship. This particular aircraft, a KA-32C, carried two main blades, one atop the other, and the propwash was considerable. It could literally blow a man off his feet. As a safety precaution, passengers were asked to kneel near the landing site, head to head, as if in a football huddle.

I thought of this ritual as the helicopter-worship ceremony and prayed loudly: "O KA-32C, we fear Thy righteous slashing blades; we bless Thy Cramp-ed seating and the priests who are Your pilots; we beseech Thee, O KA-32C, make Thyself apparent as promised in the Holy Writ of the ship's daily program . . ."

During this solemn intonation, as the clatter of the blades became deafening, I looked up to see one of the Japanese women staring at me. This woman, for reasons that remain impervious to investigative reporting, always wore a cloth painter's mask whenever we made a landing. She, in turn, seemed puzzled by my fervent prayers. We were dealing in realms of mutual inscrutability.

The *Yamal* sailed north, then anchored somewhere off the northern tip of Novaya Zemlya while I slept. When I woke and looked out my porthole, I found myself staring into an implacable wall of blue ice. The iceberg was only a few dozen yards from the *Yamal* and was about seventy feet high. It was shaped like an aggressive modern sculpture, rising on a sharp angle from a long, flat surface to a sheer wall, whose summit was a massive slab of ice that punctured the sky at a 45-degree angle. The walls of the berg were fractured and broken in the manner of granite.

The nearby coast of Novaya Zemlya looked dark through a mist that wanted to be snow. I knew that the land carried a great dome of ice, which I could barely see through the drifting mist. The weight of the glacier was something more physically felt than visually apprehended.

A great river of ice poured down a large valley from the ice dome itself, and this glacial outlet flowed directly into the bay, where it formed a wall that looked to be a hundred feet high. Tides rose and fell, eating away at the base of the wall so that occasionally enormous slabs of ice broke away from the glacier proper. The sound was that of a thunderous cracking, like a major rockfall in a small echoing canyon, and this was followed by the surging crash of all those tons of ice falling into the water and atop the ice floating below. Seabirds whirled overhead, screeching in their fierce self-righteous manner and feeding on sea life brought to the surface by the turbulence.

Early explorers postulated the presence of then unknown islands on the evidence of icebergs floating among floes of flat sea ice. My favorite description of an iceberg is history's first. In A.D. 530, St. Brendan, along with eight monks, set out from Ireland to search for "the land of the saints" in a willow-framed oxhide boat. Sailing "against the summer solstice," Brendan may have reached Greenland. In the saga of his travels, he saw "a floating crystal castle," hard as marble and "the color of a silver veil."

Our berg looked something like that.

A man on deck asked me why we weren't moving.

"Iceberg," I said, gesturing toward the blue wall that loomed over us.

"It's all ice," said the Man Who Didn't Get It.

Sea ice is never still. It drifts. It drifts—men died to discover—along a series of continuous trans-Arctic ocean currents.

In the summer of 1879, George Washington De Long, an American trying for the North Pole, sailed his ship, the *Jeanette,* through the Bering Strait, found himself trapped in the ice off Herald Island (near Wrangle), and drifted for twenty-one months before the *Jeanette* finally broke up near the New Siberian Islands. De Long and his crew dragged three small boats south across the ice until they reached open water, then sailed to the Siberian coast. One boat was lost at sea; two reached Siberia, near the Lena River delta. De Long's party died of starvation. The crew of the second boat was rescued.

Three years later, twenty-three-year-old Fridtjof Nansen, a Norwegian, read a newspaper article describing some debris from the *Jeanette* that had been found on an ice floe. No big surprise, except that the ice floe was just off southwest Greenland, way the hell and gone across the Arctic Ocean from where the *Jeanette* had broken up. It occurred to Nansen that "if a floe could drift right across the unknown regions, that drift might be enlisted in the service of exploration."

Nansen designed a ship with a reinforced egg-shaped hull that would ride up on the ice and go with the floe. The *Fram,* with sixteen crew members and provisions sufficient for five years, was deliberately driven into the ice near the spot where the *Jeanette* had been crushed. The *Fram* did not break up. It surfed on the ice, as Nansen had predicted, and drifted, vaguely north, for two years. At 84 degrees, 04 minutes north it became apparent that the *Fram* would not pass over the Pole but miss it by about three hundred miles. Nansen and Lt. F. H. Johansen set out for the Pole on foot, dragging sleds and kayaks. For a month, the two struggled over hummocks and ridges and great jumbled blocks of ice. Going was slow, and the trans-Arctic drift was now against them. In effect, Nansen was on an ice treadmill.

On April 8, 1896, at 86 degrees, 14 minutes, the highest latitude yet reached by human beings, he turned back. There was no hope of catching the *Fram,* of course, and Nansen made for the northernmost of the Franz Josef Islands, arriving at Cape Norway, on Jackson Island, in August, about four months later. He and Johansen built a shelter, where they spent a desolate winter contemplating death in the darkness.

My own brief stay on Cape Norway was a good deal more pleasant. Nansen and Johansen built their hut of rock, interspersed with moss and dirt. The remains of that hut consisted of a giant log sitting crosswise over a hole in the ground surrounded by a pile of rocks. Nansen and Johansen had found the huge driftwood log, laid it on top of their rock home, and stretched a walrus hide across for a roof. When frozen, the walrus hide was almost impenetrable; at least once it withstood an exploratory foray by a polar bear.

There were a few weathered pieces of bamboo runner from the sleds lying about. Nansen and Johansen had pulled their kayaks on sleds where there was ice; in open water, they put the sled runners over their kayaks. Just so. With very few provisions left after the winter, they had no use for extra sleds, hence the discarded runners.

It was warm, about 40 degrees, the day I visited Cape Norway.

A rocky cliff, alive with nesting birds, towered above the beach. At the summit, where there was a line of snow like frosting on a cake, a waterfall had formed. It fell through a cut of blue-green ice, then burst over a projection of rock and down a snowfield that was watermelon pink with an algal bloom. The water disappeared under a plunging rockfield, emerged downslope, then wound its way past Nansen's hut, where it formed a series of pools. The pools were connected to one another, like a stair-step fountain, and were surrounded by moss and small yellow flowers. The stream emptied out into the bay, which was choked with eroded icebergs that looked like swans and mushrooms and castles and alien battlements.

Nansen had left Cape Norway and headed south just as the sun rose in the spring of 1896. A month later he and Johansen, quite unexpectedly, ran into a British exploratory team, the Jackson-Harmsworth expedition, on one of the southernmost of the Franz Josef Islands. Nansen sailed back toward Norway with the British, just about the time the *Fram,* with all hands in fine fettle, emerged from the ice near Svarlbad—precisely as Nansen had predicted it would.

I thought about Nansen as birds swept over the sea and across the watermelon snow. I think, to some small seething degree, I despised my shipmates, as I did myself. We were traveling in comfort, if not to say luxury. The North Pole, an atavistic voice whispered, ought to be earned, at the risk of life. My shipmates and I lived in an age when technology had replaced honor.

Then again . . .

. . . glory is where you find it, and heroism isn't necessarily physical. Consider again the saga of Fridtjof Nansen.

In later life he made lasting contributions to the science of oceanography, then headed up the Norwegian delegation to the League of Nations, where his work with refugees and famine relief is credited with saving hundreds of thousands of lives. In 1922, he was awarded the Nobel Prize for this work. Nansen gave the prize money to international relief organizations. He died in 1930.

Just down the slope from the remains of Nansen's hut there was a memorial to the man: a stout wooden pole with an inscription written in Russian and Norwegian. One recent visitor had stopped to sharpen his claws on the pole.

Which brought up another matter.

With Nansen in mind, I decided that I'd speak to the tour director, see if I couldn't get the *Yamal* to stop chasing polar bears around. It seemed wise to take the hero business one small step at a time.

In a relatively ice-free bay about fifty miles from Cape Norway, we boarded Zodiacs and motored off toward a gravel spit that spilled off of a nearby island. There were walrus sunning on the spit, and several more in the water: six groups of about twelve apiece. I could hear them grunting from some distance away. Bulls weighing up to two tons showed us their huge rounded backs as they dove: backs big enough to roof a small house. The animals surfaced with a snort that sent a fine stream of spray five or six feet into the pale blue Arctic sky.

It was about midnight and the sun was golden across water and ice. The walrus swam past and stared at us, half out of the water. The beasts had tiny eyes set in jowly, elaborately whiskered faces. They had the look of well-fed Victorian gentlemen, sternly British, indomitable, intolerably stuffy. "Piffle," they seemed to say, and, "Poppycock."

We kept a respectful distance, but the walrus approached our boats—rather than the reverse—and swam nearby for over an hour, curious, it appeared. It was clear that they had never been hunted. A large bull surfaced inches from one boat and snorted in the face of a man with his eye to the lens of a camera.

"I could actually smell his breath," the fellow told me later.

"What did it smell like?" I wondered.

"Well, have you ever been to a dump in the tropics?"

Walrus eat clams, lots of clams, but according to one of the biologists on board the *Yamal,* Benoit Tullo, they do not rake the sea bottom with their tusks to get at them, a factoid I'd gleaned from one of the books in the ship's library. Not so, Benoit claimed. Study any walrus tusk, he said. They are never abraded on the inside as they would be if used for rakes. A walrus, according to Benoit, ate clams by sucking up the mollusk's siphon with its strong lips and tongue. He had seen several walrus with two broken tusks and yet the animals had always looked well fed.

Tusks are used to haul a two-ton animal with no arms up onto ice floes. They also have about the same social function as antlers do among deer.

I knew one other thing about walrus tusks, and that is: Look out for the animal with unsightly yellow blubber stains on his. This is a rogue walrus, one who has probably found a dead seal, eaten it, gotten the taste, and now deliberately hunts seals. It is said that rogue walrus may attack humans, that some learn the trick of upsetting kayaks to get at the tasty morsels inside.

The *Yamal* was running north, to the Pole. At about 84 degrees north, the ice was an incredible, unexpected fifteen feet thick, and we had slowed to five knots. The *Yamal* did not plow its way through the floes but rode up over the surface of the ice, while jagged cracks spread out from the bow in a series of sharp angles. As the ship's full weight of twenty-two thousand tons came to bear on the floe, it finally fractured, and huge blocks of ice, thirty feet long and fifteen feet thick, turned up on edge somewhere around midship, then settled back into the sea in the broken wake of the *Yamal*.

The ship did not pitch forward as the floes fractured. The bow was always riding up on new ice, and the *Yamal* held steady: so steady that I was in little danger of spilling my drink.

I was, in fact, toasting the *Yamal*'s ice master, Andrei Masonov, who was dressed casually in jeans and a ratty black sweater. He had the preoccupied air of a highly focused techno wonk as we sat in front of his computer.

"My task," Masonov said, struggling with his English, "is map route, is plan strategy." A fixed-wing aircraft had already made two flights to the Pole and back, giving Masonov a choice of four separate routes. The plane brought back a radar picture of the ice about eighty kilometers wide along each route.

Using a computer imaging program, Masonov enhanced the radar pictures along our current line of travel. The screen looked like a mass of gray clouds set against a moonless midnight sky.

Masonov laid a grid of thin red lines, latitude and longitude, over the picture and tapped a few keys. "We can make assumption about age of ice from these picture," he said, "and these assumption tell us about thickness of ice." Multiyear ice can be up to five meters thick and is deep blue in color. One-year ice is dark green and about one meter, eighty centimeters thick; new ice is light green and about thirty-eight centimeters deep.

On the computer, thick multiyear ice turns up looking white; newer ice is gray; open water is black. But radar and the computer can't read the thickness of the ice. It is only experience that can do that, and Masonov had spent twenty years comparing visuals from the bridge with computer pictures.

I asked Andrei Masonov if he hated ice or saw it as an enemy. "No," he said. "I love."

"You love ice?"

"Of course," he replied, a phrase that English-speaking Russians often use in place of an emphatic yes. "Is beautiful."

Masonov thought it best to show me. Several hours later, we were sitting in the helicopter, flying north ahead of the *Yamal,* on a three-hour ice reconnaissance mission.

At four thousand feet, the floes, these great plates of ice, looked thin, almost fragile. The sea had a vaguely *congealed* look, like the skim of fat atop a pot of chicken stock cooling in the refrigerator. The largest floes I saw covered several square miles, and they were separated by leads, thin riverlike areas of black open water. There were tiny globules of ice floating in the leads themselves.

In those places where wind and current had driven floes together, pressure ridges, sometimes twenty and thirty feet high, had formed. These ridges were often half a mile long, and they wound over the ice in sinuous patterns. Hummocks—blocky spires of ice that had formed when floes smashed together at a single point—

rose off the white plain of snow, often near the end of some snaking pressure ridge, so that the formation as a whole looked like one giant, illiterate question mark.

There was a single iceberg rising in the distance, and an officer marked it on his map. He also noted the position of major pressure ridges, the size and thickness of the floes, and sketched out the location of the largest open water leads.

Masonov, with his computer-enhanced radar pictures, had mapped the overall plan of battle, but the helicopter was an essential tool in planning day-to-day tactics.

Fifty miles north of the *Yamal*, the sky cleared and the temperature jumped ten or fifteen degrees. There were blue meltpools everywhere. It looked like the map of northern Ontario down there, like some summer place called Chain O' Lakes.

The sun was burning up a bank of clouds on the horizon. It emerged through a double halo so bright that I found myself suddenly squinting. A great slanting shaft of blinding golden light fell across the ice so that, for just a few minutes, the world below was a glittering, gaudy panorama. The meltpools were gold, flashing like mirrors in the sun. The snow was silver, sparkling silver, and there were deep purple shadows behind the spinning pressure ridges.

Andrei Masonov shouted over the clatter of the helicopter.

"You see?" he asked.

"Yes."

"Is beautiful?"

"Of course."

One night at dinner, due to a timing error on my part, I was seated with the Dreaded Couple Who Did Not Share My Political Opinions. For a change, we found ourselves discussing the matter of chasing bears with icebreakers. The man was an amateur video buff, and I had supposed—since he was wrong about most everything else—that he was in favor of the practice. "Don't like it" he said. "It's not right."

I was surprised. "You can't film much at six hundred yards," I said.

"Little shaky white specks on the ice," he agreed. "We could just tell folks it's the rare Arctic termite."

Later, I began asking around. The Man Whose Luggage Was Lost had complained to the tour director about chasing bears, as I had. Several people, it seemed, had lodged the same complaint—individually—all of us supposing that it really didn't matter to anyone else. I think I was proud of our little group.

There was, however, one strong voice in favor of getting up real damn close to any and all wildlife. "We paid good money," argued the Man Who Didn't Get It.

The *Yamal* was cracking through fairly thin ice that had opened up into numerous leads: wide black rivers winding over flat snowy fields. We were close.

I went up to the bridge and checked our position on the GPS (Global Positioning System): 89 degrees, 59 minutes. Just one more minute of latitude: about a mile. The longitude reading swung from 122 degrees (which runs through Los Angeles) to 70 degrees (New York) in about five minutes. The *Yamal* went spinning around the world in this fashion for forty-five minutes. Then the GPS scanner read 90 degrees north and nothing else.

On the bridge, people were standing around drinking champagne or pointing camcorders out at the patchy ice, at the GPS, at the captain, at each other: men and women standing camcorder to camcorder in a series of Japanese standoffs at the geographic North Pole.

But we were on thin ice here on the top of the world, and the *Yamal* circled the earth for a few more hours until the captain found a floe solid enough to be used as a dock. We were actually about four miles from the Pole itself, at 89 degrees, 55 minutes, and 79 seconds. Passengers and crew poured down the gangplank and onto the ice.

The newly fallen snow, on its fields of ice, was much lighter than the sky and it seemed as if the floor of our world was aglow, as from within. There were confused jumbles of blocky ice in the distance, and one low snaky pressure ridge that cast a faint sinuous shadow. The larger meltpools were freezing over before my eyes: surfaces ridged in static ripples so that I could read the signature of the wind scrawled in blue.

There were preparations for a party and barbecue going on at the port side of the ship. I walked around to starboard side to sit alone, in silent company with seven or eight other passengers, each of us seeking solitude, and not getting it, here at the loneliest spot on earth.

I saw the Shy Japanese Man and the Woman Who Climbed Kilimanjaro at Seventy. I wondered if they were thinking, as I was, of the people who gave their lives to get here, thinking of those who said they had made it but offered no conclusive proof: Cook, Peary, Byrd. From the party side of the boat I could vaguely hear the now familiar strains of a stand-up organ. "Those Were the Days." Polkas at the Pole.

We all gathered about to listen to one of the tour directors read a quote from Chief Seattle: Man is only a strand in the web of nature. Bob Headland, of the Scott Polar Institute, gave his estimate of how many people had stood on the ice at the Pole, including us: 2,804, he said, give or take a dozen.

Captain Andrei Smirnoff, slender and erect, with neatly trimmed white hair and a severe face, talked about the gathering as a group of people from many nations and how it cheered his heart to see all the flags flying together. And, as if all this weren't enough to be cynical about:

The happy couple came down the gangplank arm in arm while people threw colored streamers, and the two smiled helplessly as they became the first human beings ever to be married on the ice at the North Pole. The couple was Australian, and Captain Smirnoff read the vows in halting English: promises of eternal love spoken into a bitter wind. The sun was hidden behind bleak gray clouds. I stared into the sky, with the wind in my face; my eyes were tearing. From the wind, I told myself. I'd only just met the newlyweds.

Sometime later, I went time traveling four or five feet under the surface of the Arctic Ocean. I recall the complete absence of light, the familiar taste of seawater in my mouth, the incredible elasticity of time. It was all very dark, very languid, very pleasant.

Quite suddenly, however, I was walking barefoot on the ice, looking for my pants and feeling just a tad . . . irritated. The wind was unreasonable. Time was zipping right along again. Nikolai Druzdov was standing at the brink, wearing a swimming suit and about to take the polar plunge.

"Is it cold?" he asked.

"Of course," I said.

In Honduras

He Who Laughs

Once upon a time, in the past and in the future and even now as you read this, in a place not so very far away—indeed, in the Central American country of Honduras, about three days' drive south out of Texas—there lived and continues to live a monstrous fish, named Wasa, who laughs. Wasa reigns in the Cocoa Lagoon, twenty or thirty miles out of the town of La Ceiba, and is said to be allied with monkeys who howl and . . . well, what these monkeys do is not precisely unspeakable, and if they are not doing it to you—if they're doing it to someone like Grant Thompson, for instance—it's even pretty funny. Whiz, splat: Take that, eco-tourist!

There were four of us paddling sea kayaks on Cocoa Lagoon. Grant Thompson runs Tofino Expeditions, a kayak touring company out of Vancouver, Canada. He and one of his guides, Rob VanEgmont, were scouting the second largest Central American country, looking for places to take paying clients. Mexico, they felt, was saturated with kayak companies, and one of their favorite campsites in that country had just been sold to a major resort developer.

It was, Grant thought, time to move on. Scout some new locations. Costa Rica had more than its share of eco-tourism. Belize was developing a similar reputation. But Honduras, with its forbidding comic-opera reputation for coups and its proximity to various war zones, had effectively repelled tourists for decades. The country was pretty much virgin territory in eco-tourism terms. Worth a look, anyway.

Photographer Ted Wood and I were along to chronicle the scouting expedition.

We had been in Honduras for several days before we encountered Wasa and the monkeys. Flights inside the country had been extraordinarily inexpensive—the equivalent of twenty dollars or so, one way—and everyone aboard each flight crossed himself at the same time, just as the aircraft revved up for takeoff. It was like a holy drill team, and it worried me just a bit. Maybe we weren't paying enough to keep the plane airborne without divine intervention. A man with a Catholic education envisions Sister Norma, the World's Most Terrifying Nun, angrily cataloguing the tortures endured by various martyrs: sufferings we fourth graders had caused by snitching candy and fibbing to our parents. Martyrs were always crossing themselves before they were pierced head to toe with arrows or burned alive or eviscerated or fed to lions or . . .

Or maybe this was just a very, very foreign country. In 1969, for instance, tensions between Honduras and neighboring El Salvador erupted into a fierce five-day war after a soccer match between the two countries: the Soccer War.

Listen:

Soccer.

War.

A war over a game in which it is illegal to use your hands?

In addition, Honduras is a country with a history of political instability, mostly having to do with . . . well . . . with bananas, arguably the world's silliest fruit. For almost fifty years, Honduras led the nations of the earth in the export of bananas. It was a place where rival U.S.-owned fruit companies—and the CIA—had attempted, often successfully, to control the politics of the country. Honduras is *the* banana republic.

And Hondurans, I imagined, had every reason to resent visitors from the United States, yet people on the street in the major cities were easygoing, friendly, relaxed. There is a certain Latin grace about the country. In the resort town of La Ceiba, for instance, there is a shady canal where lovers stroll hand in hand at dusk and police officers drift by on mountain bikes, with automatic weapons clipped below the crossbar, while large carp circle slowly in the water below.

In the town square, caretakers throw garbage pails full of cow guts into a cement wading pool, which immediately comes alive with caiman five to seven feet long. The caiman, alligatorlike carnivores, seize the long white streamers of guts, then twist and turn, impressively, until most of them are shrouded in internal organs. A crowd of La Ceibans watches with the disinterested amusement of long familiarity. The caiman, satiated, pull themselves up on concrete slabs, and bask there in the dusk, looking smug and content with slanting catlike eyes and curled smiles.

In the Cacao Lagoon, where Wasa dwells, twenty-five miles or so from La Ceiba, there were said to be caiman as well. The water was black, a strong tea brewed out of fallen leaves and rotting vegetation. The lagoon was surrounded by mangroves that dropped branches down into the brackish waters, so that there were no banks anywhere, only a vertical wall of green. We paddled our kayaks around the verdant periphery in less than two hours.

It was Concepcion Martinez who told us about Wasa. He was our guide for the day, a young man from the nearby village of Cocoa, who often fished the black waters and knew them well. Several small, sluggish rivers fed the lagoon, and we turned our kayaks up one, which was very narrow and slow-moving. There were butterflies, sometimes in clouds of yellow and orange, and all about we heard strange birdcalls: melodic whistles and sibilant songs interspersed with various horrid strangled croaks. The temperature stood near 100 degrees and the sky above was a hazy, cloudless blue.

We were in fancy folding kayaks, double Feathercrafts, and Concepcion was paddling along in a wooden dugout. I asked if there were monkeys here, and just as Conci said yes there were, I saw a big one moving through the branches overhead. It was brown-and-orange, about the size of a cocker spaniel. And then a mother with a baby clinging to her back ran up over a nearby branch, and suddenly my eyes adjusted to the presence of monkeys. There were at least a dozen more in the bright green foliage.

"Howlers," Conci said.

And, sure enough, the monkeys began to howl, or at least one of them did. He sounded like a big, very hoarse dog with a lot of gurgling phlegm in his throat.

Ted Wood, who's heard howlers before in Central American forests—heard them from miles away—said he has always thought there was strange subaqueous quality to the sound.

"It sounds like fish laughing," he said.

"Really loud great big fish who live in trees," I offered.

"Maybe," Conci said, "they howl to tell Wasa we are here."

Wasa, according to lagoon legend, is a fish. The name, loosely translated, means "he who laughs."

"What kind of fish?" I asked.

"Big," Conci said, and he gestured to describe a fish considerably larger than I am. Apparently, Wasa is dangerous. He lives where the narrow river we were paddling flows into the lagoon and where, Conci said, the waters are *muy profundo,* very deep.

"How do you know the water is deep?" Rob asked. "Did you drop lines?"

"No," Conci said. "Everybody knows it's deep. The whole world knows it's deep." And now we did too.

"Are you afraid of Wasa?" I asked.

"Maybe," Conci said, and then he laughed. "Yes, maybe a little." He pondered the idea for a time as we drifted under the overhanging branches, with monkeys scampering and chortling overhead. "Wasa is thirty years old," he said.

"Have you ever seen a manatee in this lagoon?" I asked.

Yes, Conci said, there were manatees in the lagoon, and you didn't see them very often but—and here Conci indicated that he understood the thrust of my question—he damn sure knew the difference between a monstrous laughing fish and a manatee.

"It sounds," Grant said in English, "like something a bunch of mothers dreamed up to keep young kids out of the lagoon."

I liked the idea of myth as baby-sitter, but it seemed to me that the caiman could do that equally as well. You only had to watch them scarf up cow guts once to get the idea.

Grant and Ted, in the lead kayak, moved carefully upriver, where the water was shallow and strewn with fallen branches. The forest canopy formed a shady green archway, a tunnel of vegetation, and the monkeys were agitated, scampering overhead, keeping pace with our slow-moving kayaks.

"Back up," Grant shouted suddenly, and with some urgency. Immediately, he and Ted Wood were paddling backward, rather comically I thought, as something like rain fell around the bow of their kayak. There was more solid material as well, stuff I was able to identify as an astonishingly large number of howler-generated fecal depth charges. Our primate cousins sought to display their profound appreciation of our visit.

"The big one," Grant said later, "didn't even take aim. Just ran up on a branch and let fly—bang—like that. Incredibly accurate, considering he had to have his back to me."

We camped on a sandspit that separated the calm black waters of the lagoon from the cresting waves of the Carribean. The sun sank to our left, so that we cast attenuated pink man-shaped shadows as we set up the tents. Grant trotted out his shortwave radio and tuned into the Canadian Broadcasting System, assuring Ted and me, the Americans in the party, that we would hear important news denied us on typical U.S. outlets. It was true. As the sun sank below the horizon and the pastel sky burst into flame, we listened, not quite breathlessly, to the results of the curling championships in Bulgaria.

I tried to imagine a curling war. Disputes over corked brooms. Lumpy ice. Fighter jets screaming out of a snow-shrouded sky. Shattered limbs and field hospitals.

The lagoon mirrored the fires burning in the sky above and was fringed with shadowed gloom under the mangroves. A school of baitfish rose out of the now bloody water, flying over the surface in a panic. It was dusk, the time caiman like to dine.

Grant was talking about eco-tourism, about how it brought money into places like Honduras, which is in fact the poorest country in Central America. I contemplated the monkeys we had met that day and their excretory attitudes. Grant and I chatted about the idea for some time.

Often—in places like Mexico and Bali—resorts excluded local people, except in the capacity of busboys and chambermaids. Visitors got no real idea of the country or of how people lived. And the resorts themselves generally occupied areas that would otherwise speak to the soul. Might as well drop a putting green in the cathedral, a go-cart track in the mosque, pinball machines in the synagogue.

No, Grant thought that operations like his were the preferable alternative. Bring people in, stay in a hotel for a few nights of orientation, buy supplies from local folks, go camping on the beaches, purchase fish from local markets, leave the campsites just the way you found them. You didn't need a nation of busboys and chambermaids to travel in that fashion. You *wanted* to meet fishermen. Farmers. Fourth-generation ranchers.

We spent some moments digesting the idea.

Out in the lagoon, in the lurid sanguinary light, an egret, standing in the shallows, snagged a frog but seemed to have some trouble swallowing it. The bird's neck jerked convulsively, its beak snapped open and shut, but the frog wouldn't go down. Its back legs jerked and spasmed beyond the egret's beak.

Wasa came to mind. It wasn't exactly clear what the big fish would do if he caught you, but I imagined it was a frog-and-egret sort of scenario.

The sky began to fade until it felt as if we were covered over in a great blue-black bruise, and then it was dark. Wasa was out there, chortling away in the deep water. The monster was almost to be expected. He expressed something about wildness: sanctity symbolized, once again, as fear. Sister Norma would understand the Beast.

My flashlight beam caught two small red reflecting lights out in the lagoon: the predatory eyes of a caiman, moving silently.

And somewhere, unseen in the depths, was He Who Laughs.

This Man Cannot Speak

"You ever see *Casablanca*?" Grant asked.

We were paddling along the coastline of Honduras, moving west from Cocoa Lagoon, looking for a village called New Armenia. The people there were said to be Garifuna, a racial mix of Africans—former slaves—and indigenous Caribbean Indians.

"What about it?" I asked.

"The guy asks Humphrey Bogart why he came to Casablanca. He says, 'For the waters.' "

"Yeah?"

"And the guy says, 'There are no waters in Casablanca.' "

"Bogart says, 'I was misinformed.' "

"So," Grant said, "you see my point."

We had been misinformed about Cocoa Lagoon. People in La Ceiba, who were supposed to know, had said that it was big, that Grant could easily take clients there for a week. In fact, we had paddled around the lagoon in two hours. The rental van had cost the equivalent of a hundred dollars. We had been misinformed about the waters, and deeply hosed on the deal to boot. Which is why companies like Grant's need to do a lot of advance scouting.

A few hours later we saw people on a large sandspit that opened into another lagoon, a calm riverlike affair lined by lechiguilla, green plants that looked like a cross between lily pads and aloe vera. The plants were alive with purple flowers. As we paddled down the flower-lined aquatic lane to New Armenia, howlers in the trees above laughed like fish. Women washed clothes and children splashed about, shrieking and laughing.

A man named Raphael Arzu motioned us to shore and invited us to camp at his mother's house.

The house was constructed of thin-trunked trees crossed with smaller branches, filled in with mud, and roofed with thatch. Chickens, pigs, and ducks littered the neatly swept dirt of the yard, which was shaded by banana trees and coconut palms. A hand-lettered sign fronting the river indentified the place as Villa Hermosa, and it was, indeed, a pretty house. For a dollar a plate Raphael's mother, the estimable Alberta (Berta) Arzu, served us up a lunch on an outdoor table: rice, plantain chips that tasted a bit like fried potato rounds, eggs, and small chunks of chicken in a mildly spicy yellow sauce, heavy on the inexpensive local saffron. The egg was small and oblong, with a suspiciously leathery skin. I chewed on it for some time without making any appreciable progress in regard to breaking the skin.

Grant said that he thought the accommodations here were "cool" but not fit for FOPs, by which he meant kayaking clients Fresh Off the Plane. "A guy might do some high-pressure business at home," Grant explained, "information shooting at him all day long. But when you arrive in a foreign country, the strangeness of it, the foreignness, the kind of 'oh God' helplessness they sometimes feel, all this information at once . . . you have to settle them in a comfortable place for the first few days."

We ate some rice and contemplated FOPs while one of the hens picked insects out of the snout of a contented sleeping pig. And to my mind, there was a certain foreignness about the food.

"Uh, what kind of egg is this?" I asked Berta in Spanish.

"Iguana."

The trick, I learned, was to hold the egg in one hand and bite off a small piece of leather with the canine teeth. Pop the thing in your mouth and chew the yolk out of the leather sac. Spit out the sac. The egg was all yolk, yellow-orange in color, like that of a free-range chicken, but much richer in taste and vaguely creamy.

"This meat," Grant said, holding up a knucklelike forkful. "I don't think it's chicken."

It was, in fact, a tail section of what must have been a fairly large iguana.

"Chicken of the trees," Grant said.

In English, Ted said, "May we see the endangered species menu, please?"

I asked Berta if there were lots of iguana about, and she said that there were many, many. Because, I continued, I know that there are almost none left on some of the Bay Islands.

"Well," Berta said in Spanish, and shrugged. She looked out toward the islands. People there were very different. They were islanders, her expression said, and they went and killed off all their iguanas and acted stupid in so many other ways it was difficult to delineate them all. The imbeciles.

That afternoon we paddled down the narrow flower-lined river to New Armenia, a small town served by a gravel road. There was a rough-looking bar, a café, and a small hotel. I looked at one of the hotel rooms and heard a scraping sound above the loose boards in the ceiling. There were rat droppings on the bed, and no windows at all. It felt like the sort of place they might put you if you molested children. Not much good for FOPs, either. Personally, I liked the pig yard at Berta's place.

Back at Villa Hermosa, Raphael came by and introduced us to a thin man with an exceptionally expressive physical presence. He was in fact an involuntary mime, a man who could not speak. Raphael said he was "family," but the man was not an Arzu; he was simply troubled in some way, lived in New Armenia, was a Garifuna, and that made him "family." The only name anyone knew him by was Ganunu.

In a series of generally transparent charades, Ganunu said that people slighted him, and they wouldn't give him books, which he liked very much. The only book he'd ever had he carried with him for years, but one day it fell in the water and was destroyed.

. . . And, and . . . there was the time a man grabbed him by the arm. He showed us the man: a hulking gorillalike individual who walked in a stooped manner with bowed legs. He showed us the man's face: stern and self-important. There was something I couldn't make out on the man's shoulder and his hip. I shrugged.

Ganunu's face became a mask of frustration. He whirled, cried out in pain, looked as if he might cry. But no, wait. His face brightened. He knelt in the dirt and drew a rectangle. There was a small dot in the middle of the rectangle. Ganunu pointed to the dot, and then to the middle of his chest.

Ah. The rectangle was a jail cell. The man was a police officer with a gun on his hip and an epaulet on his shoulder. Thumbs up from Ganunu.

The police wouldn't give him anything to write with (though it wasn't clear that Ganunu could, in fact, write).

It occurred to me that Ganunu ought to have some sort of a card explaining his disability. The man agreed with me but said, in so many gestures, that no, he had no such card. I tore a page out of my notebook and, in authoritative block letters, wrote in precise grammatical Spanish: "This man is not drunk nor is he insane. This man cannot speak." Ganunu looked at the paper, then at me. His face was glowing. He shook my hand, gave me a thumbs up, did a restrained little dance, and tucked the note away in his shirt pocket.

Later, I felt the need to atone for this good deed, but the local children were no fools and decided early on that the proper and formal way to greet English-speaking people was not, in fact "How's your old wazoo?" On the other hand, *wazoo* is a fun word to say, in any language. The children and I said it quite a bit, a consequence of which is that I am now known to dozens of children in the Garifuna village of New Armenia as Señor Wazoo.

Grant liked New Armenia. The people were friendly, and the music, punta, a melange of African and salsa and reggae, was the sort of thing that made fat guys get up and dance. Berta and Raphael could arrange things for a fair price. His clients could soak up the culture. Grant and Rob paddled off down the canal looking for a grassy field to rent, a place where FOPs might feel comfortable.

Late that afternoon, while Ted and I were saying the word *wazoo* to a bunch of children, a large powerboat appeared on the horizon, and unknown men from someplace beyond the sea pulled up on a sandspit and offloaded a veritable houseful of furniture. There were several chairs, a couple of dressers, a table, and a sofa. The wind had picked up considerably, so the furniture, out there all alone on the sandspit, was partially obscured by a low-level sandstorm. It looked like a set for a Fellini film.

And then, wandering aimlessly, a small herd of cows made their way out onto the sand and wandered past the sun-blasted furniture, in the sandstorm, with the Caribbean Sea cresting five or six feet high in the background. For reasons that have never been satisfactorily explained, Ted and I felt the need to herd these cows back onto the mainland, where they belonged. We raced a kayak toward the sandspit, paddling hard against the heavy late-afternoon wind.

Ted is from Wyoming. I'm from Montana. I suppose each of us knows a little about herding cows. We'd just never done it from kayaks before. It was hard work, and I considered our plans for the future, such as they were.

Early the next day, we planned to paddle out to the Cayos de Cochinos, called the Hog Islands or the Islands of Pigs, which were somewhere over the horizon, in the distance. According to our maps, the Cochinos were not more than ten miles away, and we figured we could get there in less than four hours easy. Still, the weather had been dicey, kicking up a heavy wind and big swells in the late morning hours. Afternoons featured gusts of twenty-five miles an hour. We'd learned that much from the cows. Blinding speed is not a generally recognized bovine trait, and yet chasing an ambling herd against the wind had been a daunting chore.

I thought about cows all night and was up at four, with everyone else, packing the kayaks and cursing dully as men do when they have to get up way too damn early.

And then Ganunu was there in the dark, watching us, a question on his shoulders.

"We're going out to the Cayos de Cochinos," I explained.

Ganunu shook his head in a violent and negative manner. He pointed out to the dark sea, then to himself. I understood that he was an islander and would show me how islanders act. Ganunu lifted his head and stared down his nose at me. His face looked like he'd just accidentally eaten something the dog left on the lawn. I was scum. Dirt. A distasteful person. He turned his back on me, in contempt. He spit on the ground.

I got the impression that Ganunu didn't think the people who lived on the Cayos de Cochinos were very friendly.

The Islands of Pigs

By five it was light enough to see the breakers beyond the sand-spit. We punched through them easily enough and paddled into the open sea, which was rolling with five-foot-high swells kicked up by yesterday afternoon's winds. Half an hour later, the sun rose into a perfectly blue sky, looking for all the world like a big orange happy face. We paddled for two more hours, but the mountainous islands in the distance never got any closer until the last half hour, when our every stroke seemed to send them looming higher over us.

We made for an island with an expansive white sand beach where we had heard a Canadian couple was building bungalows to house travelers. A man in dreadlocks sat on the dock, holding his infant son. He said the owners were away and that his orders were not to let anyone land.

Well, where could we land?

Nowhere, it seemed. The whole of the Cayos de Cochinos were privately owned. Closed to folks like us. And Ganunu. The only place we could go was the island of Lower Monitor, a low half-moon-shaped spit of sand in the distance, choked with the thatched-roofed huts of Garifuna fishermen.

On that island we were met by several Garifuna men in tattered shorts, who seemed impressed that we had paddled all the way from the mainland. Further conversation revealed that, in fact, they thought we were morons for paddling from New Armenia when any child could have rigged a sail. No one ever paddled out to the island.

Tourists came, however. Most every day the motor launch,

called a tuk-tuk, brought out some young backpacking type, along with various supplies such as firewood needed for cooking, beans, cooking oil, block ice, and beer.

The men said we could set up our tents in back of the village, in the shade of some palms. Did we require food, a cook? No, but it seemed to be the expected trade-off.

Our cook, Nancy, was from New Armenia. She was another Arzu, Berta's niece, and she confirmed what we had been told: The islands were all privately owned. We were staying on the only "free place." It was basically an adjunct of New Armenia, a fishing village, where men stayed for stints of six months or so. The other islands in the Cochinos group were "private," owned by Americans and Italians and Canadians.

Lunch was one 3-ounce fish, a dollop of beans, and a spoonful of rice. So was dinner. And breakfast. It was what everyone on Lower Monitor ate. Every meal, every day. Fishing had been poor of late, due to the heavy winds. People were going hungry.

I swam out to the reef fronting the island. It was a shallow, craggy affair alive with elk horn and brain coral, with soft corals that swayed in a gentle surge: golden sea whips and purple fans. There wasn't a whole hell of a lot of fish life on this reef located a few hundred feet off a fishing village filled with poor, sometimes hungry men and their families.

A lone parrot fish, in his court-jester's garb of blue and green with patches of red, nibbled at a limestone cup of coral, trying to get at the living polyp inside. I could actually hear the crunch of coral in those powerful jaws. My shadow passed over the feeding fish and it veered off in a series of sharp angles, excreting powdery streams of chewed up limestone at each turn. The fine white sand of many tropical beaches is partially composed of this material, an idea that does not appreciably contribute to the romance of a tropical vacation. "Honey, let's wait until after midnight when everyone's asleep, then sneak out onto the beach and make love in the fish shit."

Sometime later I was sitting on the beach when a motor launch from a large scuba resort on another island landed on the beach at

Lower Monitor. A tourist couple in their early forties, decked out in fluorescent resort wear, strolled into town. I talked with the boatman, who was the resort's dive master. You could, he said, rent a room at the resort for $125 a night per person, which included three dives. People usually stayed for a week. The food was good and tonight was the steak barbecue.

And yes, he confirmed my suspicion that fish life was sparse off the village; but, he said, laws had recently been passed. Fishermen could no longer use nets. Only hand lines were allowed. "Actually," the fellow said, "they're talking about making a national park out of this island, a marine reserve. When they get rid of these people,"—he gestured toward the rows of ramshackle huts—"the fish life should recover fairly quickly."

And here we had the problem and paradox of eco-tourism in a clamshell. Get rid of the local people, who, it was clear, were overfishing the reef, thereby raising property values of the surrounding islands, which were, by and large, owned by wealthy foreigners. In time soldiers would come to Lower Monitor, the people there would be forcibly evacuated, and the wooden huts burned to the ground. The argument is that traditional fishermen could be retrained to make good money busing tables at the luxury resorts.

"More tea, sir?"

The tourist lady returned to the dive boat carrying a shell necklace. She said to the dive master (and I quote precisely here): "I gave the woman five dollars. Didn't even try to Jew her down. What am I going to do with their money? It was so funny. The woman said, 'Sank joo.' " She was amused, this ignorant harpy in a fluorescent orange halter top, that an underfed woman in a Latin American country should speak English so poorly.

On the other hand, five dollars for a few found shells strung together with a length of discarded fishing line would feed the Garifuna woman's family for a week.

Eco-tourism. Of a type.

One day, we paddled out to an small uninhabited island several miles away, a desert key where we picnicked on tortillas and jam, pineapple and coconut. The fish life was abundant here, miles from Lower Monitor. It was a tropical-island wet dream of a place, Grant said. Clients would love it. Presently, a motorboat powered up onto the beach beside our kayaks and a Hispanic man with long black hair jumped out and stomped over to where we were sitting.

The man carried a machete at his side and did not return our greetings—good afternoon, *"buenas tardes"*—but launched into an angry barrage of Spanish, the gist of which was: "This is a private island. When are you going to leave?"

We were all standing, and I didn't like the man's attitude or his machete. I moved to my right, thinking I could take him from the side if it came to that. I saw Rob drifting off to the other side, while Grant and Ted shifted about for some frontal advantage. The man was short and wiry. His eyes were cold.

"When," he demanded again, "are you leaving this island?"

Rob, who spoke the best Spanish, has the habit of repeating what was just said. Fewer misunderstandings that way.

"When," he repeated carefully, "are you leaving this island?"

Rob, I noticed, had unconsciously used the singular "you," so what the man heard in response to his question was a challenge:

When are you leaving?

No, pal, the question is, when are *you* leaving.

The machete man's eyes passed over us: four men spread out in combat formation, not one of them much under six feet tall, not one weighing much less than two hundred pounds. Bad feeling, like electricity crackling across the beach.

There is a law in Honduras, as there is in Mexico, Canada, and the U.S., that says the beach is open to the public for some distance above the high-tide line. We had been enjoying a perfectly legal picnic, but then the law didn't seem to count for much on the Islands of Pigs. The Honduran, for his part, was likely just doing his job. Fishing was a dying vocation. This guy was the occupational wave of the future.

Most people, I suspect, meekly left the beach when challenged, but the Machete Man had come on like an officious little prick, and we weren't moving, not even a little bit. The man stared at

Rob, who was smiling slightly, looking for some accommodation. The Machete Man clearly took the smile as a threat. There were no other boats on the water, only a few mountainous islands, dreaming in the distance.

The man broke eye contact with Rob, walked fifty yards down the sand, drew his machete, and began furiously hacking away at some brush fronting the beach. Biologists, I believe, would call this "displacement activity." He walked stiffly back to his boat, avoiding all eye contact, and sped off across the water without looking back.

In retrospect, I suppose Ganunu's wordless description of the islands had been our best advice. This was not the sort of confrontation Grant's clients might enjoy. We stayed around for another couple of hours, exercising our rights under Honduran law, so it was late afternoon when we started back, which meant that we had a head wind of about twenty miles an hour, right at the limit of my own ability to paddle a kayak.

Rob and I led, the wind yanking at our paddles, while Grant and Ted weaseled up behind us, drafting our kayak and using us for a windbreak. Grant was enraged: The idea of private islands and guards armed with machetes infuriated him. Screw this place. There would be no kayak tours of the Cayos de Cochinos. He was shouting about it, shouting furiously into the howling wind.

Oh, the idea of a marine reserve was a good one, sure. But look who gets the short end of the stick. Poor people. Local folks. Where's the damn justice in that? Grant wanted to know.

The place was gorgeous, the islands closely spaced and good for kayaking, but everything was private. Or resort-based. There were angry little dipsticks running around threatening people with machetes.

On the Islands of Pigs.

Pirates

Mrs. Melba Hyde-Jones, eighty, resident of the Honduran island of Guanaja, strolled through her living room, showing me various archaeological artifacts, the work of ancient indigenous Indians,

collected by her late husband, Frank. There were maize grinders
and small figurines with round faces and round eyes and round
mouths. Frank Jones was a history buff and he had written a
poem not long before he died, a poem about the history of the
island. He had said, "Melba, this one's for you."

Mrs. Hyde-Jones sat in a big wooden chair and recited the
poem—a very long work—from memory. It was about "an
earthly paradise," about Guanaja, an island alive with fish and
gulls and pelicans. The Indians who came from the mainland considered the island sacred, and warfare was forbidden.

Enter the villains of the poem. Columbus landed in the summer
of 1502, on his fourth and final voyage. Soon after, there were
Spanish galleons in the bays and blood ran in the sand and under
the trees. Peaceful Indians were taken as slaves to work in the
gold and silver mines of Mexico. Spanish ships took the spoils
back across the sea, to Seville.

Ah, but then the English began to raid the Spanish treasure
ships. By 1600 there were over five thousand pirates in the coves
and bays of Guanaja and Roatan. Blood once again ran in the
sand and under the trees. The poem strikes several triumphal
chords here, the gist of which seemed to be that the Spanish pretty
much deserved to get whacked by English pirates for what they
did to the Indians and to what had once been an earthly paradise.

The poem didn't quite say that later on, wealthy Englishmen,
who ran into trouble on Jamaica or the Caymans, might make
their way to the bay islands of Guanaja and Roatan for a second
chance in the plantation or commercial fishing business. The people of Guanaja—black and white—spoke English. They mostly
made their living on the sea. They traded with other English-
speaking Caribbean nations and protectorates: Belize, Jamaica,
the Caymans.

Then in 1859, the British ceded the bay islands to Honduras.
Most people of English heritage on Guanaja still consider this an
act of treachery. Today, the tensions on the islands are primarily
cultural: English speakers—both black and white—versus Spanish
speakers. Officially, the main town on the island of Guanaja is

called Guanaja. White English speakers—who call themselves "is-landers"—prefer the name Bonacco.

In the 1980s, piracy again played a part in the history of the Guanaja. In September 1985, Edgar Hyde-Jones, Melba's son, set out on a commercial fishing trip with a crew of nine English-speaking black men. They were approached by a boat carrying men who said they hadn't eaten in days. The hungry crew was invited aboard Edgar's boat, and were fed. After dinner the visitors produced weapons of some kind—probably Mac 10's or Uzis—and killed everyone aboard except one crewman, who leapt overboard and was miraculously rescued at sea. The incident was, of course, drug-related, and investigative agencies from the United States tracked the pirates to Colombia. They rescued another survivor, a fourteen-year-old cabin boy who, Melba said, would have been sold into slavery.

Edgar had been Melba's only son. She told me the story in a firm voice, but her eyes glistened as she spoke. She said that she was raising Edgar's daughter, who was now fourteen. Melba had never been able to tell her granddaughter precisely how her father died. "An accident at sea" is the closest she'd been able to come to the awful truth.

We sat in silence for some time. The house had been built in the 1880s, constructed of cypress imported from the United States. The wooden floors were bare and they showed over a century of traffic patterns, but they were clean and newly oiled. There was a picture of Edgar on the wall. He was wearing some sort of uniform and staring off into the distance at a future that would never happen. A clock somewhere in the house ticked off the seconds, loudly.

"Do you know why houses here are built on stilts?" Melba Hyde-Jones asked after a time.

She said malaria killed so many people on the mainland of Guanaja that over a hundred years ago, people began building on a shallow reef. "Islanders," she said with some pride, "settled a piece of water."

The town—Bonacco or Guanaja, depending on your linguistic

preference—has no roads but is intersected with canals and is sometimes called the Venice of the Caribbean. The walkways, threading between framed wooden houses and small shops, are narrow, and they cross over the canals in a series of humped-up wooden or concrete bridges. Deliveries are made by boat: ice and food and beer and clothing consignments all floating down the canals.

Windows are left open for the sea breezes, and a stroll through the town gives a taste of its life. People singing in the Catholic church, in the Adventist church; a large family gathered for dinner, heaping platters of fillets on the table; a man scolding his wife, the wife turning to leave, then turning again to deliver the last angry word; American country-and-western music blaring out of bars catering to Spanish speakers.

Even the jail is open to the breeze. One day at about sunset, I was walking down a narrow street and saw a black woman in tattered clothes shouting insults at passersby. She was slumped against a bright white wall, just below a sign reading POLICIA, and calling people "pus belly stink shits." It seemed a poor location for that activity, and I stopped to watch. Presently a hefty white policeman wearing camouflage pants and a shiny black T-shirt stepped out of the station, grabbed the woman by an arm, escorted her across the alley and into a room.

"I never stole dat ring," the woman shrieked. "I never!"

"I don' wan' hear it," the cop said mildly, "I don' wan' hear nutin' from you."

He slammed the door, which was newly painted with two-foot-high white letters reading CALABOZO. I walked by, propelled by intense curiosity, and glanced inside the calaboose through a small square window. It was like looking inside an oven, that hot, and the woman sat on a metal bunk, sweating profusely and looking miserable.

"Stink shit," she hissed in my direction—understandably, I think.

And then, only an hour later, there she was standing outside the jail, on the walkway, joking with the cop and wishing all who passed, including me, a good evening without a trace of sarcasm in her voice.

Melba Hyde-Jones asked me if I was enjoying my stay.

"Oh yes," I said.

Grant was planning on basing his kayaking business out of Guanaja. There were some good campsites on the island, and the owners of the land liked the idea of people coming in, spending money locally, and leaving without a trace.

The diving and the snorkeling were spectacular. One of the sites out by Long Key reminded me of the canyonlands of Arizona and Utah. At about thirty feet there were strange breaks in the coral heads: tunnels and canyons in the ocean. Soft corals predominated. The golden sea whips, in particular, looked like fuzzy saguaro cactus. Purple and green giant sponges reminded me a bit of barrel cactus, and the occasional mounds of hard plating coral, I thought at first, could be Anasazi ruins. But no. Too many colors: yellows and greens topped off with reds. They looked more like pagodas, or something you'd see in Tibet, if you could conceive of Buddhist architects on psychedelics. Slanting shafts of late afternoon sunlight illuminated the whole affair. And everywhere, on the whole of the reef, all the soft corals—the purple fans and yellow whips—everything swayed in a gentle surge, so that, drifting through the sinuous canyons and tubes, I felt as if I were slow-dancing with the Caribbean.

Melba told me about how the young people, sons and daughters of islanders, were leaving. Fishing didn't pay much anymore. Young people went to school in the United States, then looked for jobs there later on. No one wanted to stay and work for virtually nothing in some little island shop. The stores in Guanaja were often run by "Spaniards," that is, Spanish speakers from the mainland. Many of them were industrious. They did well, and after a time, they bought little chunks of property from islanders who might be down on their luck. Melba felt the whole place sort of falling away from her.

Had I talked with her brother, Verne, about any of this?

In fact, I'd talked a lot about it with Verne. He was strong and tireless, a rawboned tough-talking man who went to the United States at the age of fifteen and wound up working for the U.S. Army in marine transport during the Second World War, then again in Vietnam. He owned five hundred acres of agricultural land on the island and had tried to build a resort there, but got wiped out by Hurricane Fifi in 1974. He set to rebuilding, and was just about to open four years later when Hurricane Greta destroyed his newly built lodge. Verne went back to the States to make some money in construction and was flattened again, this time by a bad divorce. Fifi, Greta, and then . . . ah hell, Verne didn't even want to say her name.

At seventy-one, he was starting over.

We didn't have a lot of luck visiting Verne's land. The day was blustery, too dangerous to go all the way by boat. Verne got us to within a two-hour walk, and we stashed his boat in a deserted bay. He marched Ted Wood and me, double time, over some mountainous country that might have been the headlands of Northern California, then examined the mango and banana crop at his plantation. The water in the stream was down. Way down.

Verne blamed a neighbor above him, a damn newcomer, a Spaniard from the mainland who was burning the gullies, working a slash-and-burn agricultural system that was destroying the watershed. The sons of bitches already trashed the mainland, Verne said, and now they want to come out here and do it. It was happening all over the island. Slash and burn.

And so, on the two-hour walk out of the plantation, Verne cursed Spaniards altogether, using a term that would get you hurt bad in any barrio I knew. I liked Verne, liked him a lot, but thought I ought to say something. Nothing particularly diplomatic came to mind. When we got back to the boat, the engine wouldn't start, and Verne cracked a couple of ribs trying to work the hand crank. Then it got dark on us and started pissing down rain. There was a severe lightning storm in the distance, moving our way. We were stranded and pretty much screwed.

"Please don't go around calling people spics" is what I should have said.

Verne was in some pain, so Ted and I set off for the nearest town, jogging, in the dark. An hour later, we saw a light on a ridgetop, climbed toward the house, and met a retired couple from the United States, who radioed for help. That night, rescued, Verne, Ted, and I stayed in a small town on the mainland, in a boardinghouse owned by an ample black woman named Enola Gay.

Enola said that she was born before they named the plane that dropped an atom bomb on Japan, but she sure hoped nobody thought she had anything to do with *that*. While Enola fixed dinner, Verne said that he'd known the woman all his life, that he had, in fact, grown up with her. When Verne was a kid, he delivered milk, on horseback, and every morning there was this beautiful little girl, working out in her yard. "She was always a worker, like me," Verne said. He admired that in her.

When Verne was trying to put his resort together, Enola worked for him. Then Fifi and Greta came along, and Enola started her own boardinghouse and restaurant. She was making a living primarily, I imagine, because her fish chowder is a thing of singular elegance. My room in her boardinghouse was spare and very clean.

I woke sometime in the middle of that night. Lightning was striking nearby. The wind was booming and howling out of the east. Enola and Verne were up. I could hear them chatting in the parlor, two old friends seeking shelter from the storm.

Enola was listing the things Verne had to do tomorrow.

"Enola," he said. "I swear, I'm getting so forgetful . . ."

"Well, Verne," she said. "I think you should slow down. For your health."

"When are *you* going to slow down?"

And they laughed together while lightning struck all around. I drifted back to sleep as Verne and Enola gossiped about the people they'd grown up with.

"Was she the one who always went barefoot?" Verne asked.

A soft murmur from Enola.

"And that's her boy?"

The next morning, Enola had breakfast on the table when I got up and Verne was still talking about how the river on his land was going dry. What he ought to do, he said, was visit the governor. Talk about some *laws*. He apologized for getting so worked up yesterday, for some of the things he'd said.

So I told Melba Hyde-Jones, that yes, I'd heard Verne's opinions about the land and about various agricultural practices. I agreed with him to this extent: Slash and burn would result in a Guanaja that was literally dead in the water. The practice didn't draw paying tourists, either. You got a visit, once, from a BBC documentary film crew, and that was about it.

"But what can you do?" Melba asked. "The new people: It's their country too."

"Yes," I said. "Yes it is."

I talked a bit about Grant's project and the idea that people might pay to visit an essentially unspoiled Guanaja.

"You think so?" Melba asked. There were a couple of very good scuba resorts on Guanaja already. She couldn't see that many more people would want to come to her island.

"Hey, it's an earthly paradise," I said.

Melba caught the echo of her late husband's poem and smiled in a way that broke my heart. She was eighty years old, smarter than most, and wanted to think on the notion for a time.

We sat in silence.

Melba's clock ticked away the seconds in her century-old home.

The Lone Ranger

The highest, the most remote mountains on the mainland of Honduras form the nucleus of several national parks. We were driving along a network of bad dirt roads, looking for a way to enter the newly established Santa Barbara Park. It was steep country, very green, and the mountains were closely spaced. The land, to my eye, possessed the logic of a sheet of paper crumpled in the hand and dropped on a table.

There were cattle grazing in vertical pastures, moving under strange knobby green peaks. Pineapples grew in adjacent fields, and clear-cuts wound their way up the slopes of the higher mountains, which marched off into the distance, purple against the rising smoke of the agricultural fires burning everywhere.

The roads lacked signage of any sort and branched off to various tiny villages, where we saw horses, saddled Western-style, laden with bananas or pineapples and tied to hitching posts in front of the cantinas. Men in straw cowboy hats and Western-cut shirts pointed off in several different directions at once when we inquired about a route into the mountains above.

The road dropped back down to the country's major north-south highway, which fronted the west side of Lake Yajoa, a hundred square miles of clear waters, fringed with coffee plantations, a few resorts, and dozens of prosperous-looking farms. The lake, a seriously picturesque affair, was stocked with large and apparently exceedingly dumb bass. There were at least thirty restaurants lining the highway, each of them selling bass and only bass. We stopped at one of the upscale places, redundantly named Only Bass. They served bass with devil sauce, with tartar sauce, with garlic butter; we could have our bass fried, grilled, or baked. Everything was delicious except for the only beer on the menu, a sour imported American brand whose uniquely honest sales pitch is "It doesn't get any better than this."

Later that night, we stopped in the town of Santa Barbara and tried to get a fix on the national park rising all around in the darkness. Since the directions given in the town square all smacked of misinformation and Casablanca, we counted ourselves fortunate to run into a man named Martine Rodriguez, of the Green Heart Ecological Association, who trotted us off to his nearby office, showed us some maps, and told us that we could get into the park via the village of San José de Los Andes. The village was set about a mile high and was one of the highest settlements in Honduras. Could we get up there in a two-wheel-drive car without much clearance? Not in the rainy season, Martine said, but since it had been pretty dry lately, hey, no problem.

Which is how, the next day, we came to be irremediably stuck on a cruel boulder-strewn joke of a road at an elevation of about five thousand feet and two miles short of San José. Men from the village, returning from work in the fields, stopped and gave us a hand, as a matter of course. It was necessary to unload the van: twelve big bags, including four backpacks, three tents, and two disassembled kayaks weighing over one hundred pounds apiece. The men literally lifted the van out of some ruts and helped us push it the rest of the way to San José. While they seemed shy, it was clear that we were a source of some quiet amusement to these friendly men.

The town was set out along a sloping dusty street lined mostly by one- and two-room wooden houses. The people were mestizo, which is to say, of mixed European and American Indian heritage: Almost 90 percent of all Hondurans are mestizo. They directed us to the home of Peggy Chui, a young American Peace Corps volunteer, who lived in a small wooden house with a bucket-flush toilet, a kerosene stove, and a battery-driven shortwave radio.

We cooked dinner for Peggy and ended up talking on her porch, under a sky studded with van Gogh stars, while the lights of various fishing resorts twinkled on the shores of Lake Yajoa far below.

Peggy was working with the village farmers, developing better methods of hillside agriculture. The people of San José, she said, got bad seeds, which they sowed in poor soil. The year before, when the bean crop had come in sparse, some people had gone hungry for a time. Sixty percent of the country lived like this, Peggy said, whole villages existing hand to mouth on subsistence agriculture.

But—and this was hard for her to express exactly—the people in San José seemed . . . well, content. Happy. *Pero como* was the stoic motto: What can you do? It had taken Peggy a year to feel at home in the village, and now it was a part of her. There were evenings, she said, when a cool fog rolled up out of Yajoa and enveloped her, times when she felt as if she were living inside a glittering cloud, and the whole place felt mystical.

She introduced us to her neighbor, a man named Octivilo Ramos, who had been the chief (and only) ranger for Santa Barbara

National Park since it was established in 1987. It was an unpaid position. He was also the only guide in the area, and offered to take us into the forest for a fair price. We bargained in the Honduran fashion, which is to say, when Octivilo named a figure, forty lempira a day apiece, we were struck speechless with an agony of grief and stared hopelessly at the ground. Octivilo let us live in the silence of our unbearable pain for all of thirty seconds, then suggested thirty-five a day. Thirty-five? We stared at one another in shocked delight. Our joy was uncontainable. He couldn't possibly mean it. Thirty-five? Why, it was a miracle. We shook hands on the deal and agreed to start off into the forest at dawn the next day.

Later, after Octivilo went home, Peggy said thirty-five lemps was, in fact, his usual price, which was damn good money in San José. When people worked for others—picking coffee, for instance—the average wage in the area came to about ten lempira (a little over a dollar) a day. On our two-day trek, Octivilo would earn the equivalent of twenty-eight days of average wages.

Not many people came to San José to visit the forest, Peggy said. There had been five parties her first year, ten the next.

I suggested that while the numbers were small, visitation had doubled. Since people sometimes went hungry in the village, was it possible that some sort of trekking tourism could make up the slack?

Peggy was torn on the issue. In the best of all worlds the people of San José would improve their farming methods, feed themselves, and live as they always had. You only had to go to Copán, the country's major tourist destination, to see what San José could become. The people there, in Peggy's view, were aggressive, fixated on profit. Most of all, they didn't seem happy.

And yet . . . the poverty in San José could make your heart ache in dozens of small ways every day. Look at the children, Peggy said. There was no dentist anywhere nearby, no money to get one up to the village, and no real understanding of the techniques of oral hygiene. When the children, these beautiful children, smiled up at you, their mouths were full of rotting black stumps. So, yes, Peggy supposed, you could put in a visitors' center, charge a small fee of each trekker, and pay for monthly visits from a dentist. Thing was: Where did something like that end?

The next morning, Octivilo marched us through town, out over the coffee plantations, and up through an area of clear-cut that ran smack into the boundaries of the national park. An hour or so into the park we came upon a small canyon that had been slashed and burned.

Octivilo was a "Spaniard" Verne Hyde would have loved. He stopped there to give us a quick lecture on ecology. Whoever burned the area was planning on planting a crop, using water that would naturally flow into the area. The problem, Octivilo said, was that heavy rains later in the year would erode the gully and cause mudslides to destroy cropland below. Worse, the forest floor, littered with over a foot of fallen vegetation, acted as a giant sponge, storing rainwater that fell during the wet season and releasing it slowly during the dry. Cut the forest, he said, and the rivers—like the one on Verne Hyde's place—would begin to dry up. All the crops below, all the way to Yajoa, would die of thirst.

Octivilo said he'd known about the burn and was investigating. He was an honest, knowledgeable man but essentially a volunteer. Could he really turn in one of his neighbors. In a town of five hundred people?

The cloud forest above the burn was thick—you couldn't really see more than ten feet in any direction—and the trail was narrow, sometimes nonexistent. We passed giant hardwood trees, a type of mahogany, a hundred feet high, and the branches were hung with woody vines, with great masses of moss. Everywhere, in all the trees, there were red parasitic flowers the size of basketballs. Looking up induced a kind of vertigo: All the smaller trees bent and twisted their way toward the sun, toward a patch of open sky, so nothing grew straight up and down. There was a sense, in this dizzying forest, that every living thing longed for the death of its nearest neighbor. The mosquitoes were fierce.

Our campsite was a limestone overhang, fringed with woody vines dropped from the trees growing on the ledge above. Octivilo shared my tent that night, and he told me that there were some nonpoisonous snakes in the forest, a number of small deer, a few ocelot, and a lot of foul-smelling bad-tempered peccaries. The monkeys were gone, hunted out, but there were plans to reintroduce them.

Not everyone, Octivilo said, agreed about how the new national parks of Honduras should be administered. There was some dissension in the capital city of Tegucigalpa. One group, noting the economic benefits Costa Rica was enjoying from ecotourism, wanted to open up everything, everywhere, to unrestricted travel. Another group was more cautious and felt some areas should be preserved to protect the wildlife and the watershed. Octivilo wasn't sure which was really the right approach, but he seemed proud that Santa Barbara wasn't all that accessible to the outside world.

There were times, he said, when it felt as if he were the only person in the forest. He especially liked the winter months, when it sometimes snowed in the higher elevations. There was a very distinct line at about eighteen hundred meters. Everything below was green; everything above, white. The snow bowed down the branches of the trees, covered the red flowers, and was knee-deep on the ground.

In the morning we puttered around camp, then walked back through a forest that was shrouded in clouds. Peggy said that while we were gone, there had been a gathering of townsfolk and we had been one topic of conversation. Her friend Pedro related the story of how badly we'd been stuck, how we had to unload the van and push it up the hill. He told the story in such a way that people were doubled over in laughter. Peggy—she said she was sorry about this; she couldn't help it—then told people that the big red bags we unloaded, the heavy ones, the ones we carried, sweating and cursing two miles up the mountain: those bags contained . . . boats. Oceangoing boats. People had laughed until there were tears in their eyes.

The Ozymandias Express

The drive from San José to the ruins of Copán, located near the border with Guatemala, had been exciting in unanticipated ways.

At first we thought it was a bad accident ahead: A schoolbus blocked the roadway, and there were several plumes of black smoke rising behind. In fact, it was a protest of some kind. Lines of burning tires spanned the pavement, and men carrying sticks of varying sizes motioned us to pull over in such a way that our van, like the schoolbus ahead, blocked traffic. A man carrying a bullhorn followed the men with the sticks up and down the line of stopped cars and trucks. "Avoid violence," he shouted. "Violence has bad consequences."

The bus ahead was full of ten-year-old schoolgirls wearing white blouses and blue skirts. It was nine in the morning and already 90 degrees. The driver wouldn't let the girls out of the bus to mingle with the men on foot carrying sticks, who were being exhorted to avoid violence.

Grant, Ted, Rob, and I split up and walked down the line of cars, trying to find out what was happening. Truck drivers, who seemed unperturbed and used to this sort of thing, had strung hammocks in the shade under their trucks and were lying there scratching their stomachs and smoking cigarettes.

Rob and I sat in the shade of a maple-size tree covered over in pink flowers and chatted with an older man carrying one of the smaller sticks. Everyone, he said, was protesting recent price rises. Clothing cost too much, as did food and transportation. It was all tied in to the price of gasoline, which had doubled in the last five years.

A younger man, carrying a bigger stick, explained, quite pointedly, I thought, that the United States was behind the price jump. We were? I tried to sort out the mechanics of that, came up with several possible scenarios, and kept my mouth shut. Rob said that he was Canadian and that the U.S. was always doing that sort of stuff to him.

"The bastards," I added, temporarily Canadian.

It was a little tense for a while. Some people from a bus that was stopped behind our van walked by, carrying their bags toward the other side of the roadblock. Men with sticks menaced them, women screamed insults, and the man with the bullhorn followed behind, shouting about the bad consequences of violence.

A gentle breeze blew a cloud of black tire smoke my way. An hour passed. Two. It was edging toward noon, and was probably already over a hundred degrees in the sun. The protest, it seemed, was beginning to wind down in the heat. TV cameras had come and gone. Most of the protesters had discarded their sticks, and people were chatting amiably enough. When a man carrying a rusted automobile fender walked by, someone yelled, "Hey, are you taking your car through one piece at a time?" and everyone laughed.

I figured the protesters wouldn't let those little girls swelter in the bus much longer, and I was right. They let us go at about one that afternoon. A few hours later we drove into the town of Copán Ruinas, less than a mile from the ruins themselves.

It was a graceful place of cobblestone streets and colonial buildings, with a variety of hotels, restaurants, and cafés catering to international travelers. Tourists thronged the streets. Near a shop selling T-shirts, I saw a man wearing plaid Bermuda shorts, black socks, and black wing-tip shoes. Gee, I thought, this place is utterly unlike San José de Los Andes.

My first morning in the ruins proper, a mist was rising off the Copán River. I stood silently in the great plaza, an open grassy area dotted with several stelae, monumental statues commemorating the accomplishments of various extinct rulers. I couldn't read the glyphs on the stelae, but even in the drifting mist, the subtext was clear enough. It had been written by Percy Bysshe Shelley in 1817: Look on my works, ye mighty, and despair.

Small deer wandered toward the central court and the acropolis, an aggregation of steps and temples rising 120 feet off the grassy plain. The ruins had just opened for the day, and there were only a few other people walking in the mist. Most of them were taking notes or pictures. The place was like a great cathedral. It enforced that sort of solemnity.

There had been people living in the Copán River valley two thousand years before Christ. A city of monuments and temples and ballcourts grew up the banks of the river. The structures are smaller than those found at other major Mayan sites—Tikal or Palenque or Chichén Itzá—but it was at Copán that the culture found its fullest expression in art. If Copán was the Athens of the Mayan world, the thirteenth ruler, known as 18 Rabbit, was its Pericles.

The classic era lasted from about A.D. 465 to 800. Then, very rapidly it seems, the city fell into ruin. No one knows why. There might have been war or disease or famine or drought or civil insurrection. Some archaeologists, examining the various sedimentary layers in the riverbed, have postulated that the Copánecs simply overused their agricultural resources and that the catastrophe that devastated the classic city was an ecological one. Slash and burn.

The next day, as if to illustrate Peggy Chui's comments about the pernicious effects of tourist dollars, a local sharpy took me to the cleaners on a fast horse deal. The agreed upon four-hour ride lasted only three because "another tourist is waiting for your horse, señor." Rather than argue, I paid full price. The guide stared at the money I gave him and glared at me.

"Where's my tip?" he demanded.

Since violence has bad consequences, we stood in the town square and discussed the sexual morality of our respective mothers for a time. I don't know whether or not the man was content by Peggy Chui's definition. I did notice that he was wearing a pair of sixty-dollar Reeboks.

Later that day, I found myself back at the ruins, sitting on the ancient stones of the Mayan acropolis and contemplating the Ozymadias Express. Grant said he would take his clients to Guanaja, maybe visit New Armenia with them, but skip San José in favor of Copán, which, we both thought, tended to put things in perspective. Hey, *pero como?* You live; you do what you can—throw up your own version of a few stelae—and in the end only He Who Laughs prevails.

Misty Crossings

Earl, the weather god one of my companions favored, was in a festive mood, which is to say, it was about 65 degrees on a fine sunny October morning off the western coast of Vancouver Island, British Columbia, Canada. My heavily loaded fabric kayak was cutting smartly through the Pacific Ocean at about three miles an hour, and I was testing its performance capabilities, leaning off to one side or another in an attempt to ascertain the precise point at which the craft might capsize. This is like sitting in a chair and balancing yourself on the back two legs. People who test the performance capabilities of chairs sometimes have reason to chastise themselves.

So it is with kayaks.

Even so, I had to lean pretty far back in the figurative chair of my boat before gravity even began to exert its ponderous influence. Sea kayaks are stable in the water—not at all like river kayaks, which are maddening, tippy little sons of bitches, built to capsize for the fun of it. Sea kayaks, by way of additional contrast, also carry a lot of gear—your boat is your luggage. Such a craft is paddled in the interest of exploration and comfortable camping, not acrobatic athleticism.

My kayak was gliding over calm seas near the mouth of Esperanza Inlet, where mountains soared directly out of the sea. The land looked like Seattle, without all the Seattle. Misty green forests rose, precipitously, to angular rocky peaks. The higher summits carried a fine dusting of recent snow that sparkled and glittered in the sun. The sea was a glassy expanse: It took on the cobalt-blue color of the sky; it caught the surrounding mountains in such a way that I was paddling over the shimmering reflection of forest and snow.

It seemed a good time to lean waaaaaay back in the chair.

There were four of us out that day—four kayakers; four kayaks. Grant Thompson makes a living taking people paddling around Vancouver (Tofino Expeditions, Vancouver, Canada). Joel Rogers is a photographer who has chronicled the entire west coast of North America from a kayak (*The Hidden Coast, Kayak Explorations from Alaska to Mexico:* Alaska Books). Linnea Larson was a novice paddler. She had never been in a kayak before and saw no reason to test the performance capabilities of her craft.

On my own first kayaking trip, at Glacier Bay, Alaska, I rented a big hard-shelled sea kayak at the mouth of the bay and paddled sixty miles to Muir Glacier, a great two-hundred-foot-high wall of ice that flowed down out of the mountains and into the seawater. Killer whales patrolled the waters for errant harbor seals. One pod of these black-and-white pack-hunting wolves of the sea passed so close that I could hear them breathe as they surfaced: The glottal pop and explosive expulsion of air echoed off nearby rock walls.

I've paddled in company with killer whales and heard that same sound in the Sea of Cortez, off the coast of Baja California. There, along that coast, sheer sun-blasted rock and desert give way to a fertile sea. Pelicans and blue-footed boobies dive on schools of bait fish half a mile in diameter. Fishing is good. Clams are plentiful. Some of the reefs reach almost to the surface of the sea, and it is pleasant to drift along, watching a busy city full of tropical fish going about its business. A friend of mine refers to this activity as "kanorkling." In the distance, while kanorkling the reefs of Baja, I've seen fifteen-hundred-pound manta rays erupt four feet out of the sea, flapping their great black batlike wings.

Sometimes, on the water, near some remote island, Mexican fishermen working small boats will make a trade: a dozen eggs for a ten-pound yellow-fin tuna.

The wind in Baja generally kicks up in the early afternoon, and it is a good idea to start paddling before dawn and to set up camp about noon. The white sand beaches available to kayakers are completely deserted. There are no luxury resorts on these perfect beaches, no roads to them, no access at all except by way of kayak. Set up a tent and rig a tarp for shade. Grab an iced beer from the cooler while the tuna grills. Above, vultures wheel about, bitterly confused. These scavengers and custodians of the desert are waiting for death. I like to lift a beer in their direction and toast their patience. Be a while until soup's on, guys.

At the southern tip of the Baja Peninsula the sere, sun-blasted land rises to a granite ridge, then gives way—at land's end—to a series of free-standing rocks known as the Arches. South of the Arches, the full force of the Pacific Ocean explodes against glittering granite. The sea has ripped the stone heart out of these rocks, and one of the natural arches it has formed is 291 feet high. I recall kanorkling at the base of one of these arches, watching the sea consume land in a large and continuous underwater sandfall.

There is, as one kayaking companion suggested, "a lot of geology going on" at land's end. This elemental process is seldom so visible in time. I looked through the Arches, through rainbows of intermittent spray, out into the ocean that stretched south across the equator, vast and lonely, all the way to Antarctica. I was, I thought, at the end of the earth, and the sea was eating the land. The Arches seemed like the portals of time.

There are comparable sea kayaking explorations to be had all up and down the coasts of the Americas. In southern Chile, for instance, there are islands where tidewater glaciers pour down out of the mountains, through the tangled greenery of dense rain forests. In these places hummingbirds and parrots share the beach with seals. Hawaii and the Caribbean are fine kayaking destinations, and people have recently begun paddling the waters of the Greek Isles, of Bali and Java, of Madagascar, of Lake Baikal in Siberia.

I was thinking about this, about all these places I'd paddled, and would like to paddle, as my kayak cut through the shimmering reflection of another snowy peak. The wind across Esperanza Inlet had picked up to about ten miles an hour and the swells had risen to a couple of feet. Still fine paddling weather. The stability of my kayak had begun to annoy me. How far does a guy have to lean over until . . .

My chair, so to speak, began to fall over backward. No problem. Just whack the flat of the paddle onto the surface of the sea. The technique is called a bracing stroke, and it brings the paddler back into an upright position. Unless, of course, the paddler in question is not very good at bracing strokes. In which case he capsizes.

When your chair falls over backward, there is that awful jolt of disbelief—how could this possibly have happened to me?—followed by a sincere and fervent wish no one has seen you. Which were, indeed, my feelings as the kayak turned 180 degrees on the surface of the sea.

It was embarrassing sitting upside down in this boat, with my head pointed to the bottom of the sea, blinking furiously while my nostrils filled up with seawater.

There is, as most people know, a nifty technique called the Eskimo roll. It's a simple twist of the hips combined with a swift swirling paddle stroke. The submerged kayaker bursts up out of the sea, shakes the water from his hair, and paddles on.

Sadly, I have never been able to actually complete an entire Eskimo roll.

• • •

No one knows when the people of the Aleutian Islands first began paddling the skin boats we call kayaks. George Dyson, in his admirable history of the kayak, *Baidarka,* points out that "the skin boat's biodegradable components left archaeologists with scarcely a trace." Dyson does note that "the earliest known settlements among the Aleutian Islands date back more than eight thousand years. The skin boat might have migrated to the Aleutians from somewhere else or might have been invented there independently, perhaps in a period of post glacial isolation, as the rising sea level forced land based nomadic hunters to put their ice age-sharpened minds to building boats."

An Ice Age technology, then.

On September 5, 1741, Vitus Bering, a Dane in service of the Russian crown, sailed two 80-foot vessels into a cove on Shumagin Island, in the Aleutians. There, Bering and his crew became the first Europeans to make contact with the inhabitants of the Aleutian Islands. The people they met were paddling kayaks.

Bering's naturalist, Georg Steller, noted that "the American boats are about two fathoms [twelve feet] long, two feet high, and two feet wide on the deck . . . to judge by appearances, the frame is of sticks fastened together at both ends and spread apart by crosspieces inside. On the outside, the frame is covered with skins, perhaps of seals. . . . The paddle consists of a stick a fathom [six feet] long, at each end provided with a shovel, a hand wide. With this he beats alternately to the right and the left into the water and thereby propels his boat with great adroitness even among large waves."

This might have been a description of the Feathercraft kayak I was paddling, except that the inner skeleton was made of aluminum and heavy-duty fabric had replaced seal skin. Also, the paddler inside lacked some of the adroitness attributed to the Aleutian kayakers in 1741. I suspect that the Ice Age as a whole might have been something of a trial for me.

Not that there aren't latter-day kayakers of some skill. In the 1980s, Ed Gillet completed a California-to-Hawaii crossing in a kayak. When he arrived on Maui, only a few weeks overdue, Gillet was distressed to discover that he had been declared lost at sea and presumed dead. When he appeared on television with Johnny Carson, the host treated Gillet with the sort of amused respect our society reserves for the remarkably insane.

Indeed, in the 1970s and early 1980s, sea kayaking, according to John Dowd, was considered "an off the wall activity for a few eccentric individuals." Dowd, a New Zealander famous for his own prodigious sea voyages, is the author of *Sea Kayaking, a Manual for Long Distance Touring,* a book that is generally considered the bible of the sport. In 1980, Dowd opened North America's first ocean-kayaking shop, Eco-Marine, in Vancouver, British Columbia. And in 1984, he began publishing *Sea Kayaker,* the sport's first specialty magazine.

I had met Dowd at Eco-Marine in Vancouver in preparation for this trip, and we chatted for a while about the explosive growth of sea kayaking in the latter half of the 1980s. The sport, Dowd said, had previously been a "backyard industry, limited to dedicated and enthusiastic people who built their own boats." This, Dowd supposed, is the reason so many sea-kayaking pioneers are considered cranks and weirdos. "They are," Dowd said, "innovators." The concept of providing a service to the public at large had no appeal.

Enter Dowd and Eco-Marine, in 1980. About the same time, manufacturers like Necky and Valley Canoe Products introduced fiberglass and/or Kevlar kayaks, boats that were relatively inexpensive and sometimes quite literally bullet-proof.

The sport benefited from "new products, service, and professionalism," Dowd believes. Additionally, what Dowd calls "the technical threshold" is very low, which is to say the sport is easy to learn. I had been, for instance, able to surf my kayak over the waves thrown up by calving tidewater glaciers after a mere four days of paddling.

"A sport like windsurfing," Dowd said, "requires a lot of skill but not a lot of knowledge." On the other hand, the intricacies of sea kayaking—coastal navigation, for instance—are profound, but the entry-level skills are low.

I mentioned that I had picked up a breakdown kayak—a kayak that can be disassembled and carried in a backpack—at the Feathercraft factory, just a few blocks from Eco-Marine. There I had seen two fairly beat-up backpacks on the floor, boats that the owners had sent in to be refurbished. The names on the packs were Rick Ridgeway and Yvonne Chouinard.

Dowd wasn't surprised. "Initially," he said, "we drew a lot of hard-core climbers like Rick and Yvonne. Trekkers and backpackers came next." By the mid-nineties there were guided kayaking trips up and down both coasts of North America. I've met bankers, electricians, musicians, and paramedics sea kayaking. The sport is booming.

The cockpit of a kayak is an elongated oval. It's not much bigger around than you are, and to get in, you slip your legs into the oval and lower yourself to a sitting position. Just so. To prevent water and waves from washing into the oval cockpit, you cover it with a spray skirt. This is a kind of waterproof dress you wear snugly just above your waist. The edges of the skirt fit tightly under a cowling that projects up above the oval cockpit. There is a string to pull because you want the spray skirt very tight indeed. It needs to withstand waves crashing over the bow. It should keep you completely dry from the waist down during an Eskimo roll.

It is, in fact, so tight that you cannot just push against the kayak to get out should you happen to capsize. You have to free the spray skirt. There is a tab stitched into the skirt, and it projects onto the deck of the boat, directly in front of the kayaker. Pull the tab back, and it pops the whole front half of the spray skirt free.

Which is what I did there off Vancouver Island.

And so I was swimming, involuntarily, in 55-degree water about two miles from the nearest spit of land, and only a couple of feet from my overturned kayak. It took less than thirty seconds to flip the kayak into an upright position. I prayed that no one had seen me, but no, in the distance, I could see my companions paddling furiously in my direction. They were shouting various instructions designed to get me back in my kayak so that I

wouldn't embarrass them by drowning or by dying of hypothermia or by being battered to death in the interstices of wave
and rock.

Since the day had dawned clear and warm, and because I had
been paddling hard for an hour and half and was hot, the water
did not feel cold. Sure there was snow on the mountaintops two
and three thousand feet above, but the dazzling white peaks
against the first blue sky in days was lovely and inspirational. I
had read half a dozen books about sea kayaking and was aware
that there were several methods of "self-rescue" in such a situation. I have even practiced these techniques. A little.

The situation, as I saw it, was embarrassing but not at all serious. Grant, I knew, guides both novice and experienced kayakers
off Canada and Baja. No one on his trips ever capsizes.

Still, as my current predicament indicated, there's some small
element of risk in every kayaking expedition. It's part of the experience; part of the reason some people prefer kayaks to cruise
ships. Self-rescue appeals to the type of person who sees shuffleboard as a kind of death.

Self-rescue, unlike shuffleboard, can be effected with various
combinations of inflatable bags and paddles. With ropes. Alternately, if a victim feels strong, it is sometimes possible to just
muscle one's way back into the cockpit of the kayak. This is
rather like crawling along the top of a large floating log. It takes a
certain degree of balance.

Joel Rogers, who reached me first, steadied my kayak against
his own.

"I've just about got it," I said. The urge had come upon me to
perform a self-rescue. You don't want someone to give you a hand
up after you've just fallen over backward in a chair.

Grant Thompson arrived at about that time and suggested,
somewhat loudly, that it would be entirely appropriate for me to
accept help from Joel. I was, it seemed, being driven by the current toward a small stack of rocks about a quarter mile away.
Where the gentle-seeming swells met these sea stacks, great gouts
of spray exploded ten feet into the air. Getting caught just there

would be like having Andre the Giant pick you up and toss you into a brick wall every thirty seconds until you died. Time, Grant felt, was of the essence.

So I let Joel steady the kayak, then climbed back into the cockpit, and bailed the water out of my boat with a light plastic pump positioned between my knees.

"What happened?" Grant wanted to know.

"Tipped over," I said.

"We've been out for days," Grant shouted. "You know how to do this. How could you capsize in the middle of a crossing?"

In general, sea kayakers hug the coastline, and if anything happens, the beach is right there, a short swim away. Sometimes, however, it is necessary to navigate large bodies of water. A kayaker, for instance, might want to paddle from the mainland to an island three or four or ten miles away. Such open water "crossings" are dangerous and should not be taken lightly. The weather, for instance, can change—violently—in the space of only thirty minutes. Indeed, Joel Rogers was in the habit of invoking his own personal weather god before each crossing. "Don't kill us, Earl," he prayed. It is not clear precisely who Earl is.

"I tipped over because I was practicing my bracing strokes," I explained.

Grant stared back at me.

"Let me get this straight," he said. He looked like someone had just smacked him in the face with a dead fish. *"You were practicing your bracing strokes in the middle of a crossing?"*

It seemed the wrong time to tell Grant that his sleeping bag, which I was carrying, had come loose from my packing job and was currently sitting between my knees in a foot and a half of water. Tonight, the temperature would likely drop below freezing. There was time enough to tell him.

Up to this point, the trip had been without substantial incident. Our first campsite was a small island connected to the mainland by a sandbar, and the only clearing there was graced by an ominous purple pile of bear scat that looked as if it had been emptied out of an upturned gallon pail. The bear, it was clear, had been eating berries.

There are no grizzly bears on Vancouver Island, only the less aggressive black bears. As we unpacked the kayaks, a philosophical question that had surfaced during the planning stages of the trip reasserted itself. Grant had packed a 12-gauge shotgun in a rubber sheath. He and I and Linnea thought it best to have some defense against the bears. Joel thought that we were visitors in the bears' home; he believed that guns made you overconfident and that you didn't take ordinary care, which might result in an unpleasant interaction.

Philosophically, I agreed with Joel. And if we had problems with a marauding bear, I decided to let Joel reason with him before I fired.

While Grant prepared dinner, I trekked over the sandbar to the mainland, where a small creek flowed down to the sea. The sun was setting, but it was hidden behind thin gray clouds, and the light was a delicate pink. The tide was low, and there was only a foot or two of water at the mouth of the creek. Salmon leapt every few seconds—a flash of pinkish silver—and reentered the water with a splash that caught the setting sun and turned gray water the color of the fish itself.

About two hundred yards away, on the other side of the creek, a black bear loped along sandy banks toward the beach. The bear, a large long-legged male, ran back and forth up and down the creek, then careened off to the west. I moved up the creek, past several more purple piles of scat, and spotted two more bears—a sow and a cub—rolling around in the shallow water like children at play.

Grant had prepared a pasta dish with a freshly made marinara sauce. He used good kitchen knives, a cutting board, fresh onions, olive oil, a dozen cloves of garlic, and canned plum tomatoes, and he sipped a good zinfandel as two pots simmered on a pair of large burners.

Backpackers live poorly in the wilderness, surviving on freeze-dried turkey Tetrazzini, which tastes just like the chili mac, which in turn tastes like premasticated cardboard. A sea kayaker, by contrast, has the luxury of floating luggage. Wilderness and fine food are not mutually exclusive terms.

We settled back under the trees and listened for the wolves that still roam Vancouver Island. While Joel hung our food bags from a high limb to secure them from the bears, Grant told us about the time he tried to sell breakdown kayaks to the military. "During the Second World War," he said, "English commandos—they called them the cockleshell heroes—paddled kayaks into French ports, where they blew up a number of German ships." The military, it seemed, still saw some advantage in kayaks. Grant, acting as an agent for a manufacturer, took an ordinary breakdown kayak to a weapons show a few years ago. "The kayak had," he said, "a granola-type name . . ."

"Like Feathercraft," I suggested.

"Like that. A lightweight name. We needed to suggest that the kayak was both silent and deadly. We called it the Deadly Sea Snake."

Procurement officers suggested that the Deadly Sea Snake would benefit from an enlarged cockpit that might accommodate an automatic weapon. Late that night, in a bar, Grant spoke with a man who outlined possible military uses of an improved Sea Snake. Soldiers carrying breakdown boats in backpacks could make a HALO (high altitude, low opening) parachute jump into northern Russia. Once on the ground, they'd assemble their kayaks and paddle downriver to the nearest nuclear power facility, where they would plant remote-controlled bombs. The commandos would then paddle downriver to a pickup point. In the case of war, the bombs could be activated by satellite.

This ingenious plan struck Grant as a kind of high-level madness. The manufacturers of the kayak cited karma as a determining factor in their decision not to produce the Deadly Sea Snake.

We were in the Pacific Northwest, which is to say the dawn was usually gray and wet. We broke camp in the mist and packed everything into the kayaks. Our gear was stuffed into all manner of waterproof sacks. Long sacks, short sacks, round sacks: all of them fitting into the hatches in front of and behind the cockpit like some maddening three-dimensional jigsaw puzzle. It is said that it takes an hour to properly pack a kayak. However, if you carefully map out your loading plan, and then visualize that plan in sequence, it is possible to pack a kayak in fifty-eight or fifty-nine minutes.

Grant, who, like the rest of us, had never been to Esperanza Inlet, drew out the day's route on a nautical map. On foggy days, he strapped a marine compass to his deck in case we lost sight of land during a crossing.

And then we paddled out onto the calm gray sea, through thick fog, as a fine Pacific Northwest drizzle hung in the air. The shoreline was rocky, pitted with small coves and natural arches. The sea surged into narrow fissures, then poured out, rhythmically.

One day a small harbor seal swam alongside my kayak for a few minutes. It had a friendly doglike head and curious black eyes. Hundreds of gaudy red and purple starfish were splashed across the rocks that lay just below the surface of the sea.

We crossed over to Harbor Island in the gentle rain. The sea, in the depth of the channel, was black as ebony, spectral, under vaporous gray skies. It was like paddling over a smooth black mirror. A single loon yodeled out its mad laughter.

We lunched in an island cove and strolled along the beach to a clearing that featured a four-foot-high grassy mound about fifteen feet long. It was a midden pile, an enormous pile of clam and mussel shells left by local Indians two hundred (or two thousand) years ago.

The sun was attempting to bully its way through the clouds, and I strolled into the forest behind the midden pile, to be alone. Shafts of cathedral light fell through stands of spruce and hemlock. The forest was spooky and spiritual in about equal measure.

Archaeologists and anthropologists refer to the local aboriginal people as the Nootka. The Nootka themselves prefer to be called, more simply, the West Coast People.

The West Coast People paddled dugout wooden canoes. They

hunted whales and sea lions; they collected berries and greens; they netted salmon and herring. In the spring of certain years, they netted eulachon, a small fish that they boiled down for its oil. According to Della Kew and P. E. Goddard, authors of *Indian Art and Culture of the Northwest Coast,* "after boiling, the fish are pressed to force out the remaining oil. Formerly, the women accomplished this by squeezing the still hot fish against their naked breasts."

This, I thought strolling through the forest, is what I like about the sport of sea kayaking. It takes you to remote areas, inaccessible by any other means; it obliges you to learn something of the people who live there; and it generates aberrant sexual fantasies that might be realized in the privacy of one's own kitchen. With a good friend and some fish.

The eulachon oil was a favored condiment, like butter, and Indians from the interior trekked out to the West Coast along "grease trails" to trade with West Coast People.

There was some warfare, but not much. The island was so providential that the favored competition between various groups involved the conspicuous consumption of wealth at a feasting ceremony called the potlatch. Among the Kwakiutl, who lived just north of the West Coast People, an opposing chief might be given the seat of honor in front of the fire during the feast. The host, no doubt giggling maniacally, would then pour bowls of precious eulachon oil on the flames, causing them to flare up intensely. If the rival chief fled before the heat, he was considered to be humiliated by the wealth of the host. So he bravely sat there being grilled while a man wearing a "ridicule mask" danced about him, jeering. A ridicule mask is a representation of the human face carved out of wood. One side of the mask, however, is bare and featureless. It represents a man whose face has melted. Nyah-nyah-nah-nah-nah.

We passed Catala Island under clearing skies. There were caves in the rocky cliff walls where the West Coast People were said to bury their dead. A few hundred feet off shore, a pillar of rock about thirty feet high stood guard below the burial caves. The pillar looked statuary, vaguely human: There were ferns like a wild man's hair on its massive flat-topped head, and a sorcerer's cape of moss fell from its shoulders. We declined to explore the caves, out of respect and fear. A loon, floating at the base of the guardian pillar, shrieked out its strange melancholy laughter.

This area of Catala was an Indian reservation, inviolable, but all along the mainland, everywhere I looked, in every direction, there were clear-cut logging scars running up the slopes of the mountains. They were ugly as greed. In fifty miles of paddling along Esperanza Inlet, we were never once out of sight of a clear-cut.

I will not criticize the timber industry out of hand. I live in a wooden house, with maple floors; I work at a large wooden desk, and my product is printed on millions of sheets of paper.

Still, the responsible complaint against the logging industry is not that they're logging. It is which forests they're logging, when, and the pace at which they're doing it. Conservationists and timber industry spokesmen trot out studies by various experts to support their own point of view. A fair-minded person sometimes finds the controversy confusing.

Except along Esperanza Inlet, where ancient forests meet the sea in a kind of soaring nobility. Here, sea kayaking is a voyage of melancholy discovery; the paddler becomes, willy-nilly, an investigative reporter. He or she sees the bleak and barren hillsides, the sad mutilated lands. It is perfectly clear: The industry is going to cut down every goddamn tree that grows. It's all utterly obvious from the cockpit of a kayak: In British Columbia, along Esperanza Inlet, the forest industry is busy translating nobility into shame.

On the day that, *through very little fault of my own,* the kayak I happened to be paddling capsized in the middle of a crossing, we camped in the shadow of 2,495-foot-high Mount Rosa, one of the prettier peaks on Nootka Island. Heavy accumulations of fog hung in the ridges that rose to the summit: stripes of silver and green ascending to snow in a manner that summoned up the possibility of ethereal cogitation. It was a Zen master's wet dream.

The sky had cleared completely, and the four of us decided on a sunset paddle. To the southwest there was a reef of rocks, and beyond that, only the Pacific Ocean, stretching out vast and empty, all the way to Japan. We were paddling through calm waters, but only five hundred yards away the full force of the Pacific Ocean broke against the rocks of the barrier reef, and great plumes of spray exploded twenty feet into the air. The sun was low on the horizon and glittered through the spray, all watermelon and blood.

When we turned and headed back toward Mount Rosa, the sun lay across the water in a long golden trail. A full moon was rising behind the snowcapped mountain. I listened for wolves and heard only a freshening wind and the booming of surf.

We cooked in the wind shadow of a huge piece of gnarled driftwood, eight feet high and bone-white in the moonlight. We ate burritos and drank a cabernet, but in place of the ridicule-less potlatch I yearned for, the discussion concerned my handling of the Feathercraft during the morning's crossing. Grant thought it proper to discuss his soaked sleeping bag. I sought to deflect criticism by feigning temporary nerve deafness.

Later, I strolled along the empty gravel beach as a display of northern lights swept across the sky like luminous green smoke. This was, I realized, a campsite accessible only by kayak, and the deserted beach was a rhapsody of the sport. The stars seemed preternaturally bright. I felt in sympathy with the earth and sky, and sought to explain myself to the universe at large.

"I was just practicing my bracing strokes."

I listened again for wolves, heard only the wind, and strolled on, exploring a rhapsody by moonlight.

Malaria

I was eating breakfast on the terrace of a small restaurant in a pueblo near Sante Fe when the odor washed over our party like a fetid cloud. If stench had a color, this one would have been dark brown, thick as clay, and dense enough to cast a shadow. No one at the table sought to cast accusatory glances, because the odor was overwhelming and beyond the capacity of any one human being to produce. It seemed to have erupted out of the ground. It had, I realized, come rolling over our table from my left, where several men were gathered around an open manhole, working with a small crane mounted on a local utilities truck. The men were dragging something up out of the hole. A hint of yellow appeared above the lip of the manhole. Whatever the thing was, it was round and about the size of a volleyball . . . or, could it be? . . . a man's head.

"Oh God, no," someone said as the object came into full view. It was, in fact, a human body, still as death and dripping raw sewage. There was a profoundly shocked silence on the terrace.

The dead man was clad in a yellow rain suit. The workmen seemed unconcerned. Did they pull bodies out of sewers every day in New Mexico? What the hell kind of place was this?

And then, feebly it seemed, the body moved. An arm jutted out stiffly. The man was set down on his feet on the pavement. He passed a few words with the workmen, then lurched off toward the truck, still dripping sewage.

"I suppose," Larry Burke said, "they sent that poor guy down there to scout out some obstruction."

"Or clear it," I said.

We took our plates out of the rolling stench and into the restaurant proper. Larry Burke is the publisher of a national magazine, the man who causes many of my paychecks to be signed. We were meeting to discuss my work, which encompasses travel to remote destinations, contact with interesting people, and a reasonably liberal expense account monitored by folks who realize high-quality magazine articles often require repeated applications of alcohol. No complaints on my end: I actually like what I do for a living. To some extent, it must show. That week, I had been contacted by a daytime television talk show. Would I appear on a program the focus of which would be "people who love their jobs"? The idea made for some queasiness. What was I, another noteworthy societal anomaly, like lesbian nuns or men who wear diapers?

The thought carried a pinprick of irritation. No one wants to think he's completely aberrant; certainly not a daytime talk-show quality deviant. The truth is, there are times in my work when I'm at least as miserable as anyone else. There is, for instance, this snotty little work-related disease that keeps popping up.

I might even have mentioned the problem to Larry during that breakfast. But they dragged the guy up out of the manhole, and any complaints I had turned immediately to sewage. The man in the yellow slicker was the embodiment of a single undeniable fact: There are people in the world who have worse jobs than mine. Lots worse.

If various sewer-related topics hadn't dominated the rest of the breakfast conversation, I might have told Larry that I'm not really fit for the talk shows because I suffer from an ancient disease, a recurrent fever out of time. First described by Hippocrates in the fifth century B.C., it's now called malaria—from the Italian, meaning "bad air"—and, considered on a worldwide basis, it's probably the most common of all diseases.

Malaria is caused by certain parasitic protozoa—one-celled organisms—of the genus *Plasmodium* and is spread by female anopheles mosquitoes. (Males are blameless vegetarians, living entirely on plant juices.) The female feeds on blood. If her human victim is infected, she ingests malarial parasites along with her dollop of blood. The sexual forms of the plasmodium parasite, gametocytes, mate in the female's gut, and a fertilized sex cell forms, which encysts in the walls of the stomach. The cyst bursts after one to three weeks, spewing out what one of my reference books describes as "a large number of young sexual parasites," which sounds to me like some frightening fantasy out of the ashes of the disco inferno.

These parasites, called sporozoites, work their way into the female mosquito's salivary glands and are thus passed on to the next human she bites. The sporozoites settle in the victim's liver, where they mate and multiply, eventually spilling into the bloodstream in the form of merozoites, which enter the red blood cells and reproduce themselves asexually until the blood cells burst. The newly formed merozoites migrate to intact red blood cells, where they once again reproduce, multiply, destroy the cell, and move on. It's one big game of parasitic "Pac-Man," played for blood.

Eventually, some sexual forms of the parasite, the gametocytes, are produced. They do not mate in the human body. If the victim is bitten again, however, the gametocytes are ingested by the mosquito, a new sex cell forms in the insect's stomach, the young sexual parasites have a party, and so it goes. Bad air.

The air in the swamplands of Irian Jaya, in west New Guinea, was a miasma, muggy and thick. It was, in fact, like living inside an open wound. And there were lots of mosquitoes. The bad air was full of them. They were, I now know for a fact, anopheles mosquitoes.

My malarial sufferings are, the books tell me, fairly typical. Here's the way it started for me. Six weeks after I got home from the swamps of Irian Jaya, I started feeling stiff. My joints ached. Someone asked me why I was limping. I hadn't realized that I was. I was working on a deadline, writing, in fact, about the swamps of Irian Jaya and drinking entirely too much coffee. Was that why my urine was brown, like muddy water? Coffee, in my experience, tends to have the opposite effect.

I didn't realize for a few days that I was pissing away broken red blood cells. I felt woozy and tried to focus my attention on the problem at hand, which was my story about the swamps and the people who lived there. The tribe I had visited lived on platform houses set fifty feet up in the trees, well above the choking clouds of mosquitoes that owned the forest floor. Tribal men generally kept to the trees, but the women climbed down daily to collect food, firewood, and water. All of the women carried circular scars up and down their arms. Burning the arms with coals, I learned, was thought to be a cure for the "shivering sickness." Which seemed to be epidemic.

I sat for hours below one of the tree houses while two of our party parlayed with the men above. Waiting below during the lengthy negotiations was hateful. Six weeks later, with aching hands, I wrote about the experience: "Mosquitoes attacked those of us on the ground in thick clouds. They were very naughty and probably malarial."

In retrospect, I see now that only a very sick man could write a sentence like that last one. The next afternoon, I began shivering uncontrollably. It was 90 degrees outside, a brilliant Montana summer day, and my teeth were chattering. I'd seen people all over the tropical world in this initial stage of a malaria attack. I had it.

The chills last about an hour, and are followed by what is called the febrile stage, which starts with a feeling of intense heat, headache, and a very high temperature. Since my initial chills are fairly severe, I shake until I'm exhausted, and generally fall asleep just as the fever hits. The dreams are exceptionally vivid. Sometimes they are experienced in a vague waking state, and can be considered a form of delirium.

The febrile stage lasts around two hours and is followed by a period of intense sheet-soaking sweats, accompanied by some vestiges of headache and a feeling that the synovial fluid around every joint has been replaced by a mixture of sawdust and ground glass.

It's all over in about five hours.

A day or so later, you get to go through the whole thing again. Sometimes the interval between attacks may be longer: two, three, or four days. It all depends on the rate at which the asexual parasites are multiplying and bursting out of the red blood cells.

I was on a precise twenty-four-hour cycle. "Sorry," I'd tell my friends. "It's four o'clock. I have to go have malaria now. But, hey, let's eat at ten."

There are four varieties of *Plasmodium* that cause malaria. *P. vivax* is the most common; *P. falciparum* is the most severe and the most frequently fatal. From 1980 to 1988, 1,534 cases of *P. falciparum* among U.S. civilians were reported to the Centers for Disease Control. Eighty percent of the cases were acquired in tropical Africa, with the rest of the cases fairly evenly spread out among Asia, the Caribbean, South America, and other parts of the world. Of the thirty-seven fatalities, twenty-seven cases were acquired in Africa. A falciparum infection can, with vicious suddenness, cause liver, kidney, or respiratory failure. It may block the small blood vessels in the brain and cause coma.

Photographer Chris Rainier once told me a haunting and terrifying story about just how quickly *P. falciparum* can kill.

Several years ago, Chris was traveling in the Sudan, in company with a group of doctors from the World Health Organization who were inoculating people in remote villages. One day, at ten-thirty in the morning, a volunteer nurse began shivering in the heat. She lost consciousness two hours later. By four-thirty that afternoon she was dead.

A week or so later, Chris came down with the classic symptoms: aching bones, brown urine, chills, chattering teeth, uncontrollable shivering. The doctors told him they'd do everything they possibly could to save his life. They also suggested that he might want to write a last letter home. He had, they thought, perhaps an hour of consciousness left.

I asked Chris, who had had a very bad go of it for a few weeks, if he had actually written the letter in his allotted hour. He said he had. He couldn't remember it exactly—he wasn't feeling so hot and was a bit distracted at the time—but it read something like "Dear Mom and Dad, I was doing what I wanted to do. I love you both. Please take care of my dog."

This compares, not unfavorably, I think, with John Keats's last letter, written to Charles Armitage Brown, on November 30, 1820: "I can scarcely bid you good-bye, even in a letter. I always made an awkward bow." Keats was dying of tuberculosis and had a lot more time than Chris Rainier. He was also one of the greatest poets in the English language, and didn't, apparently, have a dog.

When my shivering started on that bright summer afternoon, I didn't know what variety of malaria I'd contracted and thought about writing the final letter.

What does a person say? How do you explain your life in a couple of pages? If that's all you have.

For a while, I occupied myself with the question of who should get copies of the letter. The list should be fairly inclusive, like, say, wedding invitations. You don't want to leave anyone out. Parents, lover, best friends—sure. Ex-wives, yeah. Business associates— okay. I had worked back through my life to a beloved high school swimming coach when the febrile stage hit and I fell completely and irredeemably asleep.

The fever dream was a bad one, full of anxiety. I was, for reasons that seemed perfectly obvious at the time, forced to occupy someone else's body. Who was this guy? He seemed to be crouched in a tower, looking down at the lawns and walkways of a busy college campus. He was holding a rifle. People were run-

ning in panic, and faint screams drifted up to the tower. Had this
yo-yo shot anyone yet? I could see a few broken windows in a
building across the way, but there were no bodies down. A SWAT
team was making its way across the lawn, toward the tower.

My problem, as I saw it, was to explain to the police that I was
not really this wacko with the rifle. I was a nice normal guy who
happened, through no fault of his own, to be temporarily inhabiting the body of a deranged sniper. "Sure," I imagined the SWAT
team leader saying just before they opened up the shotguns,
"that's what all you deranged snipers say."

The dream insisted that I come up with some more satisfactory
explanation for my presence in that particular body. What? My
mind skidded off in several different directions at once. I could
hear heavy footsteps pounding up the stairs. There seemed to be
no way in which I could adequately account for the person I truly
was.

The dream, I think, mirrored my anxiety about the last letter. If
I could just explain myself properly, maybe I wouldn't have to
die.

Since then, I've often wondered if, in some larger sense, that's
what we all think. We produce art or music or literature or philosophy or children; we make laws or medicine or history; we become saints or outlaws in our lifelong scramble to create some
living context. This, we need to say, is who I truly am. It's our one
shot at immortality.

The blood tests came back positive. "It's malaria," my doctor
said.

"What kind?"

"Vivax."

Common malaria. Not something fairly exotic, like *P. ovale* or
P. malariae. Not the deadly *P. falciparum*, either. People I know
who've survived a falciparum infection have suffered badly. During lucid periods, several thought they were going to die. By contrast, my vivax is pretty mild: a walk in the park.

But unlike my falciparum-suffering friends—who tend to go
through a single frightening incident—the vivax I have recurs at
more or less regular intervals. The parasite, like many microor-

ganisms, clings stubbornly to life. Vivax malaria is the prevalent form of the disease precisely because it withstands therapy and can become chronic.

My doctor, who doesn't have much occasion to treat malaria in Montana, consulted with a tropical-medicine expert, and together they worked out a treatment program. There was no way to know for sure if the various pills would, in fact, kill all those morozoites and sporozoites and gametocytes smooching around in my blood. And they didn't.

About six months after my first episode, I was giving a series of readings at the University of Montana, about 250 miles from my home. The malaria started shaking me at about four o'clock the first afternoon. There followed the required five hours of misery, but the next day, precisely at four, I gave my reading and felt just fine. Hey, no recurrence! A day later I was driving home, over icy roads and through a minor blizzard, when my hands began shaking on the steering wheel. It seemed I was on a forty-eight-hour cycle this time. My friend Linnea drove, and I sat twitching in the passenger seat. My pills were at home, and they would knock out the infection within twenty-four hours. Why did I leave the pills at home? Apparently, I was moaning with each exhalation of breath.

"Music bother you?" Linnea asked.

"No."

"Because, I'm sorry, the moaning's driving me nuts."

And so we listened to music at top volume, and I never did pass out during the febrile stage, but was able, in a half-waking state, to harness the fever dreams, which I played across the windshield as the wipers swept the snow away. I was in a deep green forest. Sunlight fell in shafts through alien flowers that grew everywhere on strange, unworldly trees. I may not have been precisely human, in this dream. I could fly, for one thing, and I seemed to be some sort of combination of butterfly and bird. It was strange to see this peculiar world in three dimensions and I wondered about that until I realized that I was soaring through a jungle as painted by Henri Rousseau, the jungle of *The Sleeping Gypsy*.

It was an hour and a half of exhilarating delirium.

• • •

A friend of mine, photographer Nick Nichols, once suffered a relapse of malaria in New York. He was staying at an upscale hotel, editing pictures he'd taken in Africa for a national magazine, when his teeth started chattering. By the time the house doctor arrived, Nick had sweat through the sheets on his bed. He had wrung them out and hung them over the shower curtain. So there he was, lying on a bare mattress, sweating profusely, and looking like a junkie in need of a fix.

"What seems to be the trouble?" the doctor asked.

"I have malaria," Nick said.

The doctor began asking him a series of irritating questions. Were Nick's stools black and tarry? Were people following him? Did he hear voices when there was no one there?

"I'm not crazy, you asshole," Nick screamed, "I have *malaria*."

Health professionals in America often have little experience treating the disease, which is always in a dynamic state of change. Generally, when traveling to malarial areas, it's wise to begin taking preventive drugs about two weeks before departure and to continue the regimen for six more weeks upon return. I can testify to the fact that this is not always 100 percent effective. Plasmodia are persistent, and quickly become immune to last year's preventive or therapeutic drug of choice.

One useful source of up-to-date information is the Centers for Disease Control in Atlanta, which maintains a malaria hotline with information about malarial areas and current treatments.

I've been told that anopheles mosquitoes sit at a slant on a flat surface. This may be so, but I've never been able to arrange the necessary flat surface in conjunction with a stationary mosquito. Identifying mosquitoes in this way is like trying to sprinkle salt on the tail of bird. I do know that anopheles mosquitoes are never found at altitude. One source tells me they do not occur at altitudes above three thousand feet. Bunk. I've seen people suffering what was clearly malaria at five thousand feet, while their neighbors who lived at six thousand feet seemed perfectly healthy.

That bit of anopheles esoterica was of use to me when I was searching for the ruins of a pre-Inca society in the eastern foothills of the Peruvian Andes. No use looking in the fertile river valleys: The stone huts and the great forts of the Chachapoyas people were perched on cloud-shrouded peaks, at ten thousand feet. There were stone catchments for rain, the people's only source of water. The Chachapoyas laboriously terraced the steep mountain slopes in order to grow crops. They lived this hard high-altitude life because the river bottoms were rife with malaria.

The disease might have arrived in the Americas with Columbus. A few hundred years later, Indians in the Amazon were successfully treating malaria with the bark of the cinchona tree. This is an interesting and persuasive argument for biological diversity: As we decimate forests worldwide, do we also lose the potential cure for various diseases, both those that are killing people today and those, perhaps presently unknown, that will kill in the future?

As for me, well, I still search for ancient ruins up high. I take my prescribed pills at the proper time. On my own, I've begun eating huge bloody steaks, because I think they replenish my red blood cells. I also drink the distilled essence of cinchona bark, which can be found in tonic or quinine water. Massive doses of quinine, however, may cause cinchonism, a series of symptoms including blindness and deafness. It is safer and healthier to flavor a few ounces of quinine with a shot or so of gin. The wise malaria sufferer wakes up in the morning, lying on the couch, with the overhead light blazing away. He has a headache, the events of the previous evening may not be in satisfactory focus, but he can see. He can hear. "Thank God," he says to himself, "that I thought to mix my quinine with gin."

It's not a bad life, really. I'm the only person I know who's on the steak-and-gin-and-tonic diet for his health.

The day after that strange breakfast on the terrace near Sante Fe, malaria knocked me down again. I had the pills with me, and since I was going to have to go through this episode anyway, I found that I was actually looking forward to the fever dreams. So there I was in a cheap motel, shivering in front of the television while some twitching dysfunctional tried to explain his deplorable existence to America through Oprah. "This is who I am," he meant to say, his one and only shot at immortality.

It could have been me, I suppose, telling America why I loved my job. That particular day, I would have been acceptably pathetic and just right for daytime TV: a thoroughly broken looking man, shifting in pain on his chair, shaking badly, soaked through with sweat, and babbling incomprehensibly about nifty perks—high-altitude ruins and gin and tonic and great slabs of bloody red meat.

"You got malaria on the job," the host might ask, "and you still love your work?" And in my waking fever dream, projected transparently across a sea of concerned faces, I would see a body dragged out of a stinking sewer somewhere in New Mexico, and I expect I'd say, "There are worse jobs than mine. Lots worse."

On the River of Cold Fires

The writer considered the weather and felt somehow obliged to issue a challenge to God. He was, apparently, a man who had never read the book of Job. There were several of us standing waist-deep in the icy river, cursing our leaky rubber waders, and unloading lunch gear from one of the three rafts. It was one in the afternoon, the warmest part of a cold day, and the rain, which had started earlier that morning, was falling in sheets from a glacial gray sky. It seemed biblical in proportion, this rain, ridiculously cold, and it drummed down on our heads without surcease, making us both snappy and stupid. The temperature fluttered just above the freezing mark and the downpour was so constant, so unrelenting, that my fingers weren't working well in the cold. I could see them there, fumbling redly at the end of my arms.

Funny fingers, I thought, stupidly. Aren't much good.

And then, at that point, the writer said this thing and everyone backed away from him.

I'm not being coy here. I didn't say it. There was another writer along for the trip. Aside from us—two writers—there were a couple of restaurateurs, a musician, a couple of professional fishing guides, and a real estate salesman.

All of us were slowly freezing to death, and no one was mentioning this fact. There were two women on the trip, and none of the men was going to say anything at all about the possibility of our impending icy demise until at least one of the women complained. The women, for their part, had equal and opposite concerns regarding the men. Thanks to the issue of sex, there would be no complaining on this trip.

The writer—this other writer, understand—looked up into the low gray clouds for a moment. A small stream of ice water formed and poured off his nose.

"You know," he said brightly and full of false good cheer, "God's a wimp if this is the worst He can throw at us."

And all of us sort of backed away from the blasphemer. People who had never been to church in their lives made for the bank. It was April in Montana: There are lots of things that can happen to you in this, the cruelest month, and it doesn't do to tempt fate. I had a sudden vision of Ice Age corpses frozen throughout time in the shimmering belly of some renegade glacier. Shriveled limbs. Open mouths; silent screams. An eternity of ice.

Give you an idea of how miserable it was:

We built a fire at lunch. It took a very long time to catch, longer to flame up in any satisfactory way. It took longer than the hour we had for lunch. I know that because no one got warm at lunch. The Crow Indians say that an Indian builds a small fire and stands close; a white man will build a large fire and stand far away. We were, for the most part, white men and we had built a large fire. But the ground was wet, the wood was wet, and rain kept falling from the sky. We stood very close to the large fire, breathing smoke and waiting for some warmth to develop. "This," one restaurant owner said, "is a cold fire."

"Sounds like a book title," one of the writers said. *"On the River of Cold Fires."*

"I mean it," the first man said. "You could freeze to death in front of this fire."

That's how cold it was.

The river was peculiar. Once you began, you were committed to a three-day run at the very least. It was all canyon walls and wilderness until the first feasible take-out point, sixty miles downstream. When someone in your party challenges God to make you as miserable as possible and there are a couple of days left on the trip and your fingers don't work very well, it takes an act of will to enjoy corrugated canyon walls soaring five hundred, eight hundred, a thousand feet overhead.

There was no one else on the river, because anyone who knows it well enough to float knows that late April can be unpleasant. So there were no other human beings in sight. Not for three days. It could have been Alaska. It could have been America before the white man.

The river, in fact, had been named by Lewis and Clark in 1804. They named it for the secretary of the navy in that year. It wasn't a big, important presidential river, a Jefferson or a Madison. Just a small secretary of the navy–size river, a little bit of a secret, actually, and if I were to mention its name, my companions would discuss the matter with me using baseball bats and two-by-fours. No matter that the fishing was grotesque and the weather hideous: These folks, Montanans all, believe in the Conservation of Misery.

So, for the purposes of obfuscation, I'll call it the River of Cold Fires.

We had been invited on the trip by a river guide named Jim Kent, who works out of Livingston, Montana. His first clients would hit the water toward the end of May and probably avoid any blizzards. Before that, Kent had to check his gear. Were the rafts leaking?; were the tents in good repair?; were the grill and griddle working well? It was chancy setting out on the third week of April. But, what the hell, we'd be lucky. The weather, which had been inching up into 80-degree temperatures the week before, would surely hold.

• • •

There was a black Lab along on the rafting trip, the kind of dog that joyously plunges into freezing river water to retrieve fallen ducks on a late fall day. The black Lab had the same name as the river, and he lay atop one of the softer mounds of gear strapped into the raft and cried piteously as the cold rain fell. That should suggest the measure of our discomfort. It's cold when you have to find a blanket for a black Lab.

We had about six more hours to float after the day's cold lunch, and a strong upriver wind drove pellet-hard drops of near frozen rain into our faces. The rain seeped into our clothes.

It was the worst, the coldest, and most miserable kind of weather. The temperature hovered near freezing, so the rain wanted to be snow. Soon enough, it started to fall: snowflakes the size of quarters that splashed against the exposed skin of my face.

The fish, after twenty-four hours of cold rain, were hunkering at the bottom of the river, not feeding much, not rising to the occasional hatch of mayflies. To catch trout on a fly rod in these conditions you have to throw weighted nymphs at them. These are big fat heavy flies, difficult to cast, and they go bouncing along the rocks at the bottom of the stream, where they supposedly look like the larvae stage of various insects. These insect entrées form 90 percent of a trout's diet.

Nymphing is a frustrating method of fishing, especially from a moving boat, because the fly is floated deep and the only way to tell a strike is by a sudden movement of the line on the surface. And since the fly sometimes snags on rocks, you often strike at nonexistent fish.

Every twentieth cast or so, your fly catches something on the bottom and stays there. You try to shake it loose a couple of times, but nothing happens, so you point the tip of your rod along the bad destiny of your line and just let the $2.95 fly snap off. A gift to the river. Then, in the icy rain, you get to tie another big fat woolly worm to your tippet. With numb, shaking fingers.

Because the water was dark with rain, I was using flies with white rubber legs and bits of silvery tin foil on their underside. Such flies do not imitate any known insect. Their advantage, in high, dark water, is that the fish can *see* them.

People who fly-fish—I've said this before, but it bears repeating—are rather like people who have some strange sexual fetish. "If I can't do it with whips and chains, I'd rather not do it at all." The fly fisherman says, "If I can't catch them on a fly, I'd rather not catch them at all."

Such purists regard bait fishermen as Neanderthals, spin fishermen as jerks. Some even frown on the use of un–bug-like flies such as I was using. I mean it: They actually frown at you.

It was snowing heroically. Great swirls of spring snow were spinning up the river and the flakes had given way, in the depths of the canyon, to hard stinging bits of spring snow, indistinguishable from hail.

I had caught one fish in two days, and it seemed fruitless to flog the water with my outlandish flies and offend the purists at the same time. I sat in the bow of the raft, curled against the cold. The grassy sections of the riverbanks were bright green. The snow had begun to stick in patches, so the world was the gray of the sky, the brown of the river, and Christmas on the bank.

A herd of mule deer stood on the bank and regarded us with some sarcasm. They stared at the rafts and turned inward for a herd conference: "These are the guys who challenged God to give them bad weather in April in Montana," they informed one another. Or so it seemed. A large buck gave the signal: "Let's get out of here," and they turned, springing up toward a break in the canyon wall—twenty-seven of them fleeing from bad luck until all that was visible of them was their white back ends pogoing up the gray of a rocky draw.

There was, I noticed, a snowdrift forming on my lap.

God works in mysterious ways. My reading suggests that She hasn't taken personal challenges in regard to weather quite seriously since the days of the Old Testament.

Montana's weather is changeable enough on the natch. Prudent drivers carry survival gear in the trunks of their cars eight months out of the year. A couple of sleeping bags and a bit of food can be lifesavers in a sudden blizzard. On January 20, 1954, in a mining camp near the Continental Divide at Rogers Pass, the temperature dropped to 70 below zero, a record low for the lower forty-eight states.

If Montana has the record for bitter cold, it also holds all the records for changeability. On January 23, 1916, an arctic outbreak in Browning dropped the temperature from 44 degrees above zero to 54 below in twenty-four hours. Another American record concerns a warming trend: on January 11, 1980, in Great Falls, Montana, the temperature rose from 32 below zero to 15 above in less than seven minutes.

More to the point, Montana also enjoys the meteorological oddity of severe late-spring blizzards. In the area east of Great Falls—our general location—a storm bringing 40-mile-an-hour winds dropped forty-five inches of snow on May 17, 1903. The week before, lilacs had been in bloom and people had been planting their gardens.

Sixty-six years later, on April 24, 1969, after a week of temperatures in the mid- to high eighties, 100-mile-an-hour winds driving freezing snow killed an estimated one hundred thousand head of livestock. Drifts twenty-five feet high covered spring-green grass. Certain towns were blacked out for over a month.

Indeed, according to meteorologists, unusually warm spring temperatures are a harbinger of the dreaded spring blizzard. Warm air can hold great amounts of moisture, and if a Pacific cold front is approaching—one of those big systems that extends in a long finger from the Gulf of Alaska to California—something nasty is going to happen. As the cold front moves eastward, it pulls warm moisture-laden air up into Montana from the Gulf of Mexico. When the cold front finally spills over the Rockies, it encounters that ridge of warm, wet air coming up from the south. The cold air swirls, counterclockwise, creating an intense area of surface low pressure.

All of which means that in late spring, in Montana, it is possible to get a bad sunburn on April 24 and be wading thigh-deep through a severe blizzard on April 25.

The hard wind-driven pellets of snow had given way again to fat swirling flakes that splashed against the skin like a mother-in-law's kisses. No one was fishing anymore, and those of us who weren't rowing sat still and morose, freezing in stolid stoicism. The drift on my lap was a foot deep. I wore wool socks over my gloves and a triple layer of jackets. I was shivering involuntarily, but almost numb to the cold. It didn't seem to matter much anymore.

One of the other rafts drifted by. I called to the writer, who was rowing. "A wimp, huh?"

He smiled his bright smile, full of false good cheer, and nodded upriver. We were coming into a deep part of the canyon. The storm had brought scads of wildlife down to the River of Cold Fires: There were deer and raccoon on the banks; there were beaver and coyotes. Someone thought he saw a few mountain goats on the lower ridges of the canyon wall. It was hard to tell if the patches of white were goats or small snowdrifts. There were fir and pine trees clinging impossibly to tiny niches in the canyon walls. They were all covered with a dusting of snow. Downriver, in the wind tunnel of the canyon, snow was falling in twisted ribbons, dancing toward us in a swirling glacial polka.

It was beautiful, in a savage and entirely unsettling manner. Few people, I knew, were dumb enough to risk the River of Cold Fires in the season of spring blizzards. So the sight belonged to me. It was beautiful and it was mine: the River of Cold Fires in the season of snow. I thought, This is one of those intangible things I'll own forever because I've paid for it, paid for it in equally intangible dues. The idea was wondrous cold comfort. There was a physical sensation that belonged to the idea: some strange combination of cold and inspiration. A rivulet of ice water found its way down my spine and I felt the entire surface of my flesh blossom out into goose bumps.

In Chief Yali's Shoes

"Wabintok Mabel," Chief Yali Mabel whispered, by way of reverent introduction.

He held a lit candle under Wabintok's black and desiccated face. Flickering yellow light illuminated the mouth, which was open wide in a soundless, twisted scream. It was, I understood, a privilege to view Wabintok here, in the sanctity of the men's hut.

"*Wah*," I said. The Dani expression is, in my opinion, the finest word for "thank you" in the human vocabulary.

"*Wah*," Chief Yali replied politely.

"*Wah*," a number of the other men said.

The small circular wooden hut smelled of straw, of countless fires, of singed pig fat. Wabintok himself smelled of smoke, and, yes, singed fat. He was, by some village estimates, four hundred years old. I'd never slept in the same hut with a smoked mummy before.

Chief Yali spoke with some awe about Wabintok, who was his

ancestor and a great hero of the Mabel family. *"Bintok,"* Yali explained, is the Dani word for bamboo knife. Wabintok means "Thank you, Bamboo Knife." Chief Yali's ancestor had been a great warrior, a master of the bamboo knife, in the time of ritual war, before the first outsiders came to the valley of the Dani four generations ago.

The valley, the Grand Baliem Valley, is located in the highlands of New Guinea, specifically in the Indonesian western half of the island, called Irian Jaya. The valley is a mile high, almost fifty miles long, and is home to an estimated one hundred thousand Dani people, short sturdy Papuans who, according to one guidebook "are just now emerging from the Stone Age."

I suppose that's so. Dani women wear grass skirts. The men often wear nasal ornaments made of bone. They sometimes wear feathered headdresses and paint their bodies with special-colored clay. The Dani men are phallocrypts, which means that aside from feathers and bones, they wear penis sheaths. And nothing else.

In the men's hut, where Chief Yali invited me to spend the night, the Mabel family men all said that the time of ritual war was past. It was forbidden by the government, illegal. And yet, Yali, a handsome, powerful man who looked to be in his late thirties, sported at least five small circular scars.

If there was no war, I asked in a roundabout manner, who had fired all those arrows into Yali's chest and back? Well, it seemed that while there was no war, there were battles now and again.

And so I spent the night around a smoky fire, gnawing the charred remnants of what had been a piglet a few hours before. We laughed and sang and pounded on logs and talked of glorious battles. We pledged a kind of brotherhood and spoke of the spirit each man feels in his belly and in his heart.

It seemed to me that Yali could make a hell of a living in America leading "wild man" weekends. He made me promise that I'd come back and visit him, with at least one of my wives.

Just last month, I mailed Yali a present he had desperately wanted and I had solemnly promised to send him. Certain culturally aware friends thought the gift insensitive. Such goods would "spoil" the naked Dani. Well, a promise is a promise, a brother is a brother, and screw the culturally aware. I like to think of the chief in his feathered headdress, his body paint, and his penis gourd: Yali Mabel, standing proud, wearing his new leather Redwing boots. I know what Yali said when he got the package.

He said, *"Wah!"*

Bonaire

I could see them, sitting at the bar, disappointed.

This is it? they were thinking. This is the nightlife? Crab races?

John and Chuck were winners. They had matched up such elements as "a bathtub in Paris" with the name Jim Morrison. They had identified Billy Idol videos and elucidated storylines on the basis of a single ten-second scene. They had won an MTV contest, these two New York guys in their mid-twenties, and now here they were, on Bonaire, a bucolic Caribbean island in the Netherlands Antilles lying fifty miles north of the Venezuelan coast.

There was a bar, open to the trade winds, and you could watch the sun set somewhere in the neighborhood of Lake Maracaibo, except a layer of whitish clouds hung on the western horizon every day. The sunset was muted, sickly yellow, except for the occasional purple thunderhead, so that the western sky looked like a bad bruise, slowly healing.

And now, under this wounded sky, John and Chuck picked

numbers from a hat carried by a waitress. Someone turned over a plastic bucket on the cement floor, and several crabs scuttled to illusory freedom. The one labeled "15" crossed the finish line first.

My crab, number 18, was second and earned me a free drink. Chuck and John wandered over to offer their congratulations. They were, they said, miserable. The island was like a prison. There was a dismal dearth of available fabulous babes. And the nightlife consisted of crab racing. Crab racing!

Bonaire, it seemed, was not an MTV kinda island.

Nearby Aruba was alive with glitz, with duty-free shopping, with an ambience not unlike Cancun or Waikiki. Bonaire, by contrast, was sleepy, almost drab, and comparatively undeveloped.

"Why," John wondered, "does anyone come here?" He sipped at his Amstel beer and stared at me with genuine astonishment.

"My favorite island on earth," I said.

"Why?" A chorus from John and Chuck.

"Scuba diving," I said. Chuck cocked his head in an anticipatory manner, waiting for the punch line. But there was no knee slapper involved. Just a long, convoluted story about travel and water and astonishment. It's a love story.

I was whining, as ten-year-olds will, about the fact that life was passing me by. Waukesha, Wisconsin, was too small for me. I yearned to travel, to drink in the heady aura of such exotic towns as, oh, Janesville, Beloit, Kenosha. My father, pragmatic man, suggested that I try out for the YMCA swimming team, which traveled the state.

It was, I think now, a lust for travel that fueled my preteen desire to turn myself into an outboard motor. A yellowed newspaper clipping from the time reads: "Young Tim Cahill recently set a new record in the 20-yard freestyle at a YMCA meet in Green Bay." I competed in high school and was successful enough to earn an athletic grant in aid from the University of Wisconsin. The UW swim team flew to South Bend, Indiana; to Ann Arbor, Michigan; to Columbus, Ohio. I had never been on an airplane before.

After graduation, I took a series of part-time jobs of the sort commonly attributed to authors of first novels. I was a longshoreman, warehouseman, landscaper—all that. Some of my journalism was getting published, and when the editors of a scuba-diving magazine asked me to write for them, I signed on gladly. Water was a remedy: Swimming was succor and abundance. It had afforded me some notoriety in my athletic career and paid my way through college. Now it would send me around the world. The South Pacific, Australia, the Caribbean . . .

And maybe because I was reasonably good at writing about the life of the sea—the poor man's Jacques Cousteau—other magazines began sending me to remote and exotic locales, many of which were a thousand miles from the nearest ocean.

I've been making my living in this way for twenty years. Sometimes, I think, I've gotten a little jaded.

In my third year of scuba travel, I dove Bonaire. Experts consider the island one of the three best scuba destinations in the world. This, of course, is a subjective judgment, so the other two "best" dive sights might include Truk, Palau, Australia's Great Barrier Reef, the barrier reef off Belize, the Red Sea, Fiji, the Coral Sea, or New Guinea. To my taste, Bonaire was, and remains, the pinnacle of safe hassle-free diving. Rental equipment is in good repair, dive boats leave on schedule, and dive masters are knowledgeable. Which wouldn't make a whole hell of a lot of difference if the underwater gardens weren't so spectacularly baroque.

The island, only 12 degrees north of the equator, is situated directly in the warm water reef building zone. Substantially south of the trajectory of most hurricanes, the reefs are seldom savaged by the kind of storm that has devastated more northerly islands. Bonaire, in fact, thrives (modestly) on scuba tourism. Farsighted local dive operators—Don Stewart and Peter Hughes, among others—have seen to it that the surrounding coral gardens have been protected for thirty years now.

Corals, of course, are living communities of tiny polyplike animals that have surrounded themselves with a limestone shell. Each community devises its own structure, so some corals branch out like elkhorns, some form sheets against the rock, and others look like rounded balls with curious lobelike indentations and are called brain coral. Off the beach near a place called Karpata, deep ravines run down to 120 feet; there, green "sheeting" coral covers subaqueous rocky spires, so they look like armored pagodas. Woven into the deep green of this sheeting coral are strands of iridescent purple.

A different form of coral, the soft corals—sea fans and whips and rods and fingers—sway gently. The fans, some of them ten feet high, ten feet across—are perfect examples of psychedelic macramé.

Nearly transparent trumpet fish hang head down in a forest of golden sea whips, waiting for an inattentive meal. The big clown-ish-colored parrot fish, with their horny mouths, tear away at the rocky coral—the polyp's limestone shell—to eat the algae forming there. These fish—several varieties of red and green and blue par-rot fish, some of them two and a half feet long—don't much mind divers watching them feed, though if you get above one and cast a shadow, it disappears in a series of sharp angles. Startled, the fish usually engages its waste disposal system. The finely ground lime-stone emanating from the back end of countless parrot fish has formed the flourlike white sand beaches of Bonaire.

There are shimmering clouds of foot-long black-and-blue-and-green triggerfish. Smaller tangs—gold or blue or some combina-tion of those colors—go about their business, in company with black or blue-green angel fish; with longsnout butterfly fish; with jackknifes, and sad-eyed red squirrel fish and rock hind. On a late afternoon dive, when the sky is cloudy, a single pillar of celestial light sometimes enters the water at a slanting angle, and there, amidst the coralline pagodas, with shifting schools of scenic fish on all sides, the diver feels at one with the flash and shimmer of life itself.

Liquid heaven, one diver of my acquaintance calls it.

The dive boat leaves at nine in the morning. Get up, pull on a swimming suit and maybe a T-shirt. Walk down to the pier, pick up your gear bag, which is numbered and hung on a wall leading out to the water. There are eighteen divers, suiting up en route. It is never very far to a good dive site on Bonaire.

Putting on the gear—weights to hold a body down in the buoyancy of seawater, an inflatable vest to compensate for the weights, the tank, the mask, the fins—is the most difficult physical work involved in the dive.

I am still barely awake when the boat stops at the north end of the island, where giant cactus march up sun-blasted slopes that look a little like the deserts of Baja California on steroids. The cacti are so plentiful that local farmers build highly effective fences with the thorny monsters.

Roll into the blood-warm sea. The gear renders me neutrally buoyant underwater. Inhale, and I rise a few feet; exhale, and I descend a like amount. Kick once and I am flying over rolling, multicolored reefs. My style—this compulsion to cover a lot of territory, fast—is called reef running.

I like to overload the sensory neurons with color and movement and life. Coral gardens have always snapped the thread of linear thought for me. The sensation is a timeless blast of déjà vu. I am weightless; I am flying now, yes, exactly as I fly in my dreams.

I stop to examine a truly alien being. The peacock flounder is a flat gold-and-purple-spotted fish, quite round and about the size of a 33 rpm record. The creature was born a symmetrical fish, but a few days after its birth, one eye migrated to the other. The fish swims a few inches above a sandy bottom, looking up at me, mildly, with two closely spaced extraterrestrial eyes.

And not far away is a favorite site. In a forest of swaying golden sea whips, is an alcove in the reef wall containing a flat green barrel sponge that looks like an easy chair for an underwater hobbit. A twisting purple tube sponge with several branches grows next to the chair, like a shade tree. In back of the chair there is a small white sea fan set against red and green sheet coral, like a picture on the wall. All around me, on all sides, clouds of scenic fish—purple-black damsels and golden butterflies—shift and sway, catching the afternoon light in a prismatic rhapsody.

• • •

That evening, sitting at the bar with the MTV winners, I began talking about a record I had as a kid. It was called "Bozo Under the Sea." Bozo met all kinds of fish who could talk, and occasionally we boys and girls had to turn a page in the book "or poor old Bozo is going to drown."

I did the high-pitched shivery voices of the jellyfish for John and Chuck, who chuckled politely in their miserable way. The setting sun bruised the sky, and it occurred to me that diving these reefs was like shaking hands and saying "howdy" to the ten-year-old I had once been. He's an enthusiastic little guy, constantly astounded by the world. The kid, I know, considers me a bit of a Bozo on land as well as under the sea. I don't get to talk to him much anymore.

"How much longer you going to stay?" John asked.

"A while," I said.

"Why?"

I didn't tell him that I liked diving with an imaginary ten-year-old. I didn't tell him that after twenty years, I still needed to be astonished.

Geysers

A little after five in the morning, I was wakened by the call of sandhill cranes echoing across the lake. They seemed very far away and sounded like Arabian women at war.

I was camped near the shore of Shoshone Lake, in waist-high grasses turning gold in the early autumn chill. On the hillside above, the grasses gave way to spruce, white bark pine, and lodgepole pine.

A quarter of a mile through the conifers above, the land opens up into an entirely alien world. The lushness of the forest and the marshes is gone. Stretching out for over half a mile is a gravelly white desert of hillocks and bluffs. Everywhere steam rises in silvery plumes that sway with the wind as it swirls out of the creek below and caresses the strange primordial desert above.

Mingling with the whisper and howl of the wind, there is the strange sound of splashing, of amplified gurgling deep within the earth: the profound grumblings of geysers massing to erupt. The cones, some of them four feet high, are white and twisted into primeval shapes. Boiling water erupts from these cones and engages the wind in a steamy fandango.

Yellowstone National Park contains within its boundaries fully 60 percent of all the geysers in the world. It is the largest geyser field on earth, the most active, and unlike in the thermal fields of Iceland or New Zealand, the geyser basins here have not been drained dry for use as geothermal energy.

Early white explorers sent back accounts of the boiling water and steam erupting from the earth. One East Coast publication, in 1870, rejected what now seems like a solid descriptive manuscript with the words "Sorry, we do not print fiction." And it was in 1870 that men who wondered at the supposedly fictional geysers first expressed the thought that the entire area should be set aside as a national park.

One of the largest of the dozen geyser basins in the park is located in the backcountry. It is a fairly easy eight-mile walk from the trailhead. At Shoshone Geyser Basin, there are no signs, there are no boardwalks, and almost no one goes there. Which is fine, if you believe, as I do, that awe is a fairly solitary experience.

When a geyser plays, that is erupts, it will often engage in what is called preplay. The cone will fill with water, the water will bubble and boil. More steam will escape. Some of this steam smells of hydrogen sulfide, like rotten eggs, but most of it has a curiously clean odor.

And then the geyser plays, sending scalding water boiling into the sky. The same geyser, once it is played out, may drain, the pool inside the crater sinking back into the earth with a sound that makes some people twitter in embarrassment. It is a sound familiar to the Western world since the time of Thomas Crapper, magnified somewhat by larger volumes of water.

In the geyser basin there are pools of water that may bubble or boil, but never play. Some of these hot springs are the size of a room; some are the size of a compact disc. The water color ranges from a Caribbean-blue to coppery-brown to mossy-green.

Glen Spring, set away from the basin in an alcove of greenery, is a greenish-brown pool, technically a geyser, though it plays very infrequently. Long ago, perhaps before the white man entered the park, someone or some group placed a log before Glen Spring. The log has very nearly been petrified by the flow of mineralized water. It has been there a very long time.

Indians, contrary to popular belief, were not at all frightened of the geysers. There are legends of spirits fighting beneath the earth, of spirits who created the grumble and the outbreak of hell. No fears or taboos, however, and the mineralized log seems to suggest that Glen Springs was once a form of prehistoric TV.

On the white pebbly sand, called sinter, created by the outflow of the geysers, there are the skeletons of trees; some are thirty feet high, some are sixty. The trees were overrun by sinter. They stand alone, branchless, without bark, weathered by the wind and the steam: ghost trees, casualties of a land where the spirits battle underground.

There is evidence of further casualties in the basin. The bones of elk are scattered across the sand, spread by feeding coyotes. Elk move into the geyser basin for warmth in the impossible silence of 50-degree-below-zero winter days. But the spare brown grasses in the sinter sand are grazed off rapidly so the warmth is a killing comfort.

Shoshone Geyser Basin has claimed other lives. One winter a cross-country skier was scalded to death in a hot pool. He was alone, and rangers could only guess as to what happened. The hot pools form in caverns and often build thin ledges over the boiling water, ledges that can crack under the weight of a man. The water is scalding hot. It is almost immediately deadly.

Black Sulfur Geyser is continually at play, what is called a perpetual spouter. It is positioned on the sloping bank above Shoshone Creek, so it plays almost horizontally, spitting boiling water out into the fast-flowing creek.

It is illegal to bathe in the thermal features of Yellowstone Park, not to mention deadly, but where flowing or spouting water enters a river, it ceases to be considered a thermal feature. People may bathe there, in what are called hot pots. Finding the perfect temperature is a matter of moving closer to or further from the place where the boiling water meets the creek or river. These wilderness Jacuzzis are the joy of the geyser basin. You have to find them yourself. No one tells you where they are.

The shallower hot pools are brilliantly colorful: They are green or yellow or brownish-green and take on the color of strange life forms, a kind of furry-looking iridescent bacterial slime that thrives in the scalding springs. One unnamed hot pool is perhaps eighty feet across, nearly circular, and the vent is set off toward the western periphery of the spring, like the hub of a badly set wheel. The vent itself is a creamy white, with a greenish-blue tinge, and everywhere surrounding the vent on the floor of the geyser is a layer of algae a few inches thick. Nearest the vent, where the water is hottest, the algae is light brown, and farthest from the vent, in increments, the water becomes a dark coppery brown.

A companion described the algae as living slime, a description I had previously reserved for an individual who sold me a used truck in 1983.

At sundown the plumes of playing geysers take on the color of the setting sun and a freshening wind whips the crimson pennants into drifting weightless shreds of color. At the campsite, the first stars seem preternaturally bright. As the light dies, there is the deep grumbling and hiss of a large geyser at play and this sound mingles with the loony haunting call of cranes in a twilight symphony too strange for fiction.

Family Values in the Raw

"You cannot," the fundamentalist missionary complained, "get the Dani to wear clothes. They just won't do it." The first missionaries arrived in New Guinea's Grand Baliem Valley in 1959, anxious to convert the Stone Age tribesmen who lived there. They've done all right, I suppose, these missionaries, but the question of clothing still devils the least flexible among them.

The fundamentalist sipped his tea. Aside from the "self-evident indecency" of human nakedness, he said, "it gets cold here at night." And he posed a question to me, since I had been defending the Dani's right to dress (or not) as they pleased: "Why wouldn't a man wear clothes when it gets cold?"

It's not precisely true that the Dani go entirely naked. A few days earlier, in the village of Soroba, set hard against a great cliff of gray rock, Pua, the headman, had agreed to show me how the Dani men *grow* their clothes. Soroba was a horseshoe-shaped compound composed of a dozen huts thatched with straw.

Pua led me over a low wooden barrier designed to keep pigs out, and together we walked out behind the men's hut. There were thirty or forty banana trees set against the rock wall, and nearby was a shaded area, trellised and overhung with leaves, like a grape arbor. Yellow squash hung from the vines atop the trellis. The squash—responding to the tug of gravity—grew in a long, narrow fashion. The vegetables looked a bit like giant carrots. In time, Pua said, the men would pick the squash, cut off the thick end, scoop out the seeds, bake the husks lightly, dry them for a year, and then use the gourds as penis sheaths. The gourds are secured with a bit of bark twine tied around the waist. This is the extent of male adornment in the Grand Baliem Valley, where the polite salutation "How are they hanging?" is superfluous.

The valley, nearly forty miles long by ten miles wide, is located on the western, Indonesian half of the island of New Guinea. Carved out of lush tropical highlands by the glittering cocoa-colored Baliem River, the central valley is home to an estimated one hundred thousand Dani—short, powerful people who formerly practiced ritual war to strengthen various life forces and to appease cranky ancestors.

The valley is nearly a mile high, which means the evenings are, as the missionary pointed out, quite cool. During my visit, I generally wore a light rain jacket after sunset. The indigenous Dani wore what they wore during the heat of the day: grass skirts for the women; gourds for the men.

The Dani wear gourds as a fashion statement—a defiant affirmation of their own culture. Clothes are available to them at no cost. During a short-lived government push to clothe the Dani, for instance, headmen in each village were given shirts and slacks. It was thought that people would naturally see the manifest benefits involved in clothing: the dignity of pants; the elegance of cotton T-shirts (most of which had been collected in missionary clothing drives and featured slogans regarding Ninja Turtles and muscular men in masks who fly like bats).

The effort was largely a failed one.

In the valley's central town, Wamena, a government administrative center, it is rare to see a Dani out after dark. For example: Here it is, 55 degrees, drizzling, and some poor fellow, naked except for his gourd, is standing on the side of the road, alone, with his hands clasped behind his neck and his elbows down around his chest. It's a Dani attitude of abject misery, this posture. It says, "I'm freezing." It says, "I am, at this point in time, a completely forlorn individual."

A visitor in a rented vehicle feels a kind of obligation. He picks up the gentleman on the side of the road and drives him out along a dirt path fourteen miles to the village of Soroba. The formerly forlorn Dani, whose name is Pua, invites his benefactor to dinner.

This is served in the long, rectangular cooking hut, where six different families are sitting around six different fires. It's warm inside the hut, and dry. Everyone is cooking the same thing: potatoes. The Dani are master agriculturists, and these aren't just any potatoes; they are the best-tasting potatoes grown on the face of the earth. They are huge, big enough to kill the cat if one rolled off a table, vaguely sweet, and white as snow. The Dani grow seventy different varieties of potatoes, and each kind tastes better than the last.

After dinner, everyone crawls out a low doorway and hustles through the rain, across the compound, to another large rectangular hut, where three fires are already blazing away. Family groups mingle and merge at the fires. Men sit fondly with their wives, children play, infants sleep soundly in their mothers' arms.

One man plays a kind of wooden jaw harp, modulating the sound with his tongue, with the shape of his mouth. And the rhythm suggests a song. The oldest of the women seems to be the choir director. She sings a verse, then a select few voices respond, and finally everyone joins in.

The songs are a delight, sweet or rousing or romantic, and favorites are repeated several times. At Soroba, they must do this a lot. There is a practiced harmony to the singing, a passion and a drama. Soon enough, the children are asleep. Some of the men have gone off to lie down with their wives in individual huts; others remove to the sacred men's hut for important talk.

And the visitor is left to return to his rental car. He has a room, by himself, in a cheap hotel. There is no one at the hotel to sing with, no one to sleep with, and he misses his own family. The night, he thinks, has been a celebration of simple probity and virtue. Everyone had seemed so content. The visitor drives back through the chill rain, and there are no Dani anywhere. A man would be a fool to stand around naked on a night like this. Better to go home, sit comfortably around the fire, play with your children, sing the finest songs you know, and flirt with your wife.

An evening to think about when someone asks why the Dani would choose to go naked in the cold.

The missionary had been pondering the problem for some time. He thought it had to do with the vestiges of paganism, with the sure and subtle influence of Satan.

I couldn't agree. You never see a Dani man standing on a Wamena street corner at midnight drinking cheap wine and saying "Hubba-hubba" to passing women. No, each evening's chill sends Dani people scurrying back to the warmth of hearth and home. Satan was pretty much frozen out of the equation. Going naked in the cold, as I saw it, was an expression of strong family values.

Working the Crowd

Three days of walking, and, ah, here's the outskirts of a remote village. Doesn't matter where, really. Could be Tonga or Peru or New Guinea or Rwanda or a Siberian Chukchi settlement. Time to gear up for fellow human beings. The dogs are going crazy, and they follow you in ragged packs. Walk into the center of the village. More than likely, children will form the advance guard. Dozens of them surround you. Soon enough, older people—adolescents—will develop the courage of children. The responsible adults usually come last.

And here's what happens: Sometime within the first twenty minutes of pleasant social interaction, someone will insult you. More than likely it's one of the teenage males, who will be surrounded by a knot of other young men. Could be you've concealed a slight knowledge of the language in order to test the waters. Maybe not. In any case, the kid is rattling away in the local idiom, and people are laughing. They are laughing at you.

It's a mean, denigrating laughter. The village bully has got you in his sights. He has probably called you:

A gringo son of a goat; a Zionist barf bag; an imbecile, moron, pervert, suck fish, bastard, and a floating turd, as well as the accursed spawn of filth-devouring evil. You are, according to your tormentor, a stench upon the land; a bowl brimful of vomit and urine; an illiterate dim bulb; a butt breath; the instigator of various incestuous relationships. You've been labeled a pig-dog, a snot ball, and a cow flop, not to mention a fatty, a dummy, a heretic, and a coprophaginist.

The urge, of course, is to let the assembled multitudes understand that you know precisely what is going on, and that you are not a person to be trifled with. The urge is to respond in kind and to insult the bully in idiosyncratic English. You want to get in his face—let him know that he's a sack of pus, a scum-sucking pig, a walking hemorrhoid, an idiot, and an oaf. You want to tell him, quite firmly, that he's a species of subhuman corruption, a jerk-off, a twit, a pathetic little needle-dicked shit weasel, and that you'd be delighted to introduce him to the dumb end of a baseball bat.

Such a response, in my experience, is more trouble than it's worth.

In places that lack TV, a stranger's visit is the evening's entertainment. Respond to abuse with more abuse, and the game has suddenly become that form of bear-baiting known as "humiliate the foreigner." Suddenly everyone has another insult to hurl, everyone dashing in to figuratively pull away a bit of your flesh—your equanimity, your dignity—like piranha in a feeding frenzy.

What I do—what I've done in Tonga and Peru and Rwanda and New Guinea and certain Siberian villages—is laugh right along with everyone else when the first insults start flying. There is always a moment when the bully assumes he's cornered a fool and there are more insults to endure. I continue to laugh along, just as merry as all get-out. It's smart to seem a little confused.

I look to one of the adults—someone who seems bothered by the attack—and, smiling, gesture for some translation. What are we all laughing at? The fellow may not be able to meet my eyes. He stares at the ground. The insults begin dribbling off to a muttering ambiguity, and there is much less laughter. More folks are staring at the ground. The crowd seems shamed. There is a new tension in the air.

Tension, of course, is the comedian's friend. Make them laugh here, and you've got 'em. Slapstick is universal, and you can certainly work out your own schtick, but I've found that singing "Tea for Two" in a Donald Duck voice while tap-dancing usually works. The tension is broken, the bully defused, and everyone's laughing. Now you can get on to the serious business of making friends.

The Queen Charlotte Islands:
Life and Death (hee-hee)
Tales from the Place of Wonder

A guidebook I'd paged through at a Prince Rupert newsstand had opened with an admonition that, as nearly as I can recall, read: "In the Queen Charlotte Islands, you should put your troubles and cares in your pocket, but leave plenty of room for high spirits and adventure." I'd puzzled over that bit of advice. Was I supposed to have high-spirited adventure in the same pocket that contained my troubles and cares? Why couldn't I have a couple of adventures in an entirely different pocket altogether?

As it was, I was enduring an unexpected and out-of-pocket adventure. We'd pretty much killed the bleeding last night—my head wound was taped shut—but the pain in my back was excruciating. That morning, I'd managed to hobble through thigh-deep water to get to a float plane that would convey me to the hospital in Queen Charlotte City, about a forty-five-minute flight north. I'd been hiking in the wilderness of South Moresby Island, and it doesn't really pay to be stupid in such places.

And I'd been really, really, really stupid.

High-spirited but stupid.

It was, I suppose, a good day for a flight over the Queen Charlottes. In late June, at the 53rd parallel, there were still a few patchy bits of snow on peaks that rose to three thousand feet. The sun was burning its way through a scudding layer of low gray clouds, and slanting shafts of light fell across the otherwise gray North Pacific; fell as light falls in a cathedral. The islands themselves were almost black with vegetation, except where those purely religious shafts hit them like celestial spotlights, and then the ancient mossy forests seemed to glow from within. Emerald luminescence anchored in a tenebrous misery of unrelieved gray.

From above, I could almost make out the shape of the Queen Charlotte archipelago. It looked a bit like a giant fang: the broad expanse of Graham Island in the north, then Moresby Island curving down south and east, tapering off to a point at Cape Saint James in the far south. Interspersed around these two main islands, there were over 150 others—some were little more than rocky hummocks—located, variously, 31 to 95 miles off the coast of British Columbia, Canada.

The islands were separated from the mainland by Hecate Strait, a shallow, treacherous body of water one early sailor described as a "black-hearted bitch," that seemed charged, in the sailor's opinion, with the task of "protecting the Queen Charlottes." The archipelago sits at the very edge of the continental shelf, so the rocky western headlands are pounded fiercely by the full force of the Pacific Ocean.

Back somewhere in the frosty reaches of geological time—during the Ice Age, when much of the world's water was frozen at the polar caps—sea level was much lower and the Queen Charlottes were probably connected to the North American mainland by a land bridge. Enter a few mainland species, both plants and animals. Exit the Ice Age. The land bridge was drowned in meltwater and became the black-hearted bitch we call Hecate Strait.

The Queen Charlottes, in turn, became islands—Hecate on one side, the inhospitable North Pacific on the other. These rough waters have kept the Queen Charlotte Islands isolated over the millennia since the last Ice Age. No new plants or animals. No new genetic information. The mainland species isolated on the islands have been forced to respond to local conditions, and sometimes evolved survival strategies quite different from their mainland cousins. According to Dr. J. Bristol Foster, director of the British Columbia Ecological Reserves Program, the Queen Charlotte Islands are "an evolutionary showcase."

Down there, in those undisturbed ancient forests of spruce and cedar and hemlock, there are species of flora and fauna that exist nowhere else on earth. The largest black bear in North America (*Euarctos americana carlottae*) roams the forests of the larger islands; there are subspecies of woodpecker and owl that are unique to the Queen Charlottes, along with several species of moss and flowering plants, including the alpine lily. The sheer volume of endemic species (species peculiar to one place) is, according to Dr. Foster, "astonishing." The Queen Charlottes are sometimes called the Canadian Galapagos.

That's what I'd been doing when it happened: I was hiking through the South Moresby National Park Reserve, looking for endemic species. Alone. Didn't tell anyone at the camp where our kayaks were beached exactly where I was going. Just took off. I'd made my way through the dim forests, looking for bears, for the saw-whet owl and the hairy woodpecker. I'd come across a few tiny orchids, an insectivorous plant, and any number of mosses that I couldn't identify. The Queen Charlottes are considered the moss capital of Canada, if not the world.

South Moresby is a temperate-zone rain forest, and I was trekking through country that had never heard the scream of the chain saw. The spruce and hemlock and cedar stood like monarchs, and only about 10 percent of the available light filtered through to the forest floor. The canopy above acted like a giant sponge, so the forest seemed to be dripping water even under clear skies. There was a strange green subaqueous quality to the light. Underfoot, the mosses were six inches deep and more.

There were fallen trees everywhere, covered over in moss. Spruce saplings grew out of every even vaguely horizontal surface.

Old Man's Beard, a kind of wispy green moss, hung from the branches of the living trees, and there were standing dead snags everywhere. The cedar trees, in particular, were spectacular in death: a hundred feet or more of soaring silver wood, like a monument on the land. No wonder the local Indians, the redoubtable Haida, used cedar to make their totem poles.

I was looking for woodpeckers in one particular dead cedar when the thread of linear thought abandoned me, as it sometimes does in the wild. The tree was standing at a Tower of Pisa slant. What if I were that tree? And what if I retained some shred of consciousness, even in standing death? My life span had stretched out over several centuries, and now here I was, falling, slowly, toward the forest floor. Given my life span, it would seem to be happening very fast. It would be like catching your foot at the top of the stairs: the arms windmill about; there's a brief shout; then *thump-thump-thump.*

And what did I, as a conscious cedar, have to look forward to on the forest floor? Over the span of several months—to me, the blink of an eye—I'd be covered over in moss, fungus, parasites. Insects would penetrate to my core and eat my cells from the inside out. Other living trees would colonize me with their seeds, and the saplings would suck the last living thought from my marrow.

Now, I know that this is all part of the biological cycle of regeneration. Perfectly natural. Perfectly healthy. My problem is that I tend to personalize everything. You're a tree, you fall; everything on the forest floor feeds off your body. It would be like a slow-motion horror film.

I was, in fact, indulging this eccentric train of thought when the forest right-of-way presented me with a mossy cliff wall about fifteen feet high. Easy climb. I even took my walking stick with me. I recall reaching over the top of the cliff, but then—and this seemed totally unacceptable at the time—I seemed to be falling face first toward the mute forest floor. Happily, I landed in a thick bed of moss. Unhappily, I gashed my forehead rather deeply, probably on my own damn walking stick.

I lay there for a while, assessing the extent of the damage and wondering how badly I'd hurt my back. What if I couldn't move? It would be the whole cedar scenario—that slow-motion horror film of rot and decay, with me in the lead role.

Which, I suppose, got me onto my feet and kept me moving for four hours, until I got down to the seashore, where my kayaking companions were already at work searching for me. A radio call was placed to the hospital.

And now here I was, being medevacked out of a place I considered to be an earthly paradise because I'd been stupid enough to put my adventures in the same pocket as my problems.

The Queen Charlottes—like Nepal or Tibet—are one of those places people go for emotional renewal or spiritual enlightenment. In the 1960s and '70s, the islands had been a little-known hippie Mecca; and survivalists, known as "coasties," had colonized some of their more remote areas. In those years, several timber companies were hard at work, clear-cutting the ancient forests.

There had been an acrimonious controversy. The hippies, conservation-minded locals, the coasties, and the Haida had all gathered together to stop the logging. After almost fifteen years of bitter argument, on July 11, 1987, the Canadian government saved a substantial portion of the Queen Charlottes from the chain saw when it made the southern part of Moresby Island a national park reserve. The South Moresby Reserve includes 138 islands and comprises about 15 percent of the land area of the Queen Charlottes. Gwaii Haanas, it's called: "place of wonder."

An article I read in *The Queen Charlotte Islands Observer* said there was a movement afoot to change the name of the islands to its aboriginal appellation, Haida Gwaii (place of the Haida). There was to be a referendum. After three weeks in the islands, I had a sense that it would pass.

People on the Charlottes still make a living logging the northern islands. Halibut and salmon are plentiful and many folks earn their daily bread fishing. There are about six thousand people of various ethnic descent who live on the islands. Tourism is in its infancy.

The soul of the Queen Charlottes—the wilderness of Gwaii Haanas—is available by float plane or by chartered boat. I chose to kayak South Moresby with Grant Thompson, of Tofino Expeditions, out of Vancouver, who had invited me along on a scouting trip of the place of wonder. There were ten of us in the party.

We camped, for the most part, on the southeast coast of Moresby Island. The gray cobblestone beaches were piled, at the high-tide line, with gigantic piles of drift logs that had escaped logging booms. Piled at the base of the logs, or flung beyond them, was all the flotsam and jetsam of the North Pacific Ocean. The Japanese current tosses three-year-old material up on the beach. Hawaiian garbage takes a bit longer to get to South Moresby—about five years. There were plastic detergent bottles, disposable diapers, beer cans (from Canada, Japan, and Hawaii, judging by the labels), along with treasures like the hand-blown glass balls that Japanese fishermen use to float their fishing nets.

Sometimes the beaches were covered over in a slick glaze of tiny transparent jellyfish, like small disks with protruding dorsal fins that catch the ocean breezes and give these organisms their name: by-the-wind sailors. There were broken dolls staring up from the drift logs, and huge plastic floats that boomed loudly when kicked and were handy for impromptu soccer games. Indeed, I was standing on a beach, booting one of these beach-ball-size affairs around, making a lot of noise, when my friend Linnea asked me to stop. "Shhhh . . ."

It seemed there was a bald eagle sitting atop one of the dead spruce trees that fronted the ocean. This was pretty much par for the course. There are more eagles per square mile in the Queen Charlottes than anywhere else on earth, with the exception of Alaska's Admiralty Island. I looked closer and saw that there were, in fact, two eagles, sitting shoulder to shoulder, high up in the bare branches. I got my binoculars and watched what I considered to be an odd performance. Each eagle seemed to be pretending that the other one wasn't there. Each scanned the beach and ocean, and through the glasses I could see the stern eyes, the hooked beaks, the implacable nobility. And then each of the eagles turned at the same time, and their heads collided with an almost audible thump, like two humans stooping to pick up the same sheet of paper. They regarded each other with visible annoyance, not to mention their usual implacable nobility, each of them staring fiercely at the other as if to say "You dork!"

One day we paddled several hours up to the head of Rose Inlet, where a freshwater stream ran through a grassy meadow. The tide was high, and we paddled up the meandering stream. A small harbor seal frolicked beside us for a time. The grass in the meadow was knee-high, and I could just barely see the tops of my companions' heads gliding through an undulating lake of greenery. A black-tail deer, drinking from the stream, glanced up to watch us pass. I was close enough to touch it with my paddle. The deer just stood there, watching. His attitude seemed to be one of "Yeah, so?"

That day we gathered clams, and a large bag of sea asparagus, a kind of thick-stemmed grass that grows at the edge of the ocean. We cooked up the sea asparagus with butter and garlic, wolfed down the clams, and sat, sated, at our campsite while the sun took about four hours to set.

The next day we paddled through a large flotilla of purple jellyfish the size of volleyballs, skirting a rocky island where red and orange starfish bigger than my head clung to craggy rocks just under the surface of the sea. Ahead, there was a point of land that caught the worst of the ocean swells. Booming plumes of spray exploded off the rock, and for a moment, with the sun before me, the great wall of seawater scattered the light and dozens of tiny rainbows fell across the rock.

We gave a wide berth to the rainbows and came back along this small island, a sloping hummock of rock, where several dozen Steller's sea lions were basking in the sun. The males weighed over two thousand pounds, and they grunted at us like foghorns as we passed. I'd never heard a grunt sound lordly before.

One day, a pod of killer whales passed under our kayaks, and we could hear the great glottal pop of their breathing. My friend Linnea was so excited that she kept drumming her feet on the hull of her boat. We didn't see any gray whales. A local boatman told us that the last one he'd seen had passed through over a week ago on the long southern migration.

Our campsites, just up above the drift logs, near clear fresh-water streams, were hard to leave. We pitched our tents on beds of moss a foot thick. During the long twilight hours—the sun didn't set until almost eleven—we talked about what we'd seen that day and the incredible journeys the Haida made, and still make, in cedar canoes forty feet long.

Indeed, early on, a few of us had seen some of these canoes being built.

Soon after I'd arrived on Graham Island, several of us drove from Queen Charlotte City north to the town of Old Masset, an Indian village the local people prefer to call Haida. We stopped at the White residence, a functional boxy affair, to see the canoes Morris White and several friends were making. The canoes would be paddled to a great meeting of the Northwest tribal bands at the mainland town of Bela Bela at the end of June.

Morris White, the patriarch, appeared to be in his early fifties. He spoke slowly, with a kind of throat-clearing stutter. He introduced his son, Christian, a handsome and rather cosmopolitan young man (a handshake for me, a continental hand kiss for my friend Linnea). Christian's son, a boy who looked to be about twelve, dozed on the couch while a Saturday afternoon kung fu movie blared away on a small color TV.

"Haida canoes," Morris White said, "like the ones we're building? In the olden days, Haida paddled these canoes to California." He cleared his throat.

I expressed some amazement on this point and mentioned that I had never read anything to corroborate such a boast in the historical record.

"Oh, no one knows about it," Christian said.

"The elders tell us," Morris added, "that we paddled to Chile. In South America."

"Japan," Christian said.

In point of fact, early Euro-American explorers were forever pointing out that the Haida people were fairer of skin than those in the coastal tribes. They are also bigger people, and the men still tend toward a certain Polynesian immensity. They look more like Hawaiians than coastal North American Indians.

"Hawaii?" I asked.

There was general agreement among the White men on this point. "The Hawaiians are our relatives," Christian said. "Our cousins."

We stepped out back, where there was a huge wooden airplane hangar of a barn. The Whites and three friends had been working nonstop on the ceremonial canoes for the past several months. Morris White had lost so much weight that his clothes hung loosely on his large frame. Three huge boats, each over forty feet long and made from a single cedar log, were placed upside down on oversize sawhorses. The whole place smelled like Grandma's hope chest.

The canoes, even before they'd been carved and painted with the appropriate totemic symbols of the Haida people—with the bears and eagles and beaver and ravens and killer whales—were beautiful. Works of art, built as they had been built over the centuries. Built for the rough waters of Hecate Strait. Built—who knows for certain?—to withstand the long paddle to Hawaii. Chile. Japan.

Later, over a beer in the White house, we sat chatting while Oriental people kung fu-ed each other on the television.

The Whites, it turned out, were a remarkably talented family: Morris carved silver bracelets of the type I'd seen selling for $500 apiece in Queen Charlotte City. Christian carved traditional figures out of argillite, a soft slate quarried on the Queen Charlottes. In Canada, only the Haida may work with and sell argillite. Christian's work sold for as much as $8,000 a sculpture.

Still, the Whites weren't rich people. Morris was bitter about the clever white men who somehow cheated the Haida out of their fishing boats in the mid-1950s. Worse, the forest all around them was being cut down, hundreds of millions of dollars were being extracted from the land, and the Haida people weren't being compensated. A good percentage of the population of the village of Haida was on public assistance.

"If we had lawyers and chartered accountants," Morris White said, "then we'd be a wealthy village."

Christian nodded over toward the couch in front of the television, where his young son was sucking on a Tootsie Roll Pop. "My son," he said, "is going to be my lawyer."

The boy glanced up from the television. "I said I was going to be a lawyer," he replied. "I didn't say I was going to be *your* lawyer."

Our kayak party camped for a time at Fanny Bay, near the southern tip of Moresby Island, and only an hour's paddle away from Skungwai Island (called Anthony Island on some maps). On Skungwai (Red Cod) stands the remains of Ninstints, a Haida ghost village, abandoned sometime late in the last century, where magnificent totem poles still tower against the sky. In 1981 the United Nations recognized the totemic art at Ninstints as a World Heritage Site. (Other such sites include the pyramids of Egypt and the palace at Versailles, France.)

We decided to visit Ninstints at dawn, and notified the resident Haida caretaker by radio phone from Fanny Bay.

It was a clear night when we left, with a full moon low in the sky, throwing a silver trail across calm black waters. By the time we reached Ninstints and pulled our kayaks up above the high-tide line, a fog bank obscured the rising sun. The world was pearly-gray, and wisps of mist floated low among the sacred poles. It was very still, and even the birdcalls seemed subdued.

The great cedar poles were silver-gray, and the faces carved into them—the bears and eagles and ravens and killer whales—grimaced in decay. They stared out to sea with rotting, ruined eyes.

The Haida caretaker was named Wanagun; his wife was Dja Da Unn Koo Uss, who invited us to call her Bernice. Wanagun wore gray jeans, a red sweatshirt, and sunglasses. He walked us among the poles, answering our eager questions. The totemic animals, for instance, weren't gods or demons. The poles were built fronting long wooden houses, now gone, and the carved animals represented family crests, like a European coat of arms.

Every Haida, Wanagun explained, was either a member of the Raven family or the Eagle family. There was no family intramarriage: Ravens married Eagles; Eagles married Ravens. The children joined the mother's family.

Wanagun was a Raven, and he had married Bernice, an Eagle, here, at Ninstints, in the space between the largest eagle totem and the largest raven.

That was after Wanagun, along with others, had removed over forty large spruce trees from the area. The spruce were choking out the totems, colonizing them with saplings. Wanagun figured that with the spruce gone, the totems caught more sun and wind, whose drying effects might preserve them, give them twenty more years of life.

Most of the poles, Wanagun said, were actually headstones, funerary poles. There were great men of the olden times still "buried" in the small carved boxes at the top. He pointed out a pole that had fallen and was propped up at about a 45-degree angle. The coffin lid had broken open. We could just barely make out the white rounded shape of a skull protruding from the dirt and the grasses that grew inside.

Wanagun, an articulate and informed man, was a storyteller. He told us about how the long wooden houses could only be entered by a single oval doorway. "You had to put one arm through, and then your head," he explained. And once the villagers had killed a number of enemies simply by clubbing them over the head as they entered the longhouses. "The dead people thought they were going to a party," Wanagun said. And then he laughed: "Hee-hee."

And when new poles were put up in front of the homes of important families, slaves were sometimes stuffed in the hole first and crushed to death with several tons of magnificently carved cedar. "When they tried to get out," Wanagun said, "we poked them with sharp sticks. Hee-hee."

And then there was a story about a massacre. The only survivor was a Haida boy so young that he couldn't say which coastal tribe had attacked the village. So the Haida had simply paddled up and down the coast from Alaska to Vancouver killing everyone, hee-hee. Even today, Wanagun said, some coastal chiefs refuse to meet with the killer Haida.

Another party of visitors arrived on a chartered boat, and Wanagun met them at the shore. We decided to take a walk.

Our party moved silently through mist, with the poles towering overhead. We followed a trail to the west through a tunnel of giant spruce. The ground was a series of mossy hummocks.

The trail led through old growth forest and emptied out onto a gravel-and-cobblestone beach. The ocean was misty gray, and we could see no other islands in the distance. Sea grass at the edge of the beach was covered over in dew, and we kicked holes in the mist as we walked. The trail rose through a stand of spruce, including a few giant cedars, then wound its way through a narrow rock canyon whose walls were covered over in lichen and moss.

The walls rose above us sixty and eighty feet, and they led us, willy-nilly, into a dead end, a great rounded horseshoe of stone. We found ourselves staring into two caves at the base of the rock wall. Both were shaped like an upside-down V. The rock walls on either side were festooned with woody roots snaking down from the spruce that grew at the lip of the cliffs, eighty feet above. These immense roots wound down over the irregularities of the rocks like great woody snakes, some of them as big around as a fifty-five-gallon drum.

There was a rope stretched across the mouth of the caves. We knew from Wanagun that the main cave "was where we used to burn our bodies." I hadn't been there to hear that particular statement, though I suspect it might be more accurately transcribed as "burn our bodies, hee-hee."

It was dark in the shadows of the rock walls, and the lazy, drifting mist took on a greenish hint of the forest above. We stood at the rope, and the quality of the light changed as a drizzling rain began to fall. I flicked on a flashlight and directed the beam into the maw of the central cave. There was a momentary backscatter of light, silver bright in the gently falling rain, and then we could see into the cave, which had been blackened by the smoke of innumerable fires. There were ashes scattered across the floor.

Presently, the rain let up and we could see a bit more clearly. In the center of the opening was a large boulder, shaped a bit like a pyramid, and certain projections on the rock gave it the look of a face. The sun was higher now, the sky had cleared a bit, and shafts of sunlight poured down through the trees.

The face—we decided, from our position behind the rope—was natural, not man-made. Still, it bore an uncomfortable resemblance to tikis I'd seen in the gloomy banyan forests of the South Pacific. It was eerie, and just vaguely menacing.

"I thought they buried people in those boxes on the tops of the poles," someone said.

A theory was advanced that the ancient Haida burned the bodies first, for sanitary purposes.

"Not enough poles to bury everyone," I offered. "Ten thousand years of Haida occupation? The whole island would be nothing but a stand of funerary poles."

The more satisfactory explanation was that ordinary people were cremated and that important people, chiefs, were buried on the funerary poles.

We contemplated these theories for a while, in the gloom, with the tree roots snaking down like giant arthritic hands and the stone face glaring out at us from the ashes.

This was just real damn spooky, and I'm obliged to report that we began throwing pinecones at one another; throwing pinecones and laughing out of sheer nervousness. Whistling past the graveyard.

This was wrong. We knew it. All at once we knew it. There was another long silence.

But maybe, I thought, it wasn't entirely incorrect behavior. Perhaps we had absorbed a bit of the traditional Haida outlook on life. And death. Hee-hee.

I recalled a Haida story recounted in an ethnography written by John Swanton in 1909, a book Wanagun himself used as a reference. It was a story about a bunch of naughty dead people who resided in the funerary poles that fronted a certain village. The village of living people decided to spend a day and night hunting. Every living soul left on the trip, which left the dead free to frolic. Tired of their confinement in boxes at the top of the poles, the dead all came down into one of the longhouses to dance and sing and do whatever it is that skeletons do together when the living aren't around to see. They had all night. The villagers wouldn't be back until dawn.

As dawn approached, one of the honored dead stepped on a piece of salmon skin. It stuck to his bony foot. When he tried to pull it off, it stuck to his hand. A second corpse pulled the salmon skin off and, of course, it stuck to *his* hand. Time was running out for the dead. Dawn was fast approaching now, but no one could shake the flypaper salmon skin. The skeletons were flailing about in a mad dance of angry frustration, moving faster and even faster . . .

The story now shifts to the point of view of the village people returning home in the full light of dawn. They enter the longhouse to encounter an enormous pile of disjointed bones. One envisions them standing there, puzzled beyond earthly perception, thinking, Hee-hee?

It's a traditional story, oft told in the olden days, and indicative of the Haida people's sly sense of humor. The skeletons and the salmon skin: It's the Keystone Kops, with corpses.

The Haida, I fervently hoped, might be inclined to forgive our brief bout of pinecone dodgeball. They might even have approved.

It was just after that visit that I was medevacked out. After a day of recuperation in a motel, I found myself well enough to work out of the one local bar in Queen Charlotte City. I met a young woman who dressed like a logger and talked like a hippie. She lived with her husband and child in a log cabin near Port Clemens, about an hour and a half's drive north. She had no running water or electricity, but she pitied folks who had to live all packed together like ants in places like Prince Rupert. It was pouring down rain outside, and she'd just spent three hours hitchhiking into town. A touring ballet company was performing at the community hall.

"You spent three hours in the rain," I asked, "for a ballet?"

"Probably three hours back as well," she said.

A young man in a threadbare sweater told me that there was a cosmic fusion in process here on the island of Morocco. The Haida barmaid passed by and winked. She meant to say, "This is a local fellow and we tolerate him here."

The young woman said she was in favor of calling the islands Haida Gwaii.

A mildly intoxicated white carpenter sat down and demanded to know "whoever said the Haida had no sense of humor?"

I told him that no one had ever said that, as far as I knew. And then the carpenter told me a story.

It seems that several years ago, one of the greatest of all Haida artists carved a magnificent canoe, to be displayed in a great museum. The canoe was very big, and it was covered over in exquisitely carved totemic symbols: the raven and the eagle and beaver and bear and killer whale.

The canoe had to be lowered onto its stand with a large crane, and the young operator, a white man, worked hard, arranging everything just so, because the Haida artist had a specific idea of exactly where this monumental work of art should be, how it should be placed. Important stuff, the crane operator decided, and imagined there might be some religious symbolism at work that he didn't understand. The artist would look away, ponder some internal problem, then gesture minimally: Turn it just a bit to the east. They worked together in this way for hours.

Later, when the work was done, and the canoe finally placed to the artist's satisfaction, the young crane operator was invited to have a drink with the Haida carver. They spoke for some time. The artist was, as many Haida are, politically active. He was angry at the United States at the moment: Some decision by the president of that country that would, indirectly, affect the artist and the forest that he loved.

Finally, the crane operator asked the question that had been burning inside of him for the last few hours. The artist should forgive him, he said, but he saw very little difference in the various placements of the canoe. Why had it been set just so on its stand?

"On the canoe," the carver explained, "there is a bear."

"I saw it," the crane operator said.

"Look closely," the artist said. "The bear's asshole?"

"Yeah?"

"It points toward the White House."

I hobbled back to my motel room, appreciating the Queen Charlotte Islands in general and the Haida people—hee-hee—in particular. My companions had another three days of kayaking left, and me, I had a long, lonely wait, and a bunch of packaged soup to eat. It had cost a fortune to be airlifted out of the place of wonder, and that alone, I suppose, qualifies my fall as a pretty good out-of-pocket adventure.

The Tsunami Rangers

Ugly shoulder pads.

Eric Soares was putting them on over standard cold-water kayaking gear: a wet-suit bottom and a thick nylon-pile paddling sweater under a dry suit top. The pads had come out of the box white—they were standard hockey-style shoulder pads—but Soares had painted them a gray-black to blend in against the surging sea and soaring rock of the Northern California Pacific headlands. White pads were just a lot of trouble. They stood out. Coast Guard patrols spotted them in that area where the sea batters the land. It is reasonable to assume—as the Coast Guard does—that a man paddling a small kayak through fifty-foot spumes of spray exploding off immovable rock is a man about to die.

So Soares camouflaged the pads to prevent rescue attempts.

He wanted to put himself in precisely those areas where small boats disintegrate, where men are picked up by the sea and hurled into jagged rocks, where bad timing and inferior equipment are worth a man's life.

Best to be prepared in such an environment.

In addition to the shoulder pads, Soares wore a motocross chest-and-back protector made from foam and plastic, a hockey helmet, a motorcyclist's face mask, a football receiver's gloves, elbow pads, and knee pads. He looked like something out of an Australian postapocalyptic road movie: Wave Warrior; Robo Kayaker.

There was a distant winter storm pushing 12-foot waves into Rodeo Beach, on the Marin headlands, just north of the Golden Gate Bridge. A man in an ordinary kayak had attempted the surf just five minutes ago. His boat suffered several hundred dollars' worth of damage when the first wave fell on it. It had lasted thirty seconds.

Soares's boat was a specially designed kayak, the Tsunami X-1 "Rocket Boat." Made of Kevlar, the same lightweight laminate used as armor in tanks, the boat was literally bullet-proof.

Soares settled into the X-1, buckled his seat belt, and began paddling out into the great, pounding Pacific Ocean. He was about to demonstrate the Wave Warrior's first skill: breaking the wave barrier.

The waves came in sets, five or six 8-footers followed by one great hulking 12-footer rolling in like a dream of death. Soares waited for the big one, the monster, and when he made his move, he had just four seconds to hit it right.

There was an offshore wind and it pushed against the oncoming wave, holding it upright, giving it a terrifying verticality. Soares, paddling hard, could feel the wind at his back driving him forward. The wave began to curl over at the top. Soares was pushing into the base of the wave, where the wind compressed against vertical water, and the sound was a rising howl. Propelled by his own power and the wind, Soares and the X-1 were hurled up the wall of water.

Too little momentum here, and everything goes cartwheeling over backward. And, oh, that moment when inertia dies and the boat begins its slow topsy tilt: the sensation like a sudden punch to the stomach, the knowledge of impending and total chaos . . .

. . . but the inertia was there. The wave itself was pulling shore-side water to its crest—there was a strange growl in the belly of the wave, a deep sucking howl, as of a waterfall running in reverse—and Soares was riding the power of all this upwelling water. He was "going up the falls," but the wave had already formed a tube that curled over his head. It was a ceiling of moving water suspended by its own momentum for the barest instant.

And there it was: Soares could see a thin spot, very bright, at the place where the wave had begun to curl. The lip of the wave was only a foot thick, and Soares aimed the bow of his kayak into it, straight up into the sun, so that he "punched through the light," through the very wave itself. The X-1 burst onto the other side of the wave, which moved out from under the boat so that Soares and his boat hung motionless ten feet in the air. Below him was a rainbow falling with the spray that the wind had driven back off the crest of the wave. There was a silence, and then— kaboom—like nearby thunder, the wave broke. And Soares rode a rainbow to the surface of the sea.

"You have to break the wave barrier in order to get out into the rock gardens," Soares told me. Which is to say you need to be very skillful in order to be able to get out through the surf and into those areas where a kayaker risks being crushed by water against rock.

Dr. Eric Soares is an associate professor at the California State University in Hayward, where he teaches marketing research, among other subjects. He is also a Tsunami Ranger. The Rangers are a club of about a dozen men and women who avidly don Wave Warrior gear and paddle out in bullet-proof kayaks to battle the Pacific Ocean at the point of its fullest fury.

It would seem to be a double life. On the one hand, Soares is writing a book entitled *Cost-Effective Marketing Research,* aimed at corporate marketing departments and entrepreneurs. "The premise of the book," Soares explains, "is that every company needs marketing research: I try to tell them how they can get relevant research at a price they can afford." The book is full of marketing pros and cons, ideas about controlled experimentation, random populations, control groups, and valid measuring instruments. These concepts, among others, are the meat of his university lectures. They are also the essence of his small marketing-consultation business.

On the other hand, the forty-something professor writes about his kayaking avocation in such publications as *Paddlers' News Bulletin,* wherein he sounds anything but professorial: ". . . you had to make a lot of ninja strokes to stay in the safety zone, or blow it and get creamed."

The way Soares sees it, his life fits together quite neatly, "sorta." He grew up on a cattle ranch near Redding, California, where he recalls making the business of irrigation an adventure. "I'd have to open the flumes at the main canal," he said. Then he was supposed to walk along the bank and open the rest of the flumes that diverted the water onto the ranch. Soares found it faster and more exciting to get right in the irrigation ditches and ride the floodwaters down to the next flume.

He had learned to swim at five. "I loved ice cream, and one day my dad spent a few hours tossing coins into the deep end of the local pool. I learned to open my eyes under water, hold my breath, and I got a lot of ice cream later. I guess I associated certain capitalistic impulses with some amount of risk from an early age."

Those capitalistic impulses drove Soares into the study of business and economics. His natural affinity for water kept him on the rivers—swimming, canoeing and, later, kayaking. In 1980, Soares found himself at the University of California in Santa Barbara studying for his Ph.D. He owned a kayak, but there were no rivers nearby—just the ocean, the pounding waves, and a lot of surfers. So Eric Soares, incipient Ph.D., took his kayak out into the ocean and learned the local surf dialect: He went far rad with the thumpers and dumpers when things got gnarly.

Something else. The ocean became more than just a substitute for a good white-water river. It had become a new and over-whelming passion. Once you learned how to break the wave barrier, you could paddle out beyond the breakers and hit out for a few easy miles along the coastal headlands. The cliffs sometimes rose several hundred feet above the sea, but there were always sandy coves carved into the rocky walls. Sometimes you had to ride heavy surf into shore, and that could be especially gnarly when rocky islands, called sea stacks, guarded the beach. Once you were on the sand, however, the beach was all yours. The cliffs on one side and the raging surf on the other ensured your privacy.

There was risk involved, sure, and it was like climbing a mountain in that way. Except when you got to the top of a mountain, it was all ice and snow and nothing lived there. In those coves where the ocean met the land, there were seals and otters; there was shore life in abundance. Soares felt like Captain Kirk on the Starship *Enterprise:* He was going where no man had gone before. And he could get there in less than an hour.

There were plenty of people sea kayaking in 1980, but they tended to paddle in the calmer bays or behind protected reefs. Others were braving the surf on kayaks called surf skis. These were actually sit-down surfboards—great for waves, but of limited use in exploratory forays. Unlike conventional kayaks, surf skis had no hatch, no storage capacity at all.

No, what you needed for coastal exploring was a boat that could carry a week's worth of camping gear and that could take some pretty serious rock-bashing. You wanted a bullet-proof kayak with room for your lunch.

Soares was stripping off his Robo Kayaker gear. He had broken the wave barrier at Rodeo Beach and had paddled out to the rock gardens near Point Bonita, at the northern entrance to San Francisco Bay. He had spent some time getting up close to the rocks as the breakers hit them so hard that spray burst thirty feet and more over his head. He liked "getting close to a bomb" like that, but the clapotis had been pretty good out there today too. To hit the clapotis just right, you wanted to get into the deep water, into an area where swells rather than breakers were running into some rocky island. When a good-size swell hits an immovable rock wall, water has no place to go. It drops off the rock and forms a swell that moves back out to sea. But other swells are moving in. At some point, two swells collide, and there is a powerful popping explosion called the clapotis effect. A good Wave Warrior, in proper position, can ride the clapotis ten feet in the air.

Soares likes to reverse the clapotis experience by moving into the "suck zone" next to the rock. It is a matter of some delicate timing. The swell hits the rock, and retreats. Get in there, right there, right next to the rock, in just that moment of retreat, and the bottom drops out of the sea. You fall five, six, ten feet and more.

Mistime the suck zone, however, and you may suffer the sort of rock-bashing in which a pair of ugly shoulder pads and a good helmet mean the difference between life and death. All in all, a better maneuver in a mistimed suck zone involves leaning out to sea as the next swell lifts the X-1 into the rock. Let the hull of the kayak absorb the blow. What the hell; it's bullet-proof.

It seemed inevitable that Eric Soares should meet Jim Kakuk and Glen Gilchrist. Both were coastal explorers, pushing the limits of traditional kayaking. Kakuk was a boatbuilder. Gilchrist designed boats. The three of them formed a company called Tsunami Products to manufacture—and perhaps market—the kind of boat they needed to ride the surf and the surge in coastal rock gardens. The X-1 "Rocket Boat," a bullet-proof rock basher capable of carrying four hundred pounds, is the result of several years of research and experimentation.

Soares tells his students that too many companies use market research to postpone decisions. He believes American businessmen often suffer paralysis by analysis. "We need to use tools like marketing research in a judicious manner to help us make committed decisions," he says in his lectures.

Soares has done a little of the controlled experimentation market research he finds cost-effective on the X-1. A randomly selected group of experienced sea kayakers preferred the "Rocket Boat" in rough water, and they liked it in calm conditions. However, of the seventy-two boating and wild-sports retail outlets in the Bay Area—all were visited personally—only two would sell such a craft.

"So what we need to do is create a market," Soares told me.

"This boat business relates to what I do in the water," he says. "You understand the environment, see the opportunity, and seize it."

Lisa Campbell, Soares's friend and companion, was sitting on the bow of an X-1 staring out at the breakers thundering into Rodeo Beach. She was studying the sea, looking for a "window," a set of smaller waves she might be able to handle. There were four Tsunami Rangers at the beach and only two X-1's. Lisa had been sitting there in full gear for half an hour, waiting, studying. Finally, she shook her head and gave up the boat. Not today. She had a bad feeling about the sea.

There were no disparaging comments.

"It's why I love to go out with the Rangers," Lisa told me. "They believe the first order of business is to understand the sea. And if you don't feel comfortable, don't go out."

There are a dozen active Rangers and about fifteen affiliate members. To become a Ranger, one must pass swimming and kayaking proficiency tests. Members are assigned naval ranks that are based entirely on skill. Soares is a commander, and Kakuk is a captain. While the men are perhaps equal in skill, Kakuk was assigned the higher rank on the basis of his judgment. Captain Kakuk, for instance, can be depended upon to call off a proposed sea-cave penetration if the enterprise seems too ridiculously deadly.

"The Rangers have a rule," Lisa Campbell told me. "The only excuse for not doing something is 'I'm scared.' No one is allowed to argue with 'I'm scared.'"

Soares agreed, but pointed out that having skilled friends watching you—and available for rescues—tended to mitigate the fear level somewhat. You needed those good Wave Warriors out there with you because the sport, as practiced by the Rangers, is so new. Who could have guessed, for instance, that when a swell hits a sea stack, there is often a watery cushion that rides up the rock and protects the kayak and kayaker. Soares first noticed the phenomenon when he mistimed a suck zone and got creamed by an incoming swell. "But," he told me, "I wouldn't have been in that close unless Jim Kakuk was there. I knew he could get me out."

So the Rangers exist for the purposes of camaraderie, exploration, and experimentation. Happily, they are not stingy with their personal discoveries: The Tsunami Rangers often attend kayaking clinics, where they give seminars on the proper way to enter and exit surf zones. This is done free of charge, in the interest of expanding the sport of sea kayaking without a concomitant loss of life.

The university finds the idea of marketing professors involved in marketing appealing. And far from being an embarrassment, Soares's exuberant reports in kayaking journals are seen as a way of stimulating a new market. The surf clinics are seen as a valuable community service. It all fits.

But have a glass of wine with Eric Soares. Sit there on the beach with the sun going down while the world vibrates with shifting pastels, and listen to him talk about rock gardens and punch bowls, about sea caves and churns. The guy's not fooling anyone. He'd be out in the danger zone no matter what. In the fading light, with the rumble of the sea for background music, it's not even that difficult to comprehend the nature of his compulsion.

He was talking about a kayaking trip he'd taken in the Big Sur coastal region, south of San Francisco. "Big Sur," Eric Soares said, "has some of the most incredible crystal gardens I've ever seen. There are very few rivers in that area, so you don't see much silting. The water is exceptionally clear, almost turquoise. You get next to a bomb there—bang—water hits the rocks, and it explodes into the sun: great aquamarine-colored sheets of water spiring up into peaks. And there it is—a crystal garden. Looking through the water into the sun, each drop becomes a prism. There are ethereal colors and falling rainbows, shifting crystal shards falling onto blue-green water.

"The cliffs there are five hundred, maybe a thousand feet high. The sound is a constant echoing rumble: a thunder and a murmur and a hiss. It's wave on rock, but every once in a while there's the random clapotis: a loud popping sound that's almost electrical. Like something you might hear out of a big audio speaker when a wire is misconnected. Pop! And then there's spray falling back into the ocean, and that hisses and crackles.

"All of it blends into the rolling sound of the sea, of the wind, and it's like a symphony. Every instrument is pure, it all goes together, but you never know what you will hear next.

"All the time—while all this is going on—you have to scope the sea and know where you should be for your own safety. If you want to hold in place, you might use little slapping strokes, ninja strokes, to maintain your position. And you can feel the awesome power of the ocean. You try to understand it, to use that power. Because bad timing, a lack of understanding—those can kill you. But to survive in a place where you can very easily die—there's an exhilaration that verges on giddiness.

"It's something very primitive, I guess. You have a heightened sense of life and death, and that's something you can actually smell out in those crystal gardens. The spray is like an aerator on a perfume bottle. You can smell and taste the essence of the sea in the spray. Seals, fish, the soup of organic compounds—everything. Life. There's something . . . well, sexual isn't the right word, but it's close."

Soares took a last sip of wine and stared out into the dark ocean. Far to the west, the last of the sunlight was bleeding into the sea. He might have been thinking about tomorrow's lectures or wondering which suit he'd wear to his classes. Or maybe he still saw himself out there in some glittering crystal garden: Professor Soares, Tsunami Ranger, getting close to the shimmering bombs, riding shards of light, dodging the Coast Guard in ugly shoulder pads.

Therapeutic Perambulation

Irritation, it seemed, had become the central fact of my life.

We were four days into a five-week walk across the northern region of the Republic of the Congo, moving roughly from the Sangha River to the Mataba. It wasn't the swamps or the sucking mud bogs or the tangled forest or the heat or the torrential rains that bothered me. It was the bees. Great swarms of them were ever present. There were honey bees and bumblebees and long thin waspy bees and blue-black bees and great clouds of stingless little fruit-fly-looking bees that filled the nose and mouth with every breath.

"These bees," I informed my companions, "are driving me mad."

The American biologist in charge of the expedition explained that there was precious little salt in the forests of equatorial Africa, that salt was essential to life, and that, as I tended to sweat like a pig, the bees were focused on me. In addition, I presented the largest salt surface in our party. The biologist was a wiry individual—I outweighed him by forty pounds—and our guides and scouts were, for the most part, Bambenjele pygmies, men who topped the scales at about a hundred pounds apiece, which was less than half my weight.

Our mission was to make a rough count of the animals in the uninhabited Ndoki forest—there were gorillas and chimps and elephants and leopards—and then report back to the Congolese government. Up to this point, I hadn't been able to see the chimps for the bees.

"I'm getting stung about half a dozen times a day," I complained.

The biologist advised me that the bees only reacted to dorsal pressure. "Don't touch them on the back," he said, "and they won't sting."

I tried, but the bees covered me in layers. They got under my T-shirt and stung me in the armpits; they stung me on the butt when I sat down, or on the back when I leaned up against a tree. I had to live through another thirty days of this, and I felt like screaming. The biologist said I was suffering from "insect stress."

Gradually, in the midst of this existential agony, it occurred to me that bees seldom torment a moving target. And so, for the next month, I walked. I walked an average of ten hours a day, from dawn to dusk. When the others took breaks or stopped for lunch or made camp early, I shucked off my pack and strolled down our back trail. I never stopped. I walked constantly.

Walking, I discovered, cures insect stress.

I write about travel in remote areas for a living. My doctor, who is a personal friend, likes to see me immediately upon my return. I provide an opportunity for him to treat, for instance, malaria, in Montana. After my long walk through Africa, he seemed disappointed in my physical condition.

"You look great," he said sadly. "How much weight did you lose?"

"Almost twenty-five pounds."

"Blood pressure's way down," he noted reluctantly. "Heart-beat's strong and slow."

"And I haven't had any anxiety attacks for a couple of months now."

"That's good," my doctor said, and speaking as my friend, he meant it. A year or so before, I'd made a serious mistake in love. When it all fell apart, I began having the attacks: periods of intense and unfocused fear, accompanied by a jack-hammer heartbeat, flushed skin, and hopeless depression. I didn't go out much. Tears came easily in those days.

"So you're over her?"

"I think so."

The truth was, I'd never felt better in my life.

I thought about this sudden reversal of emotional and physical fortune. The weight loss was easily calibrated. An individual weighing 200 pounds burns up about 7.8 calories per minute walking at a 4-mile-an-hour pace. We weren't walking that fast in the Ndoke, but I figured the exertion involved in crawling under thorny vegetation and wading through knee-deep mud put us somewhere on that level. So: 7.8 calories, times 60 minutes, is a total of 468 calories burned per hour. Multiply by 10 hours for a total of 4,680 calories lost per day of walking. Divide calories lost (4,680) by the number of calories in a pound (3,200) for a total of 1.46 pounds walked off per day. Given the fact that we were on low rations—rice, nuts, vegetables, and a doughy concoction of powdered root called fu-fu—a weight loss of twenty-five pounds in a little over thirty days seemed right on the money.

Dropping some excess weight tends to lower blood pressure, of course, but I felt there was more to it than that. The walking, I thought, was a kind of natural tranquilizer. Every day, about an hour into the trek, I'd drop off into a state I thought of as automatic pilot. My senses, it seemed, were preternaturally sharp. I could hear the distant pant-hoot of chimpanzees, the vaguely electronic chortle of the mangabey monkey, the scream of the crested eagle, the grunts of bush pigs, the trumpeting of forest elephants splashing in a nearby stream. Without conscious thought, I stepped over columns of fierce driver ants, and noted the acrid ammonia scent of a nearby silverback gorilla. In the visually limited world of the dense forest, I knew, without thinking about it, where everyone was; I knew my place.

Occasionally, we encountered elephant trails running in our general direction: great wide footpaths straight as any road in North Dakota. The elephants, nature's bulldozers, had cleared away the foliage that otherwise twisted around our ankles or bloodied our arms with thorns. We called these NAT paths: No Arm Touch. Walking along the elephant interstates was an atavistic pleasure. The pygmies chatted quietly among themselves in Sangha, a language I didn't know. It was, to my ear, a kind of sibilant spoken music. And above, sounding in counterpoint to our various conversations in French and Sangha and English, the monkeys, who were bedded down in the midday sun, chattered softly in the canopy. The sounds of man and monkey were not dissimilar. I felt we belonged here, and wondered vaguely about my love affair with the internal combustion engine.

In the evenings, I tried to stay awake in my tent listening for the strange humming sound of leopards beyond the fire. Every few hours, I'd hear the pygmies laughing. They never slept, or so it seemed, and they were as happy as any group of men I'd ever met.

Which hadn't been the case in the village where we'd hired them. Pygmies are the aboriginal people of the forest. They were hunters and gatherers, but about five hundred years ago, Bantu agriculturists moved in along the rivers. In the past centuries, the pygmies have gravitated to the Bantu villages, where they lead lives as second-class citizens. They are in fact near slaves, trading their lives for fu-fu and alcohol. Especially alcohol.

I thought about the pygmies. In the village, they had been dissatisfied and drunk. They wanted things that seemed to them beyond their grasp: They wanted radios and colorful T-shirts. They wanted to ride in cars and buses. They wanted jobs running forklifts for the lumber companies that were cutting down their forests. Instead, a local policeman had recently come around and burned down their small huts, made of bent-over saplings and leaves. The pygmies were told to build regular houses, like normal people. And so they got drunk and sullen, and they fought viciously among themselves.

But here, walking in rhythm with the forest, they were happy, immune to the stinging calculus of want. I listened for the leopards and realized that I, too, for the first time in some years, was delighted with my life. And why not? Compared to the Bambenjele people, my own collision with civilization and its discontents seemed minor, almost insignificant. My suffering, such as it was, amounted to little more than a matter of cultural insect stress.

And walking, of course, cures that stress.

The Monks of Apnea

"Two," the announcer said in Spanish, "four, six, eight, ten . . ."

In front of him, under bright lights, men were pulling fish out of a numbered plasticized burlap sack and transferring them, two at a time, to several mesh plastic boxes, of the type used to transport milk cartons. The boxes were later loaded onto what looked like a refrigerated truck. Above, there were five thousand people sitting on the hard stone steps of an outdoor amphitheater. Five thousand people, breathlessly watching men count fish, two by two, in Spanish.

"*. . . diez y seis, diez y ocho . . .*"

The ceremony had been going on for four hours. I felt as if I were drowning, sinking into some wavering subaqueous darkness and looking up toward a surface that was receding from me at some velocity. It was an unrelenting struggle to stay awake during this, the most public, the most visible, part of a prestigious international sporting event. I felt as if I had been condemned to some fifth-century Zen monastery and sentenced to a month of "wall gazing," that mind-numbing spiritual exercise designed to help a novice learn the essential truth that only consciousness is real, not its objects.

The unreal objects in question were fish. Mostly, the fish looked like Bermuda chub or garibaldi: hundreds of them. All these fat drab-looking fish had been taken on this, the first day of competition in the nineteenth (the promoters favored Roman numerals XIX) Campeonato Mundial de Caza Submarina: the world breath-hold spearfishing championships. Representatives of twenty-four nations were present, here in Ilo, Peru, which is on the Pacific Ocean, in the southern part of the country, down near the border with Chile. The U.S., Japan, Spain, Italy, France, Brazil, Argentina, Tahiti, and Australia were involved in the competition, along with some countries I don't necessarily associate with spearfishing: Croatia, Russia, Slovenia, Namibia, and Turkey.

"Forty-five fish," the announcer said, "for the team from Denmark." This wasn't a whole hell of a lot of fish. The audience applauded lightly. It would be hours until I learned if the United States team had similarly disgraced itself. Hours. I felt as if I had been flung into the fishy abyss, dark waters closing in around me, and enlightenment was not forthcoming.

To get to Ilo, it was necessary to rent a car in Tacna, the nearest town with an airport, and drive a hundred miles east, across a high, wind-savaged plateau on the northern edge of the Atacama Desert. Several hundred miles south of that road, one great stretch of the Atacama, the driest land on earth, has enjoyed less than one inch of rain in the past century. My road ran straight, over high desert, most of it at two thousand to twenty-five hundred feet, all arid plains and low rolling hills covered over in sand the color of sun-dried leather and cement. The steeper hillocks were ribbed with the pattern of the wind. Dust devils whirled in the distance, and occasionally one seemed to spring up out of nowhere to batter the car I was driving from the side with the booming thud of a bass drum. The car rocked sideways on its tires and the wheel twisted in my hands.

The air was gray with blowing sand and with the perpetual winter mist that hangs over Peru's southern coastal deserts. The mist, called the Garua, was curiously dry and did not condense on the windshield. The midday sun was a gray little ball that I could stare directly into without squinting.

Just before the first of what proved to be three military checkpoints in a hundred miles, I stopped to pick up a man in an expensive leather coat, carrying a clipboard. He looked intelligent and respectable. I figured I could practice my rusty Spanish on him.

The man, in fact, was a police officer, and I was allowed to work on my inflections and conjugations during a fairly mild interrogation at sixty miles an hour. He was, inexplicably, hitchhiking back and forth between checkpoints, and we played show-and-tell with my driver's license and car-rental papers while dust devils twisted in agony on all sides.

What was my business in Peru?

"I go now to Campeonato. You know?"

Happily, in Peru, they don't arrest you for speaking Spanish like Tarzan.

"The president," my policeman friend told me, "will be in Ilo tomorrow, to open the Campeonato."

So, I asked, there is no longer any trouble with the Sendaro Luminoso?

The Shining Path guerrillas, a Maoist cadre based in the southern mountains of Peru, had managed in their time to cause $22 billion worth of damage and to kill 27,000 people. In September 1992, the leader of the Shining Path guerrillas, Abimael Guzman, was captured. Since then, most of the other leaders have been killed or captured.

"Absolutely no problems," the policeman said.

Not here anyway, I thought. If what was left of the Shining Path wanted to disrupt the World Spearfishing Championship, they'd have to come down out of their camps in the forested mountains to the east, march across a hundred and more miles of empty desert, and make their way past at least three major military bases, complete with tanks, helicopters, and fighter planes. Taking out a marching column of guerrillas in this desert would be like shooting fish in a barrel.

The international spearfishing event, it seemed, was partially an effort to demonstrate Peru's military progress to the rest of the world. A pacified Peru could hold itself out to various financial markets as a swell investment opportunity.

I asked the policeman if things were better in Peru these days.

"There is more money," he said, "but the same people still get rich."

The road to Ilo rose over coastal mountains of about three thousand feet, then dropped down a steeply precipitous route to the coast. Wind-driven sand piled up on the road like heavy gray snowdrifts, and a crew of twelve men worked with shovels and wheelbarrows to clear the highway. The men's clothes were sandblasted, gray, and they wore bandannas over their mouths. What could be seen of their faces was the color of the sand and the sky and the sea. They were gray men shoveling sand in a sandstorm every day of the week, every day of their working lives.

The city of Ilo was hunkered down in a block along a desolate coastline, where heavy seas pounded against pinnacles of rock set at various distances from the shore. The sea stacks were a darker gray than the sea itself, and even on the road, five hundred feet above the shore, I could see great waves exploding against rock. Spray burst off the islets, momentary silver eruptions, bright against the dirty sky. Ilo itself looked bleak: thousands of small, square gray cement buildings huddled together before the pitiless immensity of the Pacific Ocean.

One of the outlying neighborhoods was called the City of Flowers, and it sat on a flat beach, some distance from the downtown area. There were no flowers, no gardens, no lawns. The City of Flowers was a conglomeration of one- and two-story cement houses, set square on the hard-packed desert. There was no color anywhere, not in this area, where blowing sand would peel paint back to bare concrete in a matter of months. All the houses were gray, cement-gray, and the only paint I saw was that stenciled onto every fifth building, a fading announcement advising passersby that there was CEMENT FOR SALE.

The people from the City of Flowers, from the barrio of Kennedy, from everywhere: They were all downtown. There was some kind of parade rolling down the main street, with marching bands and floats and men on horseback, who waved at the cheering crowds that lined the streets. A group of little girls wearing great tin-foil wings painted gold marched by, and because they looked more angelic than anything that ever came out of the Italian Renaissance, I imagined they were meant to be angels.

The angels marched under large, colorful, very professional-looking banners that stretched across the street. The banners, in Spanish, read: WELCOME TO THE XIX WORLD CHAMPIONSHIP SPEARFISHING CONTEST and NEIGHBOR, REMEMBER: THE TOURIST IS YOUR FRIEND and IF YOU LIVE IN ILO, WORK FOR ILO, LOVE ILO and I LOVE ILO. Love was represented by a red heart. Soldiers in full combat gear, carrying automatic weapons, manned the parade barricades.

In what looked like the town's largest hotel, the lobby was packed with sophisticated international travelers speaking Greek and Italian and Danish and Portuguese. Were there any rooms available? The desk clerk said it was to laugh. The hotel had been booked up in advance for *months*. One of the French speakers, a man named Philippe Lavarelo, stepped up to help. He worked in the French embassy in Lima, and the French were a big presence in the hotel. There was even a video team poised to document what looked like a good chance for a French victory. With Philippe's help, the clerk was able to find me a windowless basement room.

Philippe said that the French team had already been in Ilo for five weeks, scouting the waters. Since it was difficult to bring boats into Peru, Philippe had used his consular connections to secure two quick Zodiacs for scouting purposes. Most of the rest of the international teams had to make do with the slow, clunky wooden scout boats supplied by the city of Ilo. A brass band marched by outside. Somewhere down on the waterfront, a huge crowd cheered some announcement—the sound of a touchdown two blocks from the stadium.

And tomorrow, the president of Peru would arrive to open the ceremonies.

The American team didn't believe it.

"A reporter," Jon Bergren said. He was the captain of the team.

"No one covers us," Bill Ernst said.

The other team members—René Rojas, John Plikus, and Beuchat Picasso Mares—agreed.

Spearfishing was big in Europe. There is even a glossy European magazine about breath-hold events. It is called *Apnea,* a Greek word meaning a transient suspension of respiration. For the Europeans, a win in this event meant a breathless spread in *Apnea;* it meant big money in equipment endorsement. The top European divers, men like Italy's Renzo Mazzari, were international celebrities, on a par with downhill racers and top-notch cyclists. The Italian team, it was rumored, had spent $100,000 on preparations for the event.

There was a lot of international pride and prestige involved as well. Many countries sponsored divers through the military.

The American team, by contrast, had precisely nothing in the way of sponsors. Its members paid their own way, had to figure some way to take two weeks off from work, had no hope of lucrative commercial endorsements and no one at the American embassy working overtime on their behalf. The last thing they expected was coverage in the media.

It was a disparate group of athletes. Jon Bergren, for instance, had some real estate investments in Connecticut and was working overtime to survive in a bad market. Bill Ernst was a fireman. Beuchat Picasso Mares, of Miami, originally from Cuba, was possessed of an exuberant personality—you could envision him wearing one of those fluorescent ruffle-sleeved mambo shirts—and is the only world-class diver I ever met whose business card identifies him as a "world-class diver." René Rojas, originally from Chile, was a quiet, self-effacing man who ran a commercial diving operation out of California. He collected sea urchins for the Japanese market, and dove wearing a helmet. It was a one-man operation, and René said that when his topside pump gave out, the air down below got thin and that was his signal to swim to the surface. I got the impression that if René weren't a top-notch breathhold diver, he'd be pretty much defunct.

The teammates, who had all the reason in the world to act like Shriners on convention, were for the most part self-contained, even thoughtful men. Nobody was drinking alcohol, looking for nooky, or spoiling for a fight. They displayed precisely none of the dumb-ass loutishness that characterizes the downside fringe of hunting. John Plikus, at thirty, was the youngest of them. Spearfishing, it seemed, was one of those sports, like high-altitude mountaineering, that rewards experience and judgment over youth and strength.

The team, as a whole, seemed secure, even contemplative. They were chock-full of self-knowledge—or so I imagined—and appeared to be guys who had actually found a measure of enlightenment in the fishy abyss. I wondered if it was something about the sport itself that generated such calm self-assurance. These guys might have been a delegation of monks, except that they hadn't even begun to master the squirming basic human urge to kick ass in international competition.

I asked if the American team had a chance to win.

Only, it seemed, if they got lucky. The Chileans and Peruvians knew these waters and were in their home arena. The big European teams had been scouting for over a month. They had fish-finding sonar equipment, and Global Positioning Devices to locate underwater pinnacles where fish congregate. The American team had been in Ilo for one week, and they scouted the waters the old-fashioned way, which is to say they spent a lot of time swimming around with their eyes open. Since world-class divers were fairly evenly matched, scouting made all the difference in these competitions: You had to know where the fish were going to be.

What the Americans had going for them was this: the rough, cold, gray waters exploding off sea stacks; the kelp beds; the limited visibility of five to thirty feet—these were similar to conditions off the coast of New England, and off the Pacific West Coast.

I've done a little spearfishing myself, but I knew precisely nothing about spearfishing competitions. Consequently, before my trip to Peru, I had made a few calls. Bob Lea, a marine biologist for the California Department of Fish and Game, said that the state had been monitoring competition sites since 1958 and that he himself had been doing it for fifteen years. There were regulations that had to be followed, as there were in Peru, and he felt that spearfishermen had no more effect on the "resource" than hook-and-line sportsmen did. Repetitive competitions in the same area could damage a fishery, but even in Peru, with a small army of the best underwater hunters in the world working six hours a day for two days, there would be no long-term deleterious effect. It was a one-time event.

In fact, Bob Lea knew Bill Ernst. "A lot of these guys," he said, "are very conservation-oriented."

In Peru, I discovered something else about them: something admirable, and self-contained, and almost—how to put this?—almost, well, Zen-like.

I found a press office, and asked a few of the bright young people—college students majoring in communications, I imagined—where all the speared fish would go. They were, I was told, to be given away to "mothers' clubs"—groups of mothers banded together to feed their families—and to *comedores populares,* inexpensive and subsidized restaurants serving poor neighborhoods.

Was it possible to see the fish being distributed?

This was treated as an odd request. The Campeonato was about parades and ceremonies and international fellowship. It was about Peru's place in the community of nations. Why would a reporter want to watch the government give away food to poor people?

I explained—tactfully, I thought—that in my country, the government might be so interested in the ceremony or the competition that the fish would be allowed to rot. Either that, or some clever hustler—the mayor's nephew, for instance—might make a lot of money on a couple of truckloads of free fish.

One of the women said she'd see what she could do. I could come back later.

The next day, there was another parade: the military band and the angels and the men on horseback, along with teams from twenty-four nations—all of them marching down to the town's central plaza, where President Alberto Fujimori spoke. The place was packed. Even the rooftops were thronged. Fujimori never mentioned the Shining Path guerrillas, but he said that the fact that such an event could be held in Peru proved beyond doubt that the country had finally been pacified. The underlying message was, as I thought it might be, that Peru would be a great place for foreigners to invest money.

I gave several Australians a ride back to a hotel two miles out of town, where the competitors were to meet the president in a more private ceremony. I pulled into a likely spot, but a soldier tapped on my window with an automatic weapon and told me that I had to park in another lot. There were six more soldiers watching the car, a few standing on the rocks overlooking the beach, and another half dozen of them watching the road. "Geez," one of the Australians said, "they're *serious* about parking here."

The Americans posed for photos, then went up to their rooms, where they worked on their equipment. The spearguns looked to be about twelve to fifteen feet long and were powered by two lengths of stretched surgical tubing. Each team consisted of five men: three divers, an alternate diver, and a captain.

I had brought along my own gear, and I asked if I could dive with the American team during the competition. It wasn't even remotely possible. The rules were very strict. Someone diving as an observer, for instance, might have a speargun stashed underwater and would be able to pass fish to a competing diver.

"Do people do that sort of thing?" I asked.

"Oh yes," Jon Bergren said.

International spearfishing, it turns out, is a cut-throat sort of sport. Bill Ernst told me a story about an event in which a diver spent the month before a major competition illegally feeding fish in a large underwater cave. On the day of the event, he took up a position at the mouth of that cave and got quite a few fish. Not many more than nearby divers, but an hour into the hunt, all the fish in the competition area began migrating to the cave, where they had been fed for the last month. The diver cleaned them out. Nowadays, judges watched for that sort of thing.

In any case, it was unlikely I could keep up. The fact that I had once been a pretty fair freestyle sprinter, good enough to compete on the national level, didn't cut much ice.

"You could recruit an Olympic champion," Jon Bergren said, "and it would take him at least two years to start winning competitions just on the local level."

Sure, short bursts of speed were important, but the event is six hours long. A diver wants to control his metabolic processes—he wants to keep his heart beating at a low rate: forty, fifty times a minute. I thought, Great Holy Buddha on the mountaintop: It *is* a Zen kind of deal.

And there were dangers not immediately obvious. If you breath-hold dive enough, the body seems to get it. Oxygen-rich blood is not pumped to the extremities. Good divers reach a place where the body no longer screams at them to breathe. This poses a danger. In 1986, during a Florida competition, Phil Whisniwski died while trying to pull a fish he'd speared out of a cave in eighty feet of water.

Then there was the phenomenon called "shallow-water blackout." Divers hyperventilate or "pack" on the surface. They take three half-breaths, exhale three times, then take a full breath, piping in the last air through pursed lips until the lungs actually hurt. The arms are held out to the side, so the rib cage has room to expand. A full stomach takes up room that the lungs can use, and no diver eats before a competition. Some don't even eat the night before.

At sixty feet, the expansive pain in the lungs is gone. Divers are usually down for a minimum of two minutes. When they rise to the surface, they sometimes black out at about thirty feet. Kids I knew in grade school used to play "knockout" with the same gas laws—the physics of water pressure on empty lungs. Out on the playground at St. Mary's, I might empty my lungs; then someone else—maybe Armand Bruni, who was a strong kid—would squeeze my chest in a bear hug. Ten or twenty seconds later, I'd wake up on the ground, looking up into a sea of inquisitive faces. Knockout!

In shallow-water blackouts during spearfishing, upward momentum and the buoyancy of the wet suit commonly carry divers to the surface, where they pop awake, likely wondering: Is that what death feels like?

Which is an experience not generally offered in everyday adult life. Knowing one's own limitations is a form of self-knowledge. Playing around at the edge of those limitations, when the penalty for exceeding them is catastrophic if not fatal, is a form of active meditation. Forget about wall gazing: Shallow-water blackout is a flat-out real-world demonstration of the Zen dictum that only consciousness is reality. And these guys, these self-contained, semi-enlightened athletes—these spearfishermen—they were the Monks of Apnea.

So, naw, I couldn't dive with the American team. I didn't have the skill, the maturity, the spirituality. Besides, it was illegal.

Another day, another parade: bass drums and trumpets, bedraggled floats, and a dispirited band of angels trudging along in their crumpled and seriously parade-worn wings. The first day's diving had begun at nine.

The sky had cleared a bit, but there was a stiff wind driving heavy surf into the pinnacles just offshore. I could see one nearby competitor working the rocky surf-side promontory of a nearby islet. His boat—each competitor was assigned a boat—bobbed nearby. The black fins rose above the surface of the sea, then sank. Rose and sank.

It was a dangerous place to be. The diver was timing his descents to the waves that were exploding off the rocks to his back. He dove a few seconds before a ten-foot wall of water rolled over him, then likely wedged himself into a crevice in the rock wall as the underwater surge battered him. As the wave receded, the surge pulled him—and all the nearby fish—back out into the ocean. And that was when he'd do his hunting.

In spearfishing, fish are taken from a foot to ten feet away. The sport isn't about marksmanship. It's about knowing where your prey will be. The diver I was watching passed a speared fish to his boatman, and it was put in a numbered sack. His fins rose and sank as a wave powered over him.

Bill Ernst was working a kelp bed some miles from shore, in one of the three large competition areas assigned for this day. The kelp was strange: It didn't reach to the surface. You had to come shooting down through a thick canopy of leaves at thirty feet, then move rapidly, pulling yourself hand over hand through the stalks. Catch a fish, and you had to drag it up through the tangling canopy. There were about twenty species of fish it was legal to spear, and they weren't a whole hell of a lot different from fish Bill had seen in the U.S. It was tougher to avoid undersize fish: Peru had a weight limit, rather than the length limit U.S. divers are used to.

Visibility was poor: five to thirty feet. Bill told me later that he didn't see another diver. At least under water. Sometimes in these competitions, two divers will come upon a school of fish. There are two ways to handle the situation. You power into the center of the school, scatter the fish, and hope you are faster and more skillful than the other guy. Either that, or you separate and work the fringes of the school, both of you taking a lot of fish, the faster and more skillful man taking the most.

These Peruvian fish weren't particularly wary. They hadn't been hunted much. It's a lot different in places that see a lot of spearfishing pressure, like Hawaii. There you dive down into a school of fish, and when you get to where they are, they've all moved uniformly out of range. Everywhere you look, on all sides, there are fish calmly feeding twenty-five feet away. Move, and the fishless hole moves with you. From the surface, it looks like theater in the round and you're Hamlet.

Late that afternoon, people gathered at a huge stone amphitheater that was set on the beach and accommodated about three thousand people. The proud citizens of Ilo, along with small groups of international visitors—Japanese, Spanish, Greek—sat on stone benches as men with wheelbarrows rolled bags of fish along the esplanade from the docks to the beach. The bags were numbered and placed on woven mats on the sand below the flags for various countries.

The competition ended at three o'clock. Most of us in the audience had found seats at about four. It wasn't until six or so that all the fish were assembled and officials began counting them. People sat patiently watching. No one left. In fact, you couldn't leave the amphitheater—someone else would take your place. The upper deck was ringed with another two thousand people who couldn't find seats. There was polite applause for everyone: Turkey—hey, lotta nice fish, you guys—Greece, Tahiti, Brazil, Portugal, Croatia.

I reflected on the Latin American temperament. The folks sitting on these rock benches were the very same people who drove 250 miles an hour through town in pickup trucks, and in new Japanese cars and taxicabs and buses. It was, apparently, considered courteous and mannerly to honk loudly and often. People who didn't lean on the horn at least once a block simply weren't paying attention. The city was, after all, full of annoying, sometimes slow-moving pedestrians. You'd see well-dressed businessmen driving late-model cars bearing down on some ancient woman hobbling painfully across the street, and they'd blast her with the horn.

"Yo, I'm driving here, Grandma."

And yet these same people could sit patiently, breathlessly, watching men count fish for eight hours.

The Americans did okay the first day—112 fish. We were number 11, out of twenty-four countries, way ahead of Russia (30), Argentina (20), Japan (37), Belgium (47), Greece (22), and Venezuela (61). Spain was the leader with 225 fish, and France was right behind with 224 fish. Points were added for poundage, but the standings didn't change on the first day.

Back at my hotel, the French consular official was livid. France, it seems, had been disqualified. "Our captain," Philippe Lavarelo, explained, "just got into another boat. He wasn't even diving, and they disqualified the whole team. This whole thing is political. They don't like us." He was writing a letter of protest.

Jon Bergren, captain of the American team, laid it out for me. Each diver will have a list of perhaps five sites that he thinks will be productive. It may take an hour to fish out the first place. He then goes on to the next site on his list. The problem is that someone from another country may have already worked that area, and there was no way to know.

Every diver was assigned a boat, and to level the playing field, all the boats were the same size and powered by the same type of engine. The captain of each team was required to pick one of his country's three divers and stay with him and his boat.

The French had asked permission to use one of their fast Zodiacs, to accommodate their video team. The French captain, it appears, had transferred into the Zodiac and had checked various areas so as to advise his team in the matter of which sites were being fished. When Peruvian observers stopped the Zodiac, the French captain was found hiding under a tarp. Or so the competition rumor had it. (The press office would neither confirm nor deny the allegation.)

It was, Bill Ernst said, a breach of the rules, but he thought the Peruvian officials were going a little hard on the French. They should be disqualified for that day's diving, but not for the entire competition.

A Chilean diver I talked to later was all for the disqualification. If the French were allowed to compete tomorrow, on the last day of the competition, they could conceivably register a protest with the international organization, get reinstated, and have their first day's catch counted. The only way to teach them a lesson was to tell them they couldn't compete the next day.

It would also, I noted, move Peru up from eighth place to seventh, and Chile up from fourth to third. There was that, the Chilean said. But, damnit, the French were always doing questionable stuff. A few weeks ago, the Chilean said, he was scouting, diving on an underwater pinnacle. The French came by in a Zodiac and kept circling above him.

"Why?" I asked.

"Because they're *French*."

"You mean," I said, "you think they're arrogant."

Yes, that's what he meant. Exactly.

Actually, I'd had some contact with the French divers the day before. They had been uniformly pleasant, and, in fact, I owed my basement living accommodations, such as they were, to Philippe of the French embassy. It occurred to me that calling the French arrogant is a little like saying Romans speak Italian. French folks have the most euphonious language on earth, their scholars commit the most esoteric theoretics, their food is superb, their athletes are more courageous and better trained than those of any other country. They are culturally superior and can pronounce the word *ennui* in a way that lets the rest of us know how much they suffer in our presence. Arrogance is a French cultural trait, as delicious, in its way, as any bouillabaisse.

The next morning, early, my hotel lobby was in chaos. The French contingent was leaving Ilo in protest and en masse. Hey, *au revoir,* guys. I transferred from my basement hovel to a top-floor oceanfront room that had previously contained culturally superior Frenchmen.

"There is a man you could talk to," the bright young people at the press center told me the next day, "but he is very busy right now."

"What's he doing?"

"He is giving away the fish."

"But you told me I could watch him do this thing."

"Of course." Indeed, I could talk to the fish man later. He could tell me precisely how he'd given away yesterday's catch.

"Can I watch now?" I was becoming frustrated.

"Come back in an hour, please."

It occurred to me that I was being sandbagged. There might be a story here: FISH ROT WHILE POOR GO HUNGRY. Something like that. I wanted to see them give away the fish. It was either that or another parade.

I had lunch in a downtown restaurant and read the Tacna paper. The Campeonato was front-page news. Aside from the French situation, two divers had been injured in the first day's competition, one seriously. Slovenian Boris Truhacen shattered his kneecap when he rose from a dive into a fifteen-foot swell that dashed him onto a rocky islet. A single fifteen-foot wave can drop a thousand tons of water on the bow of a boat. It is a force entirely beyond human control. There was a picture of the poor guy in the Tacna paper. He was lying on a bed, his leg in a cast, looking profoundly drugged, and hooked up to what appeared to be an automatic morphine pump.

In the distance, I could hear the dismal thump of the day's first parade moving my way. A familiar-looking truck passed by outside. It was, in fact, the refrigerated truck I'd seen last night at the fish-counting ceremony.

I threw a few bills on the table and sprinted out to my car. The truck hadn't gotten very far on the narrow cobblestone street, and I managed to get up within a car or two of his bumper. When the driver cleared the downtown area—most of which was blocked off for the parade and full of pedestrians—he cranked it up to 250 miles an hour, and we went screaming into the outskirts of town, blasting our horns at children and puppies and people in wheelchairs.

Here I was chasing a refrigerated truck through a remote town in southern Peru and convinced, in my own mind, that I was the

Woodward and Bernstein of fish. The truck stopped at the farmers' market on the main road into town. Two men got out, rolled
up the back gate, and started giving away fish to shabbily dressed
shoppers.

I stood there watching for some time, chatting with folks, and
from what I was able to piece together, the Peruvians had been
extremely clever in their fish-distribution scheme. The city government was to give away the first day's catch, and the state would
be in charge of the second and last day's. Since there was some
tension between the two entities, each would struggle to distribute
the fish in a way that would enhance its standing among the organized poor.

It was a maddening development. What kind of story was this,
anyway? I couldn't dive with the competitors or even go out in a
boat to watch them. This left a six-hour hole in every day, an era's
worth of wall gazing, followed by eight excruciating hours of
public fish-counting. I had plenty of time to poke around in the
cracks and crevices of the competition, but everywhere I looked
there was a dismal lack of scandal. The contest was ecologically
sound and would have no lasting impact on the fishery in the
area. The Peruvian organizers were, well, they were parade-
crazed, yes, but they were also extremely efficient and well prepared. And now . . . now the sons of bitches were giving away
food to hungry people.

Spain won the Campeonato. Chile was second, Italy was third,
and Peru was fourth. The U.S. was tenth, out of twenty-four
countries, not a bad showing considering the team had only been
able to put in a scant week of scouting. José Vina of Spain speared
the most fish and was the individual winner. Renzo Mazzari was
sixth, which was considered a good showing. Frane Zanki of Croatia caught the biggest fish: 19.294 pounds.

Bill Ernst found me in the hotel bar late that night. I asked if he
had any complaints.

None at all. The event had gone very smoothly.

Was it the best-organized competition ever?

Bill thought for a moment and said that he supposed it was.

I finished my beer. *"Otra vez,"* I said to the barman: another time.

Bill and I chatted about the contest for a time, then he said he had to turn in. There was a big good-bye ceremony the next day. He expected a lot of speeches. International goodwill. That sort of thing.

"And a parade," I muttered darkly.

"Yeah," Bill agreed. "I think they're going to have a parade."

"Otra vez," I said.

It occurred to me that this event was something like softball—more fun to play than to watch. I told myself I'd like to do a lot more spearfishing in the future. Get good at it. The languid physicality of the sport appealed to me. There was something in the Zen of apnea I liked, something that was akin to meditation. It's probably a good thing to know your limitations, to be able to control your autonomic systems, to flirt with nirvana through apnea. An unconsecrated spearfisherman like myself could stop gazing at the walls and, instead, listen for the sound of one hand clapping in the immense wonder of the world's oceans. Dinner, after a few hours of spiritual questing, might be Bermuda chub, sautéed in lemon butter. I liked the idea of enlightenment on a plate.

The next world championship, Bill reminded me, the twentieth, would be held in two years.

"I'll hold my breath," I said.

Search and Rescue

～◦ ◦～

Park Country Search and Rescue called me out just before midnight on a cold November evening. The hunter had been missing
for forty hours. He'd been working Tom Miner Basin, in the
mountains adjacent to Yellowstone Park, tracking elk, his partner
said. It was now about two in the morning, and the temperature
had plunged to almost 30 degrees below zero. A local outfitter
had volunteered his cabin near the trailhead, and that's where we
were, poring over topographical maps, matching the terrain with
what we knew of the hunter.

He was from out of state and didn't know the Montana
mountains, his partner said, but he'd done some snow camping
on the West Coast—Mount Rainier, I think. The guy went up
alone, just to test himself in the snow. He was a highly
trained security guard at the sort of facility terrorists target,
and he kept himself in shape. We knew that while he didn't
have a tent or sleeping bag, he did have matches, good

boots, warm gloves and a good hat, and had dressed in woolen layers.

His partner said he was the type of guy who pushed himself, who didn't give up. They'd come across some elk tracks in the snow two days ago, and our lost hunter thought he could run the animals down. His partner waited at the trailhead until long after dark. Then he drove down into town and notified the sheriff.

Our team called the man's wife. You hate to do that—wake them up at two in the morning to tell them a loved one is missing in bitterly cold weather. And yet you have to know as much as you can. You have to figure out what your man is likely to do. The hunter had told his wife there was no way he could get lost. "All you have to do," he had said, "is walk downhill to the river." Near Tom Miner Basin, there are lots of ways to go downhill into places that lead straight back up into the spine of the Gallatin Mountains.

So that's what we had to work with: tough guy, in shape, no quitter, some experience in the snow. I had a good feeling about this one. Mostly, after forty hours in 30-degrees-below-zero weather, they don't make it.

Our team was working from what we call the PLS—place last seen. Usually, after a day and a half, we'll find lost folks within a radius of about three miles of the PLS. For this hunter, we'd stretch the radius out to five miles. We figured our man must have followed the elk until it got dark on him that first night. The animals were moving south and west. We eliminated unlikely elk habitat, and established two or three areas where the man might have stood as the darkness fell on him. If he was disoriented and tried moving downhill, he could have ended up in only a few places.

In the morning, we'd send snowmobilers out into the areas where we least expected to find our man. It's tough searching for someone on a snow machine, and we don't put much faith in them. A horseback team would ride the search area diagonally, looking to cut tracks. A fixed-wing aircraft would overfly the basin.

Everything we knew about the hunter's personality, and the behavior of the elk he was tracking, suggested that the topography of the land would funnel him into an area several miles away, at the top of an old logging road, somewhere near eight thousand feet. That's where we'd set up our base camp. We called in the county snowplow to clear the road. I saw it lumbering by the outfitter's cabin, its yellow revolving light casting eerie stroboscopic shadows on the snow. At dawn, we'd dispatch half a dozen teams of two each to search the area on foot. That's what I'd volunteered to do. I'm what they call a ground pounder.

At four that morning, I laid out my sleeping bag in a back room and tried to get a few hours of sleep.

We live in a world in which nothing that happens is our own fault. Slapstick has outlived its day. A slip on a banana peel isn't funny anymore—it's a lawsuit. Take Chiquita Banana to court on that one. We have all become victims.

Which, I think, is why some of us venture into the wilderness. We do so because it's not safe, and there's no one to blame but ourselves. You can get hurt out there, which is precisely the point. Wilderness is a way of taking back control of our lives.

When I first moved to the mountains almost twenty years ago, I lived on a remote ranch along a body of water called Poison Creek. The previous owner, an old-time cattle rancher named Don Hindman, had kept a thirty-acre portion of the land where he built a house in the shadow of the Crazy Mountains. Don was my mentor, and I used to walk the mile or so to his house every few days to visit and listen to stories.

One warm October day, I walked up to Don's house in my shirtsleeves. He asked if I'd considered the weather. Mountain weather, he pointed out, is frenetically variable. Temperatures can change 50, 70, even 100 degrees in twenty-four hours.

So, my mentor told me, even if you're only walking a mile on a sunny fall day, it's worth your life to be prepared. "Wear a coat," Don advised, adding, in his kindly avuncular way, "you imbecile." During my first years in the mountains, I did a lot of these imbecilic things. Obviously, I survived. That's why it's called dumb luck. I figure I owe something to the wilderness, and that something is called Search and Rescue.

Tom Miner Basin, in south-central Montana, is just north of the 45th parallel, about halfway between the equator and the North Pole. The mountains that rise on all sides reach altitudes of eleven and twelve thousand feet. To the west are the Gallatin Mountains; to the east, the Absarokas; to the north, the Crazy Mountains and the Bridgers.

For the most part, these mountain ranges are either managed wild lands or designated wilderness areas. They stretch into the adjoining states of Wyoming and Idaho and comprise the largest essentially intact ecosystem in the "temperate zone" of the Northern Hemisphere. Called the Greater Yellowstone ecosystem, the rugged glaciated mountains, high benches, and rolling prairies encompass millions of acres of state forest, national forest, and national parks, including Yellowstone National Park, Grand Teton National Park, and the 900,000-acre Absaroka-Beartooth Wilderness.

If I walked up into the mountains I can see from the front door of my house in town, I could hike seventy very rough miles until I even crossed a road. It ain't Disneyland out here, and the wilderness is not tolerant of mistakes.

There was, for instance, a young man who took a fatal fall near the summit of a mountain in the Beartooth Wilderness. In his tent, we found a bag of psychedelic mushrooms and a notebook full of swirling spiral designs, which contained this terrifying note: "I think I can fly."

One year, two eighteen-year-old college coeds set out on a day trip to a lake at nine thousand feet. They were novice backpackers, and it was only five miles from the trailhead to the lake. They assumed they could walk ten miles in five hours, easy, but they hadn't calibrated three thousand feet of elevation into their plan. When it got dark, they stayed where they were, as they had been taught to do in a backpacking course. (Lost hunters, by contrast, usually strike out cross-country, and tracking them sometimes turns into a foot race.) We found the young women and got them down to the trailhead before dawn. Two sets of very happy parents were waiting there, and I felt about as good as I ever have in my life. The two girls were young enough to be my own daughters.

It doesn't always work out that well. A few years earlier, I was called out to search for two elk hunters in the Pine Creek Drainage. The men were friends, recent arrivals from Oregon, and not used to Rocky Mountain weather. They were hardworking fellows, barely scraping by on low-paying jobs, and both had families to feed. An elk—or two—would get them through the winter. They were meat hunters and honorable men.

The November day they set off dawned bright and clear. It was about 28 degrees above zero that morning. The men were dressed in cotton: denim jackets; denim pants. One of them had thought to wear a hat.

By sundown that evening, the temperature had dropped fifty degrees. A blinding snowstorm had closed down the entire county.

Why hadn't the men come out ahead of the snow? We tracked them for the better part of a day. The going was slow at first. Tom Murphy, our best man tracker, started from the trailhead, where the men had parked their vehicle. They had walked uphill, through wet snow that was now covered over with the light airy snow that fell during the storm. It was necessary to crawl along the men's direction of travel, blowing powder—blue smoke, we call it—out of the tracks in the older hard-packed snow.

Early the first afternoon, the tracks said, the men had shot an elk. Apparently they tried to drag the 600- or 700-pound animal toward their vehicle. It would have been sweaty work, even in the cold. Their cotton clothes were likely soaked.

Sometime late that afternoon, as the temperature dropped, they must have realized they were in trouble. They left the elk and tried to walk out. But the blizzard was on them, and they appeared to be disoriented. Their tracks, easier to follow now in the deep newly fallen snow, veered off from the place where their vehicle was parked. They began moving downhill, but the heavily wooded slope steepened precipitously. The forest was dense with trees, thick with down timber.

It must have seemed hopeless in that storm, in the dark, with no lights. The snow was knee- and thigh-deep, and the men left tracks like post holes. Twice they stopped and tried to light a fire. Both times they failed. It was 25 degrees below zero that night.

We stood looking at the burned matches and the green living boughs the men had tried to ignite. The down trees on either side would have provided plenty of tinder, but the men tried to burn green pine boughs instead. They were experienced woodsmen— former loggers—and knew how to build a fire. While they had been working with the elk, hypothermia had ambushed them. We could see it in their tracks—in their lack of coordination and their confusion, in their stumbling pace, in the bad decisions they made, in the few cold ashes of their failed fires.

One set of tracks led over a fallen tree and stopped. The man had fallen backward, and was caught in a sitting position, with his arm entangled in the branches of a living tree. He died there, in that place, and his sweat-soaked clothes were frozen stiff on his body.

Another set of tracks approached the fatal tree, and there was an indentation in the snow where the second man had sat down. The two must have talked there, in the dark, with the snow falling all around them. They must have known they were dying.

We found the second man half a mile away. The tracks in the snow said that he sat down, smoked one last cigarette, then pitched over and died.

To this day, I'm haunted by those tracks. Several times over the past few years I've dreamed of those men and of that last conversation.

I was trying to sleep in the outfitter's cabin when I saw the yellow light on the snowplow moving back down the gravel road leading to town. In another few hours, I'd be out pounding the ground, looking for the lost security guard. I needed to sleep, and just as I was dozing off, some bozo started hammering on the front door. I heard someone mutter and stir. There was the sound of a door opening.

A sheriff's deputy said, "Oh man, are we glad to see you."

And a man's voice—raspy, exhausted—replied, "You think you're glad?"

We kind of like it when the lost hunters find us.

I stoked up the woodstove, and our man sat in front of it for fifteen minutes before we could get the frozen boots off his feet. There were no signs of frostbite. The guy would keep all his fingers and his toes. He'd built a few fires, he said, but they hadn't kept him very warm. He'd been working on a new plan—two fires: one at his back; one at his front—when he saw the strange yellow light flashing on the snow far below. He'd run, stumbling, down the steep snow-slope, but the plow was gone long before he got there. He'd followed its track down the logging road and knocked on the door of the first cabin he saw. Which was where we were.

The man called his wife. I had the feeling, from listening to his end of the conversation, that she was crying. His partner walked around shaking our hands. He kept saying, "I can't believe you sent the plow right to him." We were sort of proud of that ourselves.

Later, just at dawn, I took a short walk in the snow and stood overlooking the Yellowstone Valley. Our lost hunter had been pretty good out there, and I tried to see the sunrise through his eyes. Far below, I could mark the course of the river by the fog rising off fast-moving water. The air glittered with tiny floating crystals of ice, called diamond dust, and when I looked into the sun, it was haloed in rainbows. The last few days had been a matter of life or death for our guy—for all of us—and that, I thought, is both the secret and the terrible beauty of wilderness. It was going to be an absolutely splendid day, and we had no one to blame for that but ourselves.

Among the Karowai: A Stone Age Idyll

It was, I suppose, a single piece of ineptly executed and cynically fashioned art that sent me fleeing five hundred miles upriver, back into time, and deep into the malarial heart of the swamp. The people I wanted to meet—it was only later that I would come to know them as Karowai—lived a Stone Age life and knew almost nothing of the outside world. They were, some said, headhunters, cannibals, savages. If so, they still owned their own lives.

Which didn't seem to be the case with the people who lived in the administrative center located at the mouth of the great river that drained the swamp. It was only my second night in the town of Agats, and it was raining, again, here on the southern coast of Indonesian Irian Jaya, the western half of the island of New Guinea. Torrential rain hissed into the Arafura Sea, and it pounded down onto the slick brown tidal mudflats. This area, known as the Asmat, is named after the region's most famous inhabitants and is the world's largest swampland.

The electricity in the town dimmed, sputtered, and died. It was 100 degrees at eight in the evening, and the wooden boardwalk, set fifteen feet above the mudflats, was slick and treacherous as I followed a man who called himself Rudy past darkened and shuttered clapboard buildings. There were fine things Rudy thought I needed to see. Artifacts I should buy.

Rudy's aboriginal art shop was another clapboard affair, and rain thundered down on the galvanized-tin roof of the place. The electricity in the town blinked on for a second—a flash of sickly orange—then coughed piteously and died for the night.

This was not unexpected, and Rudy carried a flashlight. He was an Indonesian but not a native inhabitant of Agats. Rudy came from Java, the capital island of the Indonesian archipelago, a short slender man with burnished golden skin and straight black hair. He wore a lime-green polo shirt with an alligator over the place where his heart might have been, and his shirt was open to display a small gold Playboy bunny hanging from a thin chain around his neck.

Rudy was in the business of selling native Asmat art. The Asmat are Papuans, sturdy black people related to Australian aboriginals and thought to be linked to the "Java Man" who lived over half a million years ago. The word *Papuan* derives from a Malay word, *papuwah,* meaning "frizzy-haired."

Throughout the whole of recorded time—and as recently as the 1960s—the Asmat people were the most feared cannibals in the southern swamps. Head-hunting formed the core of a complex system of survival designed to appease various malevolent spirits. Art was essential to that life, and the Asmat were master carvers. Their ancestral columns—which look a bit like totem poles as envisioned by Giacometti—were delicate, flowing poems of war and revenge. Asmat carvings, coveted by collectors, are included in the permanent collections of the Museum of Primitive Art and the Metropolitan Museum in New York.

By the 1990s, tribal warfare was very nearly a thing of the past, and the spiritual impetus that fashioned Asmat art had been degraded. Javanese sharpies like Rudy hired villagers to hack out sad, uninspired pieces that could be sold to unwary visitors, most of whom came off adventure cruise ships.

Rudy's darkened shop was filled with carvings piled one atop the other and marked with tags that read SHIP, PRICE, CABIN NUMBER. Broken pieces lay in a pile and occupied a corner of the shop. The replications of ancestral carvings, the bis poles, had been fashioned quickly, out of soft wood—not the traditional ironwood—and the spirits did not dwell in them.

Rudy sensed my growing irritation and turned the yellowing beam of his flashlight onto a squat wooden carving he imagined I might be inclined to purchase. I stared at a blocky chunk of wood, coarsely chiseled to represent a man and a woman locked in a carnal embrace. The soulless figure was as crude as something scrawled on a bathroom wall and had nothing to do with the delicacy of traditional carving that did, indeed, sometimes encompass copulatory scenes. Rudy's dying light illuminated the clunky travesty and lingered on splotches of black paint meant to represent pubic hair.

"Sexy," he whispered.

I thought for a moment of Michael Rockefeller, who had visited the Asmat in 1961 as part of a Harvard Peabody expedition, and returned soon after to purchase art for an exhibition in the United States. Rockefeller planned to visit some of the more remote villages near Agats, but his boat capsized in a fierce tide and was driven out into the Arafura Sea. His two Asmat guides swam to shore, where they summoned help. Rockefeller and a Dutch art expert, René Wassing, stayed with the overturned boat. The next morning, Rockefeller, tired of waiting, left Wassing with the boat and began to swim toward shore, which was four to seven miles away. He was never seen again.

Rockefeller was a good swimmer, and he had rigged up a flotation device out of two empty jerricans. There are sharks in those waters, as well as man-eating crocodiles. The tide was also very heavy.

Nevertheless, at least one local missionary believes Rockefeller was a victim of ritual cannibalism. Had he made it to shore, Rockefeller would have washed up near the village of Otsjanep.

At the time Irian Jaya was a Dutch colony, and some years earlier Dutch police investigating a head-hunting incident at Otsjanep had killed the local chief and four others. The Asmat believe that a man killed in war will not rest until avenged by the death of an enemy. Rockefeller, naked and defenseless, would have been seen as a representative of the "white tribe."

Whatever the truth of the matter, it can be argued that Michael Rockefeller died for art.

Rudy moved in close to the sad, sorry copulation figure, trained his light on the genitals, and said again, "Sexy."

It was not a piece to die for.

"Rudy," I said. "I gotta get out of here."

I wanted to go upriver. Back in time.

The boat was a forty-foot-long dugout, no more than three feet wide, and powered by a 40-horsepower kerosene Yamaha engine. My traveling companion, photographer Chris Ranier, had wanted to get out of Agats very badly. He is best known for his documentation of endangered and disappearing cultures, and Agats was a town where you went to the Asmat museum because traditional culture was, as they say, history.

We had no radio in the big dugout, only a bit of rice, one spare propeller, and two burlap bags full of trade goods. Our guide, William Rumbarar, was a Papuan from the nearby island of Biak, and it was William who hired two local Asmat boatmen to accompany us: Conrados Kamau was a slender clever man, good with engines, and Stef Metemeo was a short muscular gentleman with an infectious smile, who functioned as the Minister of Morale for our trip back in time.

There were plenty of Javanese guides available in Agats, but the native Papuans seemed to distrust all Javanese out of hand, reason enough to choose a Papuan guide. And William, for his part, knew his stuff. One recent book on the Asmat, for instance, suggested that there were neolithic peoples living in tree houses only a few hundred miles upriver and that these Stone Age tribes were friendly and welcomed visitors. William had been there.

"Gone," he told us. "All modern now." By which he meant

that the people had come down out of the trees and that they now lived in clapboard houses with tin roofs. The children all went to school, the adults went to church, and everyone wore missionary-clothing-drive T-shirts and shorts. It wasn't that my book was incorrect: All this had happened in the five years since it was published. "Change is very fast now," William said.

That change—the homogenization of humanity—seems to be the direction of history. There is a certain sad inevitability about it all. For the upriver people in the Asmat, it happens like this: Missionaries come, followed by the government in the form of soldiers and policemen and bureaucrats. And then the multinational developers arrive, hard on the heels of the government, and they promise a better life to anyone who wants to log the forest and farm the waste. Perhaps the development would involve mining or petrochemical exploration, but the result has always been the same. Everywhere. The living culture is entombed within museums.

Still, William explained, if we wanted to go farther upriver, deeper into the swamp, he knew of some people who still lived in the trees, people who used stone tools and were largely ignorant of the outside world. If this was, in fact, the case—the irony wasn't lost on me—I would be an agent of the changes that offended my romantic notions of human diversity. I would personally entomb some of the living culture in prose, and Chris would document it on film. Perhaps, several generations down the line, young people in the Asmat would study his photographs in an attempt to understand what had happened to them.

"How far upriver are these people?" I wanted to know.

"Past Senggo."

Senggo? Where had I read about Senggo? I paged through the best and most recent guidebook I had been able to find, *Irian Jaya,* by Kal Muller (Periplus Editions, Berkeley, California). The book, published in 1990, said, "Some unacculturated ethnic groups live in the jungles upriver from Senggo." Very good. However: "Cannibalism is frequently reported and surely practiced here."

"Who are these people you know upriver?" I asked William. He said, "Care-oh-eye." Karowai.

Muller's book didn't have a lot of encouraging things to say about Karowai hospitality. It said, in fact, that they were cannibals. The Dutch Reformed Church has been proselytizing among the estimated three thousand or so Karowai for ten years and has yet to celebrate a single baptism. One missionary, the Reverend Gert van Enk, calls Karowai country "the hell of the south." Van Enk himself, according to Muller, "is not allowed into most of the tribal territory, and if caught there would be pin-cushioned with arrows." Confirming other sources, van Enk says that cannibalism is still common among the Karowai. A death is believed to be caused by witchcraft, and a culprit (or scapegoat) must be found, killed, and eaten by the relatives in revenge. This leads to a never-ending cycle of cannibalism.

"You sure this is, uh, safe?" I asked.

William said, "Oh yes, very safe, no problems, don't worry." And then his body was shaken by a sneezelike convulsion followed by a series of helpless, high-pitched wails. It was, I understood after thirty seconds or so, the way William laughed.

The rivers of the Asmat, seen from the air, are milky-brown, the color of café au lait, and they meander drunkenly through varying shades of green in great loops and horseshoes. The water comes from the central highlands of New Guinea. It flows from glacier-clad peaks fifteen thousand feet high, and plunges through great canyons into the flatland swamps, where it forms dozens of interconnected waterways that empty into the Arafura Sea.

The Asuwetz River (also called the Baliem) is a mile wide near Agats, on the coast, and at low tide the banks are a sloping wall of slick brown mud twenty feet high. Mangrove trees, buttressed by high exposed roots, brace themselves against flood tide.

Women in long, thin dugout canoes that were the same gray-brown color as the river stood to paddle against the flow of the river. Thirty years ago, the handle of a paddle would be carved in the visage of an ancestor's face. That ancestor would have died in war and the paddle would have served to remind everyone of the necessity for revenge.

None of the paddles I saw were carved in this way. Such artwork is now against the law, part of the Indonesian government's push to finally end head-hunting.

Upriver villages consisted of several poor huts set on stilts above the swampy ground. Some of the villages were arranged around rectangular houses 150 feet or more long, called yews. There were doors evenly spaced along the length of the yews, one for each family group, though only men are allowed inside. In past times, head-hunting raids were planned in the yews, and the Indonesian government sent soldiers in to burn most of them down years ago. The upriver longhouses, however, were too remote to attack and exist much as they must have centuries ago.

At the Asmat village of Kaima, we pulled into the beach fronting the yew. Mean, slinking skinny little dogs battled pigs loudly for garbage under the yew. Women and children sat on the porch, weaving string bags made from orchid fibers.

One of the men issued a sort of command, a grunting hiss. Instantly the women and children were gone, clambering six feet down notched poles to the ground. Suddenly there were several dozen men standing on the porch. They wore shorts in varying degrees of repair, and some of the men sported T-shirts with such cryptic messages as JEAN-CLAUDE VAN DAMME—KARATE. A few of the men stood with their arms crossed over their chests, a defiant and aggressive stance in this culture.

We stopped because the chief here was said to possess five human skulls. We wanted to talk with him about the skulls, about the old ways, about the time before the missionaries. The men of Kaima, for their part, saw three strange Papuans, expensively dressed (shoes!), and two white men. It was unlikely that much good could come of such a visit.

There was an uncomfortable aura of suspicion and distrust. Conrados talked with the chief, a powerful-looking man of about thirty-five with fine, regular features and wary eyes. The chief was wearing yellow shorts and dried rattan strips around his considerable biceps.

I hunkered down by one of the dozen hearths in the yew. There were beautifully carved spears against one wall, some polished black ironwood bows, a variety of arrows with different bone points for different prey, and at least one polished but uncarved drum near each fire. All the woodwork was finer by far than any of the carvings I had seen in the boardwalk shops of Agats.

Conrados squatted by my side and explained that the chief might, in fact, have one skull. The chief didn't know for sure. Because of the missionaries and the government, he didn't know. For 20,000 rupiah (about $10) he could look.

"Tell him it's 20,000 rupes only if he finds the skulls."

The chief disappeared. The rest of the men stood around silently. They didn't talk with Conrados. I glanced over at the finely carved weapons. It was all very uncomfortable. We seemed to frighten the men of Kaima just about as much as they frightened us.

Presently, the chief returned with the improbable information that he couldn't find his skulls. Misplaced the pesky buggers. There were, he told Conrados, too many people around for him to be able to find his skulls. The missionaries. The government.

We had already seen an illegal Asmat skull outside of Agats, in the village of Syuru. It was a twenty-minute walk from town over a wide, well-maintained boardwalk set variously five and fifteen feet above the boggy ground. After about ten minutes, the wooden walkway began to deteriorate precipitously. There were missing planks, rotted planks, broken planks, and then no planks at all, only a few sticks. One of these broke under my weight, and I grabbed at something that held and then swung there for a moment, like a kid on the monkey bars.

Syuru was a small, traditional village of thatched-roofed huts on stilts. There were no boardwalks in the village itself, only a series of half-submerged bark walkways. As I wobbled my way over narrow tree trunks—small children took my hand to steady me in this process—a humming, murmurous sound I had been hearing for some time began to separate itself into individual moans and wails.

An important man had died the day before. Now the women

had covered their bodies with ashes and soot. They would mourn in this fashion for seven days. The sounds were coming from several houses at once. Wailing and moaning would build to a crescendo and then subside for a moment. Suddenly a loud voice from one of the houses—sometimes it was a man's voice; sometimes, a woman's—would shout out a hoarse, anguished speech in Asmat. I had no translator, but I imagined the words were something like: "He was a good man; he worshipped his ancestors, he fed his family and now he's gone." And the moaning and wailing and shrieking would start all over again.

In the swamplands of the Asmat, all the dead return as ghosts, but those improperly mourned can be malevolent. They can make a living relative's life hell. A cranky ancestor strews banana peels across the path of life. Literally. People in the Asmat don't fall down without a reason.

When someone dies, a proper show of grief makes a favorable impression on the recently deceased, who can then protect his descendants from all those evil spirits that populate the netherworld.

The yew at Syuru was separated from the village proper by the boardwalk. The night before, Conrados, a local Asmat, had spoken to the men of Syuru. Here the men were expecting us, and there were no women on the porch in front of the dozen doorways. It was 9:00 A.M. and most of the children were in school. It was a good time to talk heads with the guys.

The yew was two hundred feet long, at a guess, with high rafters, and there were at least fifteen fires, all set in a row, in the center of the structure and neatly spaced along the length of the floor. Only a few of the older men were present, and when a couple of schoolchildren stopped on the boardwalk to see what was going on, a thin muscular man in threadbare gray shorts ducked through the door. He stood on the porch and said "Scram" in Asmat. The sound, the same one I heard in Kaima, is a grunting hiss. The children hurried off down the boardwalk without looking back.

The men squatting around the fires in the yew wore shorts, and they smoked clove-scented Indonesian cigarettes called kreteks. This smell mingled with the odor of woodsmoke and singed pig fat. No doubt human flesh—locally called "long pig"—had been cooked over these fires in past generations.

An older man in faded beige shorts smeared his face and chest with white ashes. He put on a feathered headdress made of bird-of-paradise feathers and produced a fire-blackened human skull from the bag. It was all very surreptitious, and there was a good deal of looking around, because we were engaged in something everyone knew was illegal. The sounds of mourning, across the way in the small huts, rose to another tormented crescendo.

I noticed that the skull lacked the lower jaw, which meant it was the trophy of a head-hunting raid. The skulls of powerful ancestors, sometimes kept as safeguards against evil spirits, are invariably intact, the lower jaw lashed to the skull with strands of rattan. Head-hunting trophies, on the other hand, are invariably missing the lower jaws, which are detached and worn on a necklace: a fearsome emblem of proficiency in war.

The man with the skull—no names: the missionaries; the government—demonstrated the value of the powerful skull. He rolled out a palm mat and lay down with his head balanced atop the blackened skull. It did not look like a comfortable way to nap.

During sleep, I had read, a man is most vulnerable to the evil influence of the spirit world. Therefore it is wise to keep a skull nearby during sleep. Men formerly slept in the yew using the powerful skulls of their ancestors, or their enemies, as pillows. Across the rotting boardwalk, a man's rich baritone voice called out a long, sing-song lament. And then, from twenty houses, the sobs and shrieks and wails began anew.

I stared at the man on the mat, whose eyes were closed and who might have actually been asleep. He seemed perfectly serene.

We were well above Kaima and had been motoring against the current for ten hours. Here, about 250 miles upriver, the villages generally consisted of a yew and four or five huts. They were separated, one from the other, by twenty or thirty or fifty miles.

There had been two short afternoon rainstorms, tropical down-pours accompanied by rumbling, ominous thunder. The sky was all rainbows and bruised Wagnerian clouds. The forest overhung the river and it seemed to me, in my ignorance, all of a piece: unvariegated greenery.

The river was flowing down to the now distant sea at about three or four miles an hour, but it looked sluggish, weighted down with brown silt, and its surface was a viscous brown mirror reflecting the overhanging greenery and the operatic sky. Yellow leaves, like flowers, floated among the reflected clouds. A swirling mass of neon-bright blue butterflies swept across our bow in a psychedelic haze. The world felt like the inside of a greenhouse, and the air was heavy with moisture and the fragrance of orchids.

A snowy egret kept pace with the boat, and blue-gray herons, looking vaguely prehistoric, rose from the banks of the river in a series of horrid strangled croaks. In the forest, cockatoos screeched loudly enough to be heard over the laboring of our kerosene engine. The cockatoos bickered among themselves: ridic-ulous, self-important dandies with their white feathers and marching-band topknots.

Chris and I bickered with a good deal more dignity, I thought. He likes to sing, and has a completely monotonous voice, which is entirely beside the point. The point is—and this can't be stressed too strongly—*Chris Ranier gets the words wrong.*

"Wooly wooly, bully bully . . ."

"Chris."

"What?"

"It's 'Wooly bully, wooly bully.' "

"That's what I was singing."

"You weren't. You were singing, 'Wooly wooly, bully bully.' "

" 'Wooly wooly, bully bully'?"

"Yeah. 'Wooly wooly, bully bully.' Not 'Wooly bully, wooly bully.' "

" 'Wooly bully, wooly bully'?"

In the midst of this perfectly asinine conversation, William erupted in a convulsive sneezing snort, followed by a series of high-pitched wails. And then Stef and Conrados buried their heads in their hands and wailed, as if in helpless grief.

" 'Bully bully,' " Chris sang, " 'wooly wooly.' "

I moved to the bow of the boat and sat sulking about this insult to Sam the Sham when what appeared to be the soggy brown remnant of some flood-felled tree suddenly disappeared from the surface of the river with a faint splash and a swirl of bubbles.

Crocodiles were once plentiful in these rivers, and local people considered them something of a bother. One famous beasty took up residence near the Asmat village of Piramat and killed fifty-five human beings before it, in turn, was killed in 1970. The animal was twenty-three feet long.

These days, crocs are seldom seen in the larger rivers. They were hunted for their hides in the late 1970s, and now, William said, they are usually found only in narrow backwaters, deep in the swamp.

Just before sunset we passed a village where a thin, attenuated man who might have been painted by El Greco paddled out to sell William some fish in exchange for a quarter-pound of tobacco. It cost another quarter-pound of the stuff to buy a large black bird with a blue mane like a stiff doily that ran from just above its eyes to the back of its neck. The bird was about the size of a large duck. It had bright red eyes with black pupils. William said that the bird was a mambruk and that it was going to be our dinner. I thought: I can't eat this. It would be like chomping down on the goddamn *Mona Lisa*.

The water took on the impressionistic pinks and yellows of a pastel sunset, so the reflected greenery on its surface was alive with color. Our wake, in the pink-yellow water, was for a moment blood-red.

There was a half moon already rising in the pastel sky. A huge bat, the size of a goose, passed overhead and was silhouetted against the moon. These mammals, sometimes called flying foxes, are nothing like the horrors in Grandma's attic. They're actually kind of cute, with velvety foxlike faces, and they fly in straight lines or great curving swoops, beating their wings slowly, with eerie deliberation, like pelicans. I caught the acrid stench of ammonia—bat droppings—and guessed that the flying foxes probably roosted in some nearby trees. And then there were hundreds more of them, passing across the moon, in the final dying of the light.

The river was milky in the moonlight, incredibly bright against the black forest that blotted out the sky to either side. Stef knelt in the bow of the boat, watching for floating logs and fallen trees. It seemed to me that some of the logs simply swam away, though the rippling lunar ribbon that stretched out ahead of us set the mind whirling through various fandangos of fancied dread.

Senggo, the only upriver settlement marked on most maps, was a neatly arranged village of about twenty houses arranged face-to-face across a muddy raised-grass track flanked by irrigation ditches on both sides. The place was quite "modern" by William's definition: clapboard houses; tin roofs; a two-story residence; two homes with glass windows; latrines built over deeply dug trenches; large, adequately drained agricultural projects; a resident missionary; and even a policeman available to stamp and sign our *surat jalan* (literally: travel letter) in exchange for only a very minor bribe.

No one seemed particularly concerned when I told them we were going upriver to see the Karowai, though nuances of meaning were a bit difficult to discern with my Indonesian vocabulary of about a hundred words.

"*Karowai bagus orang-orang?*"

No, they're not good.

"*Karowai tidak bagus orang-orang?*"

No, they're not bad.

"*Apa?*"

They're Karowai.

The storekeeper—he stocked bottled water, Lux soap, canned corned beef, sardines, margarine, T-shirts, towels, and shorts—welcomed us into his home, where we slept, sweating, on rattan mats as clouds of mosquitoes had their bloody way with us.

A goodly number of roosters spent the entire evening practicing for the dawn, so we were up before first light and back out onto the river at sunrise. A horde of schoolchildren stood on the dock and shouted good-byes. We had spent almost twelve hours in the company of dozens of people. The Stone Age was only a few more days upriver.

William spent several hours teaching me to finally see the swamp. The tall trees? The ones over there that grow from a single white-barked trunk and have elephant-ear-size leaves? Those are called sukun, and the Karowai eat the fruit, which is a little like coconut.

Stands of bamboo often grew on the banks of the river, in a green starburst pattern that arched out over the water. Banana trees also grew in a starburst pattern of wide flat leaves. They reached heights of seven or eight feet, and yielded small three- and four-inch-long bananas.

Rattan, a long tough vine used to lash homes together, to string bows, or to tie off anything that needed tying—the local equivalent of duct tape—was identifiable as a slender leafless branch, generally towering up out of a mass of greenery like an antenna.

Sago, the staple food, was a kind of palm tree that grew twenty to thirty feet high, in a series of multiple stems that erupted out of a central base in another starburst pattern. The leaves were shaped like the arching banana leaves but were arranged in fronds.

When sago trees are cut, William explained, the trunks are split open and an ironwood stick is used to pry out the pith, which is forced through a fiber screen to separate the fibrous material from the sappy juice. The juice is a sticky blue-gray starchy fluid, about the consistency of library glue, and the Karowai eat it every day of their lives.

The pith is pounded into a starchy extract that looks like a ball of chalk. It can be baked into a kind of doughy bread. A single sago tree yields about seventy pounds of starch. Karowai villages are located near large stands of sago.

So—sukun, rattan, bamboo, banana, sago—the forest was no

longer a mass of unvariegated green. Naming things allowed me
to see them, to differentiate one area of the swamp from another.
I found myself confirming my newfound knowledge at every bend
in the river. "Banana, banana," I informed everyone. "Sukun,
sago, sago, rattan, sago, bamboo . . ."

William, like any good teacher, seemed proud enough of my
accomplishment for the first half hour or so, then the process
began to wear on him. I was like some five-year-old on a drive in
the country, pointing out every cow in the pasture to his weary
parents.

A river lunch: one nice hot sun-baked tin of dogfoodlike corned
beef with a rather mournful looking cow on the label, a little of
last night's rice, a couple of pygmy bananas. Mash it all up in a
bowl, and watch the egret above, impossibly white against the
blue of the sky and the green of the sago.

When the outboard began to splutter, Conrados stopped
abruptly, in midriver, and began to tinker. It was unbearably hot,
well over 100 degrees, and I broached the idea of a brief swim.
The possible presence of crocodiles was debated. I reminded
William that there were hardly any left. He reminded me that
we had seen at least one the day before. Stef, standing on the
gunwale of the boat, settled the debate with a front flip into
the silt-laden brown water, and then, somehow, we were all in
the river, splashing each other like children, surely immortal
(it couldn't happen to *me*), and secure in the knowledge that the
resident crocs would take someone else, a fact that would certainly sadden those of us who survived. And besides, it was *incredibly hot.*

Sometime later that afternoon, after Conrados cured the
Yamaha, we traded a length of fishing line and a dozen hooks for
what William assured us was *the* local culinary treat: two pounds
of fat sago beetle larvae wrapped in sago leaves and secured with
a thin strip of rattan. The maggoty-looking creatures were white,
with brown heads, and about the size of my little finger to the
second knuckle. William mimed popping one into his mouth,

nodded, made a yummy-yummy sort of face, and sneezed out his good-natured laugh.

He apparently thought I'd be horrified at the idea of eating bugs. In point of fact, I'd rather eat bugs than that damn beautiful bird we had devoured the night before.

We passed men standing on rafts of five or six large logs, stripped of the branches and peeled of their bark. The logs were roped together with thick strands of rattan. Further upriver, the rafts were larger: twenty or thirty or even eighty logs. Sometimes there was a small A-frame shelter made of sukun sticks and sago leaves on the rafts.

The logs, I learned, were floated down to Senggo from here— one man said it would take about four days—where they were purchased by "men from Java" for 5,000 rupes apiece, about $2.50.

At the next raft, one of the larger ones, William had Conrados turn back, and we picked up one of the loggers, a thin young man named Agus. He was wearing a gray, tattered T-shirt and shorts. He was, William explained, one of his Karowai friends and our local contact.

The Karowai village, situated on a bend of the river, was a minia-ture Senggo: just a few houses on stilts facing one another across a raised path, and a flooded-out field of yams where a few men with metal shovels were digging drainage ditches. It occurred to me that cannibals aren't generally interested in yams. A blackboard in one of the open-sided buildings probably functioned as a commu-nity center and school. The men, about a dozen of them, wore shorts, and the women wore knee-length grass skirts. There were no tree houses in evidence. It seemed, all in all, a fairly civilized sort of place here in the hell of the south.

And the people, once they learned we had tobacco to trade for a place to sleep, welcomed us as brothers. Chris and I were as-signed a private room in the men's house, but I felt like wandering around a bit. I saw Agus chatting urgently with a local man who wore an earring fashioned from the silver pull-tab from a soft-drink can. The pull-tab glittered in the slanting light of the late afternoon sun. The man nodded several times, then dashed off, at a dead run, into the forest. The entire encounter had looked vaguely conspiratorial.

Stef cooked a dinner of fried catfish, along with a healthy portion of sago beetle. The larvae were fried brown in the pan. They were crisp and sort of fishy-tasting on the outside, probably because they had been sautéed in fish oil. Inside, the larvae were the color and consistency of custard. They were unlike anything I'd ever eaten before, and the closest I can come to describing the taste is to say creamy snail.

The people in this village, I told William after dinner, weren't the Karowai I had read about in Muller's book.

"Change is very quick now," William reminded me. Two years earlier, just after Muller published his book, the government had instituted a program designed to stop ritual warfare among the Karowai and to get people to stop eating each other. They had summoned all of the Karowai chiefs and provided transportation down to Senggo, where everyone could see the tangible benefits of civilization, like canned corned beef and Batman T-shirts. If the chiefs would agree to end their deadly feuds, the government would help them. It would provide agricultural experts, and it would help the people build grand towns like Senggo. We were, William explained, staying in one such town.

There were, however, still people who lived in the trees. They built their houses deep in the swampy forest, well away from the river, which meant well away from the government and well away from the missionaries. Tomorrow we'd take a nice little stroll through the swamp and meet them. William said that Agus lived there, in one of the tree houses. When he wasn't logging.

"Where?" I asked. "Which way?"

William pointed off in the direction that the pull-tab man had taken. And it became clear to me that Agus wanted his relatives to know that we were coming. The message was probably something like: "Yo, we got honkies; hide the heads."

• • •

We didn't actually stroll through the swamp. The forest floor was a mass of knee-high grasses, spongy marsh, and low bushes. The understory hid an uneven surface, full of brackish potholes and unexpected tussocks. The exposed roots of the larger trees humped up out of the ground in a series of ankle-breaking traps: It was much easier, all in all, to simply walk on fallen trees that happened to point off in the right general direction, and it was not easy to walk on the fallen trees at all. The larger ones were slippery with moss and the smaller ones tended to crumble under my weight.

I thought, As soon as we get through this shit, we'll be on the trail. About an hour later, it occurred to me that this shit *was* the trail. Fallen trees were the equivalent of Agats's wooden walkways.

William cut me a good walking stick, which was helpful. I liked the stick and thought of it as a scepter, a symbol of dignity: Behold, it is Tripod, Mighty Jungle Walker.

Prolonged log walking is a bit like riding a bicycle: speed equals stability. And I was, in fact, moving pretty fast on a large mossy log that spanned the narrowest section of a deep foul-smelling scummy black pond when William and Stef and Conrados and Agus all began screaming, "Sago, sago, sago!"

"I see it," I called back. The sago tree was at the end of my log, on the bank of the pond, and I leaned out to grab it, because I was going just a little too fast.

"Tidak!" No!

The trunk of the sago palm, I discovered to my regret, is the vegetable equivalent of a porcupine. They are thorny sons of bitches, sago palms, extremely uncomfortable to grab for stability on mossy logs, and I had to listen to William sneeze about this prickly lesson, on and off, for over an hour.

And, of course, it rained on us. And then we could see the arc of a rainbow through the trees, and then it rained again, and suddenly we were in a large clearing surrounded by tall white barked trees 150 feet high. In the middle of the clearing, fifty feet in the air, was a house with open sides and a thatched roof. The

main support, set directly in the middle of the floor, was one of
the white-barked giants that had been cut off at the fifty-foot
level. The corners of the house were supported by convenient
smaller trees and stout bamboo poles. The floor, I could see, was
made of crossed sticks of sukun, and the thatch was sago frond.

There was a bamboo ladder up to about the twenty-five-foot
level and that gave way to a thick rounded pole with notches for
steps. Agus shouted some words in Karowai. Someone shouted
back from above. There seemed to be a bit of negotiation going
on. Mosquitoes in thick clouds attacked those of us on the
ground. They were very naughty, and probably malarial.

And then I was clambering up the bamboo ladder and making my
careful way up the notched pole. There were nine people sitting
on the platform: two infants, two nursing mothers in knee-length
grass skirts, two little boys about three and four, one boy about
nine, and two naked men, each of whom had a leaf tied tightly
around his penis. There was no one who might have been a
grandmother or grandfather. Anthropologists who have studied
tree dwellers on the nearby Brazza River figure the average life
expectancy of these seminomadic hunters and gatherers is about
thirty-five years.

One of the men, Samu, wore a ring of bamboo in his nasal
septum and a double ring of rattan through the sides of his nostrils. He was, William said, the chief of this house. Three families
lived here, and each of the three men had two wives.

The tree-house platform was rectangular: about twenty feet by
twenty-five. The bones of several small fish hung from the ceiling,
secured by rattan strings. I saw no human skulls, but there were
dozens of arrows fitted into the ceiling and piled in the corners.
There were two fires—a men's fire and a women's fire—and both
were built on beds of small rocks over a reinforced triple-thick
area of flooring. The children sat with the women, around the
women's fire.

Agus and William continued to negotiate with the Karowai
men. We were not the first white people these tree dwellers had

ever seen. The year before, William had brought in two European groups, seven people, though no one ever stayed for more than a few hours. We wanted to hang out for a day or so, stay the night, shoot the shit. Which complicated matters.

In his two previous visits, William had learned precisely what the Karowai require in terms of trade goods. The swamp here does not yield good stone, and in the very near past, the Karowai had had to trade with outside tribes for stone axes. We had steel axes for them (I could see another steel ax set in a corner of the platform, next to an ironwood bow with a rattan pull-string and a set of arrows made from reeds and tipped with sharpened bone).

Aside from the axes, the Karowai were pleased to accept fishing line, metal hooks, salt, matches, rice, and tobacco. These were acceptable gifts, much admired and appreciated. We were welcomed to stay the night. They didn't accept credit cards here at the Karowai Hilton.

Samu, as headman, got first crack at our tobacco. He packed the rough-cut leaf into the end of a narrow bamboo tube, which fit into a wider tube that was etched in geometric red-and-white designs. He put the wide tube to his mouth, placed the narrow end against a hot rock, inhaled, then rocked back onto his heels. His face was beatific.

One of the women, Pya, reached up into a string bag hanging from the roof of the house, fished around a bit, and came up with a white ball of sago pith, which she dropped onto the embers of her fire. After a short time, I was offered a piece the size of a tennis ball. The food had the consistency of doughy bread and was very nearly tasteless. The term *half-baked* kept clattering through my mind, but I smiled and complimented Pya on her culinary skills. I used one of the few words of Karowai that I knew.

"Manoptroban." Very good.

It was the first word I had uttered in the tree house, and as soon as it tumbled out of my mouth, I wanted to call it back, because it was, of course, a lie. The older of the two men, Samu, stared at me. His expression was that of a man whose intelligence had been insulted. Sago? Good? People eat this soggy crap every day. All the time. They do not sit down for regular meals, but eat only when they have to, because there is no pleasure in the taste of sago. They eat it because there is nothing else. Good? It's not good, you imbecile. It's sago.

I felt chastened and reluctant to say anything else, maybe for the rest of my life. It was better to just sit there and pull sago thorns out of my hand with my teeth.

The Karowai exchanged a few words. There was a failed attempt to remain dispassionate, and then all of them were laughing. The laughter was aimed at Chris and me. This familiar teasing and testing of strangers seems to be a universal human trait, and Chris, in his many travels, has learned to defuse it by laughing right along with everyone else. My strategy exactly. Soon enough the laughter became genuine, and we were all giggling and poking one another in the hilarity of our mutual insecurity.

There was a nice breeze fifty feet above the ground, and no mosquitoes at all. Chris asked William if the Karowai live in trees to avoid mosquitoes. William transferred the question to Agus, who was learning Indonesian, and Agus—although he knew the answer—respectfully asked Samu. Samu nodded and said a single word in Karowai.

And the answer came back—Karowai to Indonesian to English: "Yes."

There was a very long silence.

Samu finally added that it was also safer in the tree, by which he meant, I think, that in this boggy flatland the tree house had the military significance of being high ground. A single man with a bow and a sufficient supply of arrows could hold the fort against any number of similarly equipped attackers. There were even strategic holes in the floor, places where a skilled archer could pick off anyone foolish enough to try to hack down the columns that support the house.

"So there's still war?" I asked.

Samu's reaction might have been a case study for Psychology

101: Here, students, is a man about to tell a lie. The chief shifted his gaze, he stared at the ground, he coughed lightly and occupied himself for some time bringing up a great gob of phlegmy spit that he lofted off into the forest below.

"No," he said finally. No more war.

William took a hit of tobacco from Samu's pipe and attempted to defuse the situation with what he took to be an innocuous question. Where did Samu get his penis leaves? There was a string bag full of them hanging from the roof.

Samu fidgeted uncomfortably, stared at the ground, coughed again, spat again, .nd finally allowed that he didn't actually recall where he got the leaves.

I thought: God knows, Samu, your secret would be safe with us. The pure hard fact of the matter was that Samu would likely lose his leaves to one of the massive timbering operations now just cranking up in the Asmat. Indeed, only three years earlier Agus had lived in this very tree house. Now he had given up his penis leaf for shorts and a T-shirt that read PIECE. It was a simple, sad irony: Agus, having encountered civilization in the person of William two years ago, was now cutting down the forest that had fed him and his people for centuries.

Agus used the money he made to buy steel axes. Generally, the Karowai move every two years, after they have exhausted the local sago. It takes about a month to build a new tree house. With a steel ax, the process takes only two weeks.

The Karowai didn't like coffee or tea, but they craved tobacco. Traditionally, they had smoked dried bark.

And rice! When William fixed Agus his first bowl of rice, the Karowai had burst into tears, it was so good. It was William who had brought him all these things, awakened him to the world as it existed beyond his village: showed him steel axes and rice and matches and canned corned beef. And though Agus and William were about the same age, Agus called his benefactor Father. He was a sweet man, Agus, ambitious and bewildered at the same time. He wept every time William had to go away.

"I get the leaves," Samu said by way of accommodation to the question that had been asked some time ago, "from the trees." He nodded out toward the forest.

And then there was another long silence. Several hours' worth of it. The Karowai seemed perfectly comfortable just sitting around, smoking, enjoying their company in a haze of tobacco smoke and self-contained neolithic composure. I, on the other hand, felt constrained to fill up the fleeting hours with productive activity. To that end, I spent a good deal of time scribbling in my notebook:

I. Karowai culture
    A. Inappropriate comments
        1. Eat me.
        2. Sago is good.
    B. Inappropriate questions
        1. Been in any wars lately?
        2. Where you guys get them dick leaves?
    C. Inappropriate subject matter
        1. Cannibal jokes
    D. Appropriate behavior
        1. Sitting in a hunkering squat
        2. Smoking
        3. Spitting
        4. Being silent
        5. Keeping the fire going
        6. Tending to the fussy child or infant
        7. Smiling dreamily for no particular reason

About midafternoon, unable to sit still any longer, Chris and William and I took a walk through the swamp to visit one of Samu's neighbors. It was another hour or so to a second clearing, where there was another tree house, which was probably only thirty-five or forty feet high. Our host was named Romas, and he had a pair of what appeared to be red toothpicks sticking out of the top of his nose. The toothpicks were, in fact, bones from the wing of a flying fox, colored reddish-brown in the smoke from the fire.

There were fish bones hanging from the ceiling, as in the first Karowai house, along with a turtle shell and a number of pig jaws hanging from a rattan rope. We had a long conversation about these trophies, which seemed a little anemic to me. The fish looked like ten-inchers, little guys, but the Karowai-to-English translation suggested that they were, in fact, the remnants of memorable meals. When Samu came to visit, Romas said, his neighbor always noticed a new set of bones. And the needlelike bones, going dark red in the smoke from the fires, became an occasion to engage in hunting stories. They were, these pathetic remains, conversation pieces. Interior decorating.

Against one wall was a war shield, four feet high, decorated in geometric designs, colored white and red. Next to the shield were several bows and several bunches of arrows, all of which were unnotched and unfeathered, so that when Romas allowed me to fire one off into the forest, it began to wobble after only fifty feet or so. The arrows do not fly true for very long, which is probably not much of a problem in the forest, where there are no long vistas.

Some of the arrows were tipped with cassowary bones. Cassowary are ostrichlike birds whose powerful legs end in claws that are capable of disemboweling a man. Next to the armaments were several seven-foot-long tubes of bamboo that contained drinking water.

The men in the tree house assured me that we were not disrupting them in the least and that they were doing what they ordinarily would be doing, which was precisely what everyone in Samu's house was doing. Romas reached into the embers of his fire and pulled out a bug that looked a good deal like a large iridescent grasshopper. He stripped off the wings and popped it into his mouth, like a piece of candy.

I was given a wooden bowl of the blue-gray glue that is sago sap. Sago, in fact, was all I'd had to eat over the past twenty hours. It wasn't unpleasant, just tasteless, and I fully understood why a man who had eaten nothing else in his life would burst into tears over a bowl of rice.

Romas said he hunted wild pig and cassowary. He also ate bananas, cassowary eggs, insects, and small lizards. The only sure thing to eat, however, the only dependable crop, was sago. Sago sap. Sago pulp. An endless diet of sago.

It rained three times that afternoon, and each downpour lasted about half an hour. In the forest there was usually a large-leafed banana tree with sheltering leaves where everyone could sit out the rain in bitter communion with the local mosquitoes.

Just at twilight, back in Samu's house, where everyone was sitting around eating what everyone always ate, a strong breeze began to rattle the leaves of the larger trees. The wind came whistling through the house, and it brought more rain, cooling rain, so that, for the first time that day, I stopped sweating. My fingers looked pruney, as if I had been in the bath too long.

Samu squatted on his haunches, his testicles inches off the floor. The other man, Gehi, sat with his back to the wall, his gnarled callused feet almost in the fire. It was very pleasant, and no one had anything to say.

After the rain, as the setting sun colored the sky, I heard a gentle cooing from the forest: mambruk. The sky was still light, but the forest was already dark. Hundreds of fireflies were moving rapidly through the trees.

William rigged up a plastic tarp so the Karowai could have some privacy. Chris and I could hear him chatting with Samu and Gehi. They were talking about tobacco and salt, about steel axes and visitors.

Chris said, "I don't want them to change."

We watched the fireflies below. They were blinking in unison now, dozens of them on a single tree.

"Do you think that's paternalistic?" he asked. "Some new politically correct form of imperialism?"

"I don't know," I said.

But I thought about it. I thought about it all night long. When you suspect that your hosts have eaten human flesh in the very recent past, sleep does not come easily. It seemed to me that I was out of the loop here, not a part of the cycle of war and revenge, which was all just as well. I had expected to meet self-sufficient hunter-gatherers, and the Karowai were all of that, but they wanted more. They wanted steel axes, for instance, and did not equate drudgery with any kind of nobility.

I tried to imagine myself in an analogous situation. What would I want?

What if some alien life force materialized on earth with a superior medical technology, for instance? They have the cure for AIDS, for cancer, but they feel it is best that we go on as we have. They admire the spiritual values we derive from our suffering; they are inspired by our courage, our primitive dignity. In such a case, I think I'd do everything in my power to obtain that technology—and the hell with my primitive dignity.

I thought about Asmat art and what is left in the world that is worth dying for. I thought about Agus, who wept over his first bowl of rice and whose first contact with the outside world set him up in the business of cutting down the forest that had fed him all of his life.

I thought about the butterfly I had caught when I was a child. My grandmother told me to never do it again. She said that butterflies have a kind of powder on their wings and that when you touch them, the powder comes off in your hand and the butterfly can't fly anymore. She said that when you touch a butterfly, you kill it.

Butterfly; Karowai.

Sometime just before dawn, I heard a stirring from the Karowai side of the house. Samu moved out from behind the plastic tarp and blew on the embers of his fire. Gehi joined him. The two naked men squatted on their haunches, silent, warming themselves against the coolest part of the forest day. Presently, the stars faded and the eastern sky brightened with the ghostly light of false dawn.

A mist rose up off the forest floor, a riotous floral scent rising with it, so I had a sense that it was the fragrance itself that tinged this mist with the faint colors of forest flowers. The mist seemed the stuff of time itself, and time smelled of orchids.

As the first hints of yellow and pink touched the sky, I saw Samu and Gehi in silhouette: two men, squatting by their fire, waiting for the dawn.

ABOUT THE AUTHOR

TIM CAHILL lives in Montana and spends much of his "at home" time at a cabin on the edge of the Absaroka-Beartooth Wilderness. He shares his life with the redoubtable Linnea Larson.